New Directions in the Study of Justice, Law, and Social Control

CRITICAL ISSUES IN SOCIAL JUSTICE

Series Editor: **MELVIN J. LERNER**
University of Waterloo
Waterloo, Ontario, Canada

New Directions in the Study of Justice, Law, and Social Control

Prepared by the
School of Justice Studies
Arizona State University
Tempe, Arizona

Plenum Press • New York and London

Library of Congress Cataloging-in-Publication Data

New directions in the study of justice, law, and social control /
  prepared by the School of Justice Studies, Arizona State University,
Tempe, Arizona.
      p.   cm. -- (Critical issues in social justice)
  Includes bibliographical references.
  ISBN 0-306-43292-7
  1. Sociological jurisprudence. 2. Justice.   I. Arizona State
University. School of Justice Studies. II. Series.
K376.N49   1990
340'.115--dc20   89-23237
                                                             CIP

© 1990 Plenum Press, New York
A Division of Plenum Publishing Corporation
233 Spring Street, New York, N.Y. 10013

Printed in the United States of America

Contributors

Richard L. Abel, School of Law, University of California, Los Angeles, Los Angeles, California 90024

David Altheide, School of Justice Studies, Arizona State University, Tempe, Arizona 85287

Donald Black, Department of Sociology, University of Virginia, Charlottesville, Virginia, 22903

Richard A. Cloward, School of Social Work, Columbia University, New York, New York 10025

Albert K. Cohen, Department of Sociology, University of Connecticut, Storrs, Connecticut 06268

Andre Gunder Frank, H. Bosmansstraat 57, XG Amsterdam, Netherlands

Marta Fuentes, H. Bosmansstraat 57, XG Amsterdam, Netherlands

John Hepburn, School of Justice Studies, Arizona State University, Tempe, Arizona 85287

John Johnson, School of Justice Studies, Arizona State University, Tempe, Arizona 85287

Gary T. Marx, Department of Urban Studies and Planning, Massachusetts Institute of Technology, Cambridge, Massachusetts 02139

Sally Engle Merry, Department of Anthropology, Wellesley College, Wellesley, Masachusetts, 02181

Michael Musheno, School of Justice Studies, Arizona State University, Tempe, Arizona 85287

Laura Nader, Department of Anthropology, University of California, Berkeley, Berkeley, California 94720

Stephen Pfohl, Department of Sociology, Boston College, Chestnut Hill, Massachusetts 02167

Frances Fox Piven, Ph.D. Program in Political Science, Graduate School and University Center of the City University of New York, New York, New York 10036-8099

Peter Schmidt, Department of Economics, Michigan State University, East Lansing, Michigan 48823

Ann Dryden Witte, Department of Economics, Wellesley College, Wellesley, Massachusetts 02181

Marjorie Zatz, School of Justice Studies, Arizona State University, Tempe, Arizona 85287

Preface

The publication of this anthology culminates what began as a Visiting Distinguished Scholars Lecture Series sponsored by the School of Justice Studies. When Dr. John M. Johnson was awarded the Arizona State University Graduate College's Distinguished Research Award for 1986–1987, the School faculty voted to use the accompanying stipend to bring several scholars to campus. Each visiting scholar was commissioned to present an original paper on contemporary issues in justice and to meet with graduate students and faculty during a week-long visit to campus.

This collection of essays promotes wide-ranging conceptions of justice. As first conceived, we sought to bring an interdisciplinary perspective to the study of justice as a way of intellectually extending the current focus of research and teaching. As it developed, the collection permitted us to reflect on our own instructional program in law and the social sciences and to promote a conception of social conflict and control which includes social, political, economic, and legal controls.

Several persons at Arizona State University have been integral to the completion of this anthology. Dr. Brian Foster, dean of the Graduate College, provided support and encouragement for the Distinguished Scholar Lecture Series. Kim Chambers, coordinator of graduate programs, and Kay Korman, administrative assistant, were invaluable in maintaining contact with and coordinating the on-campus activities of the visiting scholars. The staff of the College of Public Programs' Auxiliary Resource Center—Marian Buckley, Keith Campbell, Tammy Stein, and Mary Cullen—were most helpful in word processing and editing the manuscript. Their efforts are greatly appreciated.

Contents

Peter Schmidt and Ann Dryden Witte

CHAPTER 1

New Directions in the Study of Justice, Law, and Social Control

Michael Musheno, David Altheide, Marjorie Zatz, John Johnson, and John Hepburn

Introduction

In the spring of 1986, we invited several distinguished scholars to write these essays on justice, law, and social control. In part, we initiated this project to reflect on the directions of our interdisciplinary Ph.D. program, which focuses on law and justice in society. More fundamentally, our goal was to encourage research on justice and injustice that could be integrated with the study of law and society or inquiry that focuses on social control, social change, conflict, and its resolution.

An important reason for examining justice as an integral part of law and society inquiry is that agents of the market and the state appropriate concepts of (in)justice for their own control purposes. Their cooptation of (in)justice represents a threat to both individual freedom and collective struggles for greater emancipation. For example, when do formal claims about the manifestation of justice mask the further deprivation of liberty? When are assertions of injustices rendered against society more accurately portrayed as struggles for societal emancipation? These are fertile questions for scholars interested in the social transformation of law and society.

Studies of justice and injustice, deviance and diversity, as well as

MICHAEL MUSHENO, DAVID ALTHEIDE, MARJORIE ZATZ, JOHN JOHNSON, and JOHN HEPBURN • School of Justice Studies, Arizona State University, Tempe, Arizona 85287.

equality and inequality, have increased over the past two decades. The following essays reflect this trend. They also extend this work by focusing on new questions and revealing new problems. They introduce an inquiry of law and society that is sensitive to issues of (in)justice, and convey the importance of interdisciplinary studies of social control, conflict, and change.

In contextualizing the essays, we have avoided the temptation to construct a single vision of what they communicate about the study of justice, law, and social control. Instead, we offer a brief appraisal of how the authors converge and diverge in articulating the following concepts: justice, law, social control, social structure, social conflict, and deviation. Also, we introduce 12 theoretical themes that unite the ideas of two or more of the essayists. Before turning to these concepts and themes, we provide brief summaries of the essays.

Summaries of the Chapters

Richard Abel's "The Contradictions of Legal Professionalism" examines the influence of legal professionalism on lawyers. His timely analysis focuses upon the behavior and relationships of lawyers and their clients (as individuals and producers and consumers of legal services), the market, and the state. Abel shows how the practice of law is influenced by its Western capitalistic environment. Professionalism in the practice of legal justice is a chimera for the perspective of "just us," a position that allows lawyers to ignore obvious problems of injustice by concentrating only on those identified by the profession. The "just us" perspective leads lawyers away from confronting the problems inherent in their profession. Abel points to some of the contradictions of legal professionalism, such as unequal access to the law. This is especially evident under advanced capitalism, particularly in the United States, but comparative data from other "first world" capitalist nations are introduced to extend and limit the observations.

Donald Black's "The Elementary Forms of Conflict Management" shows the structural underpinnings of the meaning, nature, and consequences of conflict management. Black's comparative analysis suggests that specific social and cultural contexts guide the form and options for conflicts and their resolution. Forms of conflict management (self-help, avoidance, negotiation, settlement, and toleration) are analyzed, along with subtypes and the "social fields" in which each is most likely to be found. His approach on self-help includes an analysis of discipline and rebellion as well as vengeance. His other forms of conflict management entail the study of responses such as litigation, strikes, feuds, riots, beatings, and torture, as well as ridicule, scolding, gossip, and suicide.

Richard A. Cloward and Frances Fox Piven's "Why People Deviate in Different Ways" suggests why some people deviate in socially constructive ways and others in socially destructive ways. They say that an analysis of deviant behavior requires us to understand deviancy as a subset of all social behavior. They point to the importance of interdisciplinary research, since single-discipline research can explain only part of the problem under investigation. Following Edwin Sutherland, Cloward and Piven argue that the following precepts guide analyses of why people deviate as they do: Deviant behavior is complex social behavior that "should be susceptible to explanation in terms of the same sociological perspectives that explain conforming behavior." The social forces that regulate behavior include (1) social ideas, (2) social resources, (3) social norms, and (4) social reactions. These operate in cumulative and interactive ways.

Albert Cohen's "Criminal Actors: Natural Persons and Collectivities" shows how social scientific efforts cast crime and deviance as morally repugnant features of individual lives produced a reified conception of rule violations. This has made it difficult to understand and deal with collectively inspired violations, some of which were not even against the rules! Cohen develops an interactional conceptualization of collectivities in order to incorporate them as actors into criminological and sociological theory. All crimes are the product of interaction among a plurality of participants (e.g., those engaging directly in the criminal act, victims, and the audience to the act). The attribution of agency, whether to "natural persons" or "collectivities," is an example of the social construction of reality according to certain rules. The task for criminologists, says Cohen, is to figure out what these rules are for a given social system. Similarly, there are rules for determining who/what is a "natural person." This too is a social construction. These rules are what he means by "structural frames." Crimes both of collectivities and of natural persons are "outcomes of interaction processes interpreted in light of structural frames that govern the processes themselves." The frames differ between natural persons and collectivities.

Andre Gunder Frank and Marta Fuentes's "Social Movements" interprets the origin and significance of social movements that promote social change in response to injustice. Based on the belief in the primacy of economics, this chapter examines large-scale social movements. It delineates their characteristics and connections. Various types of social movements have in common "the force of morality and a sense of (in)justice in individual motivation and the force of social mobilization developing social power." Most of the "new" social movements emerging around the world are not new, they argue. Rather they share features with much older, and geographically dispersed, social movements. The strength and importance of social movements is cyclical and related to long political, economic, and ideological cycles. Some social movements compete with one another, while others overlap in membership or permit coalitions. Although most social movements are viewed as more defensive than offensive, Frank and Fuentes see them as perhaps the most important agents of social transformation. In addition, the discussion of various third world, feminist, and peace movements, raises ethical and moral questions regarding the power role of intellectuals.

Gary Marx's "Fraudulent Identification and Biography" explores the ways in which justice is used as a facade for inappropriate state dominance and/or the machinations of personal self-indulgence. Fraudulent identity and biography in the United States is related to concepts of accountability and authenticity. Marx tells us to anticipate the ironic consequences of inordinate efforts to promote order and reduce conflict: more disorder. As more of our life is subject to accountability, and as more techniques are devised to ensure a predictable context (wherein performance stands for competence), opportunities for fraud abound. The growth of fraudulent identification and biography is tied to "expansions and contractions in opportunity structures associated with the rise of industrial society and the welfare state." Marx suggests a variety of dimensions useful for related studies of fraudulent identity. These are integrated to form heuristic typologies. He is concerned with the conditions under which the use of fraudulent identities is most likely and, conversely, with those which serve to constrain their development. The study is geared toward industrialized, technological, and capitalist states, yet his approach is applicable to other technologically advanced societies.

Sally Engle Merry's "Law as Fair, Law as Help: The Texture of Legitimacy in American Society" addresses theoretical issues of law as ideology. She explores the relationship between authority, legitimation, and domination in the context of the varied uses and views of law. The chapter examines "the texture of legitimacy" for U.S. citizens in light of data from three small urban areas that differ in their class composition. Merry argues that legitimacy "depends less on a vision of the law as just and fair than it does on an understanding of the law as pervasive, powerful, and, from time to time, effective." She describes how formal mediation efforts are necessarily intertwined with perspectives about law and justice. These emanate from everyday life experiences, including language, culture, and politics. Contexts of experience are mediated by contexts of meaning, which are embodied in actual disputes. She demonstrates the variation in cultural meanings of law, when legal and other agents of social control are used by people with problems, and when people use alternative forms of dispute resolution. Variations in the views of law and legitimacy are identified on the basis of class, race, gender, and experience in court.

Laura Nader's "The Origin of Order and the Dynamics of Justice" critically examines the relations between law, order, and justice. The context of order hides certain parametric decision rules for defining, recognizing, and suppressing disorder. Order is not descriptive; it is a piece of political phenomenology. Disagreements are most evident between those who see the existing social system as just and those who see an unjust social system being sustained by social inequities. Nader argues that the debate concerning issues of law, order, disorder, justice, and injustice lacks an adequate test of the assumptions about the assumed connections between law and order. Better understandings of the relationships between social structure and social order are needed. She also examines the power embedded in the control of the definition of deviance in her analysis of consumer complaints. Where defective and dangerous products are sold, it is the complaining consumer who is perceived to be "the deviant," rather than the producer of faulty and hazardous machinery. She maintains: "When people clamor for justice, they are driven by a sense of injustice that leads them to want to transform the social structure." Nader uses cross-cultural data to illustrate the extent to which alternative mechanisms of dispute resolution are activated and the impact of these attempt to counteract injustice.

Stephen Pfohl's "Terror of the Simulacra: Struggles for Justice and the Postmodern" depicts social life as awesomely indexical, showing how our language, everyday experience, and intellectual understandings are mutually constituitive of one another. A way of seeing is also a way of not seeing. Claims to define a situation are also ways to enact that definition. Images of the world produce that world. He asserts that the contemporary, modernist context is now defined in such a way that future scenarios will likely reproduce modernist logic. His poetic analysis of the struggle for justice in advanced capitalist societies focuses on dominant constructions such as hierarchical structures. In addition, his examination of the "electronically narrated story of our time" shows how the practice of creating and disseminating ideas can be seen as another form of conflict. The struggles for justice, says Pfohl, are "heterogeneous but convergent efforts to deconstruct [hierarchical] institutional social apparati . . . so as to reconstruct . . . relations of power-reciprocal social exchange" out of the existing "re-

lations of economic, political, heterosexist, racial, and imperial hierarchies." As an exemplar of postmodernist deconstructionism, Pfohl's
essay nevertheless embodies the long-standing tensions of the Enlightenment ideals that have served as ideals for justice in Western
societies.

Peter Schmidt and Ann Dryden Witte's "Some Thoughts on How
and When to Predict in Criminal Justice Settings" provides an example of how assumptions about crime, criminals, opportunity, time,
and other variables can be invoked for purposes of social control and
regularity (i.e., efficiency). The standardization, manipulation, and ev-
isceration of social context and temporality can be accomplished for
a practical purpose. As the title suggests, this chapter discusses the
role of prediction in criminal justice decision making. Emphasis is
placed on ethical and methodological criteria for deciding when and
how to make such predictions (of, for example, recidivism). They use
a relatively new survival/hazard modeling technique to make predictions of which groups of prison releases are likely to return and which
are not. While they agree more on the "how" of prediction, they are
less certain, and indeed, in conflict, on the "when" of prediction. This
is as much an ethical as a methodological problem.

Concepts

Key concepts for enhancing the study of justice, law, and social
control are apparent in the collection. We will focus mainly on the
three major concepts of justice, law, and social control as well as their
relationship to the basic concepts of social structure and social conflict and deviation.

Justice

Our authors employ different meanings of justice.With a few exceptions, they approach it as the breach of justice and explore sources
of injustice. Abel focuses on legal justice, derived from proper legal
procedure and complete delivery of legal aid. The contradictions leading to injustice are the structural relationships underlying the practice
and delivery of law that discourage full delivery and adequate representation for most clients. Justice, for Black, can be fruitfully studied
from the management of conflict. Access to, and availability of, multiple forums of conflict management appear essential for responding
to injustice and ensuring justice. Frank and Fuentes point to people's

response to injustice through the activation of social movements in their pursuit of justice, and the relevance of considering appropriate means of justice. They stress the structural sources of injustice around the world and the efficacy of struggles for justice via structural conduciveness.

Cloward and Piven emphasize that individual and collective deviance are reactions to structural injustices. As in the work of Frank Fuentes, justice is portrayed as a process of struggle by political deviants usually engaged in larger social movements. Merry approaches justice from the perspective of the people she studied, noting that they view law and avenues of dispute resolution as tools for redressing grievances. Contrary to metatheoretical work on dispute resolution mechanisms, she finds evidence that people are not mystified by the institutional structure of dispute resolution, including the formal legal process. Nader suggests that justice in society transcends the narrow focus on the legal system and the law. It includes assessments of the distribution of goods and benefits as well as access to avenues for alleviating inequities. She says people are concerned that social arrangements work to promote symmetry rather than asymmetry.

Pfohl finds justice elusive when the world he sees confuses fantasy and reality, when images that mask injustice are promulgated by controllers for mass consumption. Justice is a feature of the knowledge process. Learning how reality is constructed must be fundamental to the struggle for justice, especially how concepts such as benefits or commodities are constructed and used. Marx provocatively plays with this conceptualization of justice by assessing the nature and pervasiveness of fraudulent identity in our age. He suggests that knowing the truth about the other person's identity is basic for justice; when trust is undercut by systematic reasons for, and successful evasions of, personal misrepresentations, then the most taken-for-granted features of the social order are shaken.

These varied treatments of justice raise basic issues. The concept of justice, for example, may be used as a facade for state dominance of machinations of self-indulgence. In contrast, the concept may serve as the catalyst for collective political deviance and associated social movements in their confrontation with injustice, or as the reason for providing social welfare for the public at large.

Law

Traditional conceptions of law play a secondary role for most of our contributors because, with a few exceptions, they see law as a reflection of other definitional and political processes. This is encouraging because it advances us toward a realization that law and legal institutions have made a historical claim to appropriate the concept of justice. In the process, these have altered ideas about other possibilities. According to Abel, law is meaningful when it is enacted through technical competence and professional guidelines. In Cloward and Piven's framework, law is the formal sanctioning process that is less sensitive to the injustices that produce deviant behavior. For Black, law as governmental social control is but one form of conflict management and, therefore, only one response to injustice. Despite the intent of most law to rationalize life, conflicts, and control, it has not replaced informal social control. As for Nader, rather than viewing law more generally as governmental social control, she focuses on formal law. Formal legal rules and the nature of sanctions are grounded in the social structure. They thereby reflect many of the same inequities and assumptions seen in human association in everyday life. Merry suggests that law may not represent socially legitimated rules so much as law is legitimated because it is a practical mechanism for getting things done.

Legal equality, for example, has been used as an ideal for justice via law. Ironically, this abstract ideal has often been used for advancing state domination rather than for altering existing inequities. Like the concept of justice, law can be employed for a variety of means.

Social Control

Social order follows from people's acceptance of assumptions and rules that they did not author. These are embedded historically. How people reflexively recognize this embeddedness of formal and informal social control is a key issue. Schmidt and Witte, for example, who focus on the organizational control of people, harmonize with others about ethical issues surrounding such activity; authenticity and inauthenticity have consequences. Abel implies that social control involves clinets' reliance on lawyers who are guided by economic and marketing considerations. As lawyers become the main medium through which disputes are resolved, the marketing scenario is perpetuated as citizens become "clients." For Black, social control consists of the various processes used to manage conflicts. These processes arise naturally among the members of a particular group. The social setting is reproduced with each conflict event, as well as the mode of its resolution. In addition, the way of managing conflict helps define the nature of the conflict. Cloward and Piven see this informal control as a process of achieving conformity and producing deviance in terms of rules, roles, and relationships.

On the other hand, Cohen, in an interesting twist, suggests that people's assumptions and interpretations about appropriate individual or collective agency and identities leads us to look for certain regularities and not others. Thus, frames of expectation guide one's focus. Moreover, Marx argues, when people recognize that an identity is official and can have negative consequences for individuals, in trade for more efficient social control, then incentives and skills for deception will be created and diffused throughout the social order. For Nader, the nature and extent of compliance and reciprocity is the foundation of social control. Pfohl finds control machines in the cultural production process. He amplifies the widespread understanding that a way of seeing is also a way of not seeing. Until discourse is developed for reflecting on our incapacity to see how we are produced, argues Pfohl, we will continue as products not of our own making. One implication is that more "objective" measures will emerge, to use information for purposes of both informal and formal control.

Social Structure

Most of our contributors look to various contexts of action for understanding the form and emphasis of rules, order, and legitimacy. That "social order" is an interaction order linking people, organizations, institutions, and nations to a past, present, and future not of their own making is implied by social structure. An essential part of social structure for Abel is the pattern of social actions that regulates the rights, duties, and obligations of lawyers for their clients. Economic and marketing considerations lead lawyers to do specific work on certain kinds of cases of particular kinds of people. From Black's perspective, social structure refers to the social characteristics of a conflict, or to how the conflict is situated in social space. A social order reflexively produces itself as conflict is managed.

Social structure is functionally interdependent with several other complex elements for Cloward and Piven: Ideas, resources, norms, and reactions to behavior flow from patterned hierarchical role relationships. For example, women do not deviate in the same patterns as men because they have not had the same kinds of resources for collective action. Laura Nader goes further in explicating social order and social structure because her focus is on the process by which people accept relationships and activities as legitimate, and whether or not they comply with routine patterns and expectations. One point she stresses is that less hierarchical social organizations exact more compliance because people have a stake in the activity as theirs. This may include structural modifications to hierarchy such as leveling, by which differentials are not unilateral but are task-specific (e.g., older brothers have authority over younger children, but all children inherit equally). When injustices are attributed to pervasive inequalities in hierarchical relationships, Nader suggests, compliance and legitimacy will be increasingly problematic. The opportunities and possibilities provided by structural arrangements involve regularity and routine. However, it is still essential, Pfohl cautions, to have a way to articulate the process that seems natural and orderly.

The problems with focusing on what is taken for granted are especially acute when technologies of control are embedded in social structure. Thus, Pfohl suggests, we must develop a discourse for reflecting on how we produce ourselves as social actors. Marx cautions that an expansion of technology has been accompanied by more sophisticated modes of control, which in turn produces a transformation of deviance.

Social Conflict and Deviation

Social conflict arises from grievances, according to Black, such as forms of deviation in everyday life. Individual and collective action against rules is a feature of ideas and resources in Cloward and Piven's essay. This leads agents of social control to react through stigma and repression. Cohen's analysis of deviance suggests that images of agents as individuals rather than collectivities have severely limited our capacity to understand deviance, crime, and social problems. His suggestion for exploring the "ecology of legitimation" is central for clarifying issues of justice even though, paradoxically, this may enhance social conflict. Nader reminds us that social orders do not like to be disturbed. Loyalists often reserve the most shrill criticism and negative labels for those who complain; they become the new class of deviants.

It is important to consider Laura Nader's contention that disorder may reflect and, indeed, promote changes relevant for justice. The most global perspective among our authors is that of Frank and Fuentes, who see economic cycles underlying organized deviance in the form of social movements. The economy and organized political movements are reflexive. Social change occurs when modes of conflict management change, because they reflect the social structure.

Thematic Emphases

A number of themes emerge from the chapters.

1. *Justice is not an objective condition but a varying perspective on rights, duties, and responsibilities.* The meanings attached to justice and injustice are problematic, often reflecting the ethics and morality integral to any culture. Some of the authors show how experiencing injustice serves to mobilize people to undertake social change. As the study of dramatic social change (such as the "American" and other revolutions) reveals, what may be deviance to agents of social control is political protest to the participants.

Much inquiry has pointed out the injustices of existing social relationships, particularly with regard to the processing of criminal offenders. These studies move beyond that focus to suggest how transformative change proceeds. Both Nader and Frank and Fuentes suggest that *injustice sparks people to collective as well as individual action.* This theme is also suggested by Merry in her explanation of why people mobilize to use the legal system to their benefit. Further, Abel, Nader, and Frank and Fuentes suggest that transformative change is usually initiated outside the legal order, and its success, according to Frank and Fuentes, is dependent on the effort being well timed with cycles of the larger social order. The idea that legal professionalism can be transformed into a societally beneficial endeavor is dependent on timing too, as suggested by Abel.

2. *The pursuit of individual and collective freedom from social control produces contrasting definitions of deviance.* Marx and Pfohl raise the issue of the demands on individuals and collectives to conform versus the desire for freedom. Such an issue asks us to entertain questions concerning domination of the individual versus the greedy self-indulgence of the individual. Phrased in this manner, domination by social control agencies and agents can be viewed as deviant, as can the indulgence of the individual. Yet social control agents can also be viewed as benign when they allocate various types of social welfare, as can individuals when they create new forms of social welfare through deviant action. Such actions show that deviance is socially negotiated and may carry positive or negative labels. Analyses by Merry and by Nader examine the ways in which deviance or violations may be reactions to injustice. This raises the question of how defendants can become plaintiffs in their attempts to redefine who is the source of negative deviant action.

The discussions of collective action by Piven and Cloward and by Nader present some of the conditions under which diverse activity is defined as a form of prepolitical protest or as positive deviance. And the social movement essay by Frank and Fuentes implicitly asks which social factors influence action as being viewed as deviant, normal, or political. The study of the negotiation of intent and consequences is paramount. One of the critical factors concerns the type of means used in obtaining new benefits and burdens. And the more general control of the definition of long-term consequences of diverse action remains crucial to our understanding of freedom and deviance.

3. *A paradox of control exists.* Different agencies and agents of social control produce their own claims to legitimacy, efficiency, productivity, fairness, ethics, and morality. They thereby define which instances are excluded by one or more of these criteria. Social control agencies often restrict debates on alternative arrangements of justice. And the state with its bureaucratic agents further confines such debates by keeping crucial points of justice from reaching public forums. Personal identity has social and organizational foundations that can be manipulated by local agents of social control. Marx refers to control in several ways, including formal regulations (e.g., licensing of persons for certain occupations), storage of large data bases on persons (IRS, FBI) increased benefits available to citizens (e.g., welfare, retirement, Medicare, veterans), and how these pertain to fraudulent identification. Cloward and Piven use the generic concept of social relation to include both formal state response and informal public response. Cohen refers only to government sanctions and imposition of criminal penalties.

4. *Social structure shapes law and options for resolving disputes.* Several analyses show how the interaction of two or more units are involved in claims, disclaims, and perceptions about justice. Issues of justice are represented in official information and records. Many are derived from actors' definitions of situations. The situational meaning of an experience as unjust reflexively turns to routines, norms, values, and sanctions that transcend particular situations. Some of these definitions are attempts to transcend situational morality and ethics. With some essays, we learn what some of these definitions are, and how they are applied in particular instances. In other essays, it is suggested that people do not understand the relevance of justice for a situation. Indeed, a common theme in several essays is the way social life is organized to normalize the description of an action as something other than justice.

5. *There should be an emphasis on social deviation rather than individual deviance.* Three of the essays represent a movement away from the study of individual deviance and the processing of individuals as violators of state rules. The origins of this shift away from the dominant ideas of American criminological theory can be traced back

to at least the 1940s, in the pioneering work of Edwin Sutherland, with many others following and extending these ideas since then. The three essays here can be located in this minority criminological tradition. Cohen challenges traditional theories that focus on the individual as a deviant actor. He points the way to the study of deviant collectivities. Marx argues that forms of deviance are being transformed as a function of social change, particularly owing to changing technologies and the expansion of bureaucratic controls. He suggests new forms of deviance to explore (fraudulent ID and biography) and sees deviance more broadly than legal rule breaking, following the earlier lead of Edwin Lemert's research and its acceptance by Howard Becker. Cloward and Piven push deviance inquiry further by suggesting that we should undertake interdisciplinary research of why people deviate from, or conform to, the social order in different ways, collectively/individually, constructively/destructively.

6. *Justice, law, and social control are problematically related.* Many scholars now challenge the convergence assumption about law and society. They offer new constructions of pluralism and argue that the social structure does not determine the modes of conflict regulation available in a particular social sphere. Nader and Black argue that social structure determines the prevailing system of law (or social control). Specifically, Nader suggests that the conventional linkage of law and order levels and obfuscates other empirical realities. She suggests that the relationship between law and order should be cast to include justice: social order/disorder and justice/injustice. For Nader, deviance as an official violation of order, if not law, may actually entail a different order. However, Cloward and Piven pose a challenge to this view by claiming that plural forms of deviation may emerge from the same social level. They see control reactions as a critical dynamic in the form deviation takes. Merry's chapter challenges the convergence notion of legitimacy, arguing against the view that the legal order only mystifies and therefore mirrors the social order.

7. *State domination involves an increased reliance on rule creation and control of agendas for rule use.* Nader, Frank and Fuentes, and Pfohl remind us that the enactment and interpretation of sanctionable rules and guidelines presumes a higher authority. In the modern state, such an authority may (1) enforce rules (2) provide formats for such rules, (3) generate private agendas for rule making, and (4) provide for the enactment of additional rules to reinforce those with little compliance. A careful look at the nature of the state and state control is in order, a task that can only be alluded to here. Several chapters note the increase in mandates against behaviors that presuppose literacy (originally a feature of a format for freedom!) Signs pro-

claiming "no" and "not" now mark off the cultural landscape. Several of the contributors observe that state domination of the individual is now considered more important than the interests of the individual. Everyday life is a fundamental source of data for the study of justice.

8. *Control of the definitions of justice and injustice is power.* Injustice is experienced in the breach of expectations about rights, duties, and responsibilities at a particular time and place. Social control agents often try to redefine such experiences as nonproblematic. Abel reminds us that clients experience the main purpose of law and the primary perspective of professionals when they approach legal institutions. Those without resources have cried out for justice, but, as Nader reveals, their actions have been largely ignored or redirected to ineffective forums of social control. Merry nicely illustrates that legitimacy is a feature of everyday life experiences and perspectives; for some people, law is pervasive, powerful, and occasionally effective, rather than merely just. For others, following the work by Frank and Fuentes, law is a reflection of attempts to stymie change. The subjects as well as the practitioners of legal rationality recognize that there is something crucial in the relationship between hierarachy and injustice. In this regard, victimology is a study of lived injustice, which calls forth visions and vocabularies of compliance and change.

9. *Public information and imagery about justice and injustice are mediated by social control agencies and mass media and reflect organizational practices.* Inequalities do not automatically produce inequities; it is the way the former are appraised and defined, on the one hand, and the nature and sanctioning of claims-making about the latter, on the other hand. Abel points to the impact of meritocratic images and practices in the legal profession, and how merit systems often disguise rather than reduce injustices as mediated by social control agents. Pfohl argues that fantasy is offered as a substitute for truth and justice in social life. True images, he maintains, are not visible because they are obfuscated by pseudoimages cast in familiar formats, which are often nondiscursive and taken for granted as the necessary rules and logic for social order. Cohen's appraisal of individual and collective deviance poses a similar issue about familiar discourse. Rule violations are recognizable through forms of discourse including language and imagery about disorder and crime. Crime has been cast historically as individual to individual. It is thus difficult to consider a group of individuals collectively, as an entity culpable of wrongdoing, if individual acts cannot be demonstrated conclusively. The image, the idea, the law, the evidence, the public outrage, and the definition of victims are joined through assumptions about knowledge and communication that essentially constitute the circle of understanding and

action. One implication is that justice cannot be understood only in
the breach. It is important to gain an awareness of how justice and
injustice now are presented, as well as the underlying rules, logic, and
procedures for producing such images. Another implication is that
comparative studies of collectives judged culpable under formal law
are greatly needed.

10. *Techniques of control reflect ideology.* A central point in the
sociology of knowledge is affirmed in several of these essays: Power
is knowledge. This often means that we seek problems for which we
think we have solutions, and, conversely, the application of techniques manages those problems. Abel, Marx, Nader, and Pfohl illuminate distinctive contexts of knowing as features of enacted power,
the process through which we follow and respond to a definition of a
situation that we did not author. There are often inconsistencies in
personal, occupational, and state ideologies. The spirit of the law, for
example, might be just, but the practice of law, as Abel reminds us, is
to do something else, including managing cases, making money, and
having a career. Thus, the law is mediated and essentially realized
through means that, simultaneously, have nothing and everything to
do with law. If procedural changes involve technical considerations,
then the idea that necessitated the procedure in the first place now
takes second place to the technical rationality.

Marx reminds us that, as people become aware, come to understand, and are capable of deconstructing the control apparatus, they
may create a mode of discourse for freedom-through-deception. This
usually means doing conceptual and behavioral transformations about
guilt/innocence, pleasure/pain, justice/injustice. To obtain their ends,
people have learned to feign crying, yelling, pouting, or aggressing.
Now they incorporate modern, technical forms of deception. It is not
enough to be skilled at using the structure and guidelines discur-
sively, although that may be an initial step. The power of technique
also contains possibilities for liberation on terms such as those engen-
dered by situational morality and ethics. The problem is to place justice frameworks alongside the order routinely represented. For example, Witte and Schmidt illustrate how rationality of prediction and
control becomes sensible and sanctionable within a context of prisoner control. When researchers operate under the definition of an agent
of social control, the issue is not the nature of punishment, prison,
and rehabilitation, but cost-effectiveness, or how likely an individual
is to commit another crime.

11. *Researchers can develop encompassing perspectives for understanding justice and injustice.* Our distinguished scholars generally agree that notions about justice flow from the cultural context and

social structure that gives them meaning. Yet they would also agree that such contexts do not determine all frameworks for elucidating justice. They are able to obtain a perspective on perspectives, without foresaking a passioned commitment to creating a more just social order. Implicit in some of their pronouncements, however, is a caution to intellectuals to recognize that group membership slogans, partisanship, or ideologies infuse and define empirical observation. Abel, Black, Nader, and Marx challenge incorrigible propositions that would, for example, present a simple and coherent argument from an analysis of a problem to its solution. These writers deal in paradox and complexities. They suggest that an understanding of how social order promotes certain inequities does not necessarily mean there are simple ways to avoid them. With their discourse for justice, what are the realistic and obtainable goals of justice?

12. *Understanding social structure is fundamental to attempts to promote justice in the form of liberty and responsibility.* In attempts to strike a balance between liberty and responsibility, most of our authors point to the necessity of understanding relevant parts of the social structure. While the essays here remind us of just a few of the injustices in the world around us, there is relatively great agreement on the concept of injustice, particularly as more encompassing injustices emerging from structural inequities are examined. Such agreement is even institutionalized in the written constitutions of nations throughout the world, which attempt to reinforce the balance between liberty and responsibility. These extraordinary written similarities reflect agreement on some of the sources of injustice, including the "existing relations of economic, political, heterosexist, racial, and imperial hierarchies." They speak to the reduction of injustice. Yet injustice persists and often proliferates. This volume advocates placing the study of justice in its historical, political, economic, and philosophical foundations.

CHAPTER 2

The Contradictions of Legal Professionalism

Richard L. Abel

The lineaments of the contemporary American legal profession profoundly shape the functioning of the legal system and the quality of
justice it produces. Legal specialists play an indispensable role in mediating the interaction between Americans and their laws. This is not
true of all legal systems; rather, it is one manifestation of the highly
developed functional division of labor characteristic of technologically advanced societies. In many technologically simple societies, such
as those of precolonial Africa, all adult males were eligible to perform
the roles of lawgiver, legal decision-maker, legal representative, and
unaided litigant (Abel, 1973). Futhermore, much legal interaction was
entirely unmediated by specialists. Claims were asserted and resisted
through self-help, direct negotiation between the parties, or informal
sanctions. In the contemporary United States, by contrast, most forms
of self-help are outlawed, inequality between adversaries discourages
negotiation, and informal sanctions tend to be ineffective (Abel, 1984).
At the same time, most lay judges have been eliminated, lawyers dominate legislatures and administrative agencies, and it is both difficult
and uncommon for a layperson to appear in court without legal representation (Ziegler & Hermann, 1972). A layperson may even encounter major obstacles in mobilizing the law proactively without legal
representation—whether negotiating a contract, making a will, transferring property, creating a trust, obtaining permission to develop land,
or filing an income tax return. Recently, it was suggested that the several million undocumented people eligible for permanent residence

RICHARD L. ABEL • School of Law, University of California, Los Angeles, Los Angeles, California 90024.

under the new immigration law will constitute a windfall for lawyers (Applebome, 1986; May, 1986).

If legal specialists have become indispensable, however, they vary greatly in their training, structures of practice, and organization (Abel & Lewis, 1988a, 1988b). Americans parochially tend to identify the legal profession with private practitioners. Yet in most civil law countries there are many more judges, prosecutors, state attorneys, house counsel, and legally trained civil servants than lawyers in private practice (Abel, 1988c). In Norway, for instance, private practitioners are less numerous than lawyers employed in either the civil service or the private sector. In Germany, the magistracy (including both judges and prosecutors) is more than half the size of the privately practicing profession. In Belgium, private practitioners are less than a third of all lawyers (Abel, 1985a, Table 4).

All accusatorial systems tend to magnify the role of the magistracy at the expense of private practitioners. But sometimes, for a variety of reasons, the state may go even further to suppress private practice. In the early 19th century, Norway nationalized the entire legal profession for several decades, making lawyers' services available to all citizens without charge (Johnsen, 1988). During the interwar years, governments in both Japan and Germany sought to reduce the number of private practitioners and to restrain their actions in order to suppress challenges to Fascist hegemony (Blankenburg & Schultz, 1988; Haley, 1982; Reifner, 1982; Rokumoto, 1988). Third world countries like Mozambique have made all lawyers public employees in order to facilitate state planning, equalize access to justice, and reduce the perceived costs of legalism and litigiousness (Isaacman & Isaacman, 1982). And of course the socialist world offers little scope for private law practice (Shelley, 1984).

An awareness that all legal specialists, and especially private practitioners, play a limited role in many other legal systems reminds us that their centrality in the common law world is culturally and historically specific. But there can be no doubt about that centrality. In England in 1984, 86% of solicitors holding practicing certificates were engaged in private practice (Abel, 1988b, Table 2). In New Zealand in 1981, private practitioners outnumbered judges more than 36 to 1 (Murray, 1988, Table 2). And in the United States in 1980, more than two-thirds of all lawyers were in private practice, while only 4% were in the judiciary (and many of these were clerks, not judges) (Curran, 1986). Thus, it is not just legal specialists who mediate between American citizens and their legal system but specifically lawyers in private practice.

One important set of questions about this mediation concerns the distribution of legal representation: Who is assisted in what kinds of matters by which lawyers? I have addressed these issues in the past—particularly the ultimate question: Is it possible to achieve either formal or substantive justice if legal resources are allocated by the market, in whole or part (Abel, 1979, 1981a, 1985b)? Although I will touch on this below, I want to frame the present inquiry differently. Lawyers, first and foremost, are an occupational category. Furthermore, they are an occupational category that sought to attain the status of a profession and largely succeeded. The question I want to pose, therefore, is: What difference does it make—to lawyers themselves, to their clients, and to the larger society—that they aspire to the ideals of professionalism? Although I have been extremely critical of the way in which bar associations use the ideology of professionalism for purposes of mystification, and I have emphasized, perhaps exaggerated, the failure of lawyers to live up to their pretensions (Abel, 1981a, 1981b), I do not mean to deny the power of ideals to shape both aspirations and behavior. In this chapter I will consider the influence of the professional ideal on the work of lawyers, their dedication to the pursuit of justice, their concept of personal freedom, the relation between individual lawyers and clients and between producers and consumers of legal services viewed as collectivities, the relationship of lawyers to the market and the state, and the capacity of lawyers to construct collegial communities and resolve the tensions between equality and privilege.

One of Marx's central tenets—the alienation of workers under capitalism—has become an article of faith among many (both workers and students of work) who otherwise dissociate themselves from Marxist theory and practice. Most Americans experience work as subordination and meaningless drudgery, whose only goal is survival or, for those lucky enough to earn larger pay packets in shorter hours, the means to realization outside work—in the family, as consumers, and during leisure hours. "Thank God It's Friday" is the cri de coeur of the alienated worker. Perhaps the greatest attraction of the professions, therefore, is their claim to offer unalienated work. This is not an empty boast: Job satisfaction is significantly higher among professionals (Report of a Special Task Force, 1973).[1] Lawyers are no exception. They derive intrinsic satisfaction from exercising technical skills painfully acquired through years of study. They take pride in their craft, in the quality of their performance—perhaps especially in those

---

[1] A group of dissatisfied newspaper reporters offered an ironic illustration of this by seeking to have themselves classified as nonprofessional employees in order to claim overtime, because it was assumed that professional employees work unlimited hours without additional pay ("Suit Studies," 1986).

aspects that permit display and encourage competitiveness. Indeed, lawyers may be sufficiently enamored of their role to sacrifice material advantage in order to preserve it. Swiss lawyers in the canton of Geneva recently debated whether to liberalize their ethical rules to allow them to seek lucrative work as counselors to multinational corporations. Prominent members of the bar opposed such reforms, arguing: "We look with nostalgia at the lawyer who rises in a hearing to undertake the defense of someone. This is one of the most magnificent aspects of the profession: to fight against injustice with talent and honest. This, truly, is the role of the lawyer" (quoted in Bastard & Cardia-Vonèche, 1988). The fidelity to role inspired by the capacity of lawyers to find joy in their work also benefits society by encouraging high-quality performance—not out of fear of punishment for sloppiness but because a job well done is its own reward.

All legal work does not partake of these qualities, however. First, pleasure in technical skill easily can degenerate into the fetishism of technique. Indeed, one of the standard caricatures of the lawyer— whether the visual images of Daumier or the verbal descriptions of Dickens—is the legalistic pedant. The environment within which students learn and lawyers function encourages the kind of tunnel vision that sees trees but never forests. The classroom interrogation, student law review editors' anxiety about finding authority for every statement and checking every citation, the bar examination's preoccupation with black letter rules, the large law firm's perfectionism (bankrolled by its wealthy clients), and, of course, the constant fear that an adversary will take full advantage of any slip—all of these produce an obsession with detail.[2] What else but endemic compulsion neurosis could explain the 60- to 80-hour weeks that many lawyers routinely devote to their work even when no superior demands it. The Nazi slogan *"Arbeit macht frei"* should be a salutary warning that work may become just as addictive and enslaving as any other activity.

Professionals may endow their work with interest only by consigning others to intense boredom. Lawyers enjoy the luxury of intellectual stimulation because they are able to delegate the endless drudgery to subordinates (whose alienation is increased by serving

---

[2] Some of the earliest and best descriptions of the "legal personality" can be found in Riesman (1951, 1957), a lawyer turned sociologist. When I was an undergraduate I once praised David Riesman, whose course I had just completed, to Paul Freund, whose course I was then taking. Freund replied dismissively that Riesman had written nothing worthwhile since the articles on group libel he had published as a graduate fellow at Columbia Law School—thereby confirming Riesman's characterization of lawyers and explaining his decision to become a social scientist.

others who appear exempt).[3] In any case, much of the importance that lawyers attach to their work does not express its intrinsic value or challenge but rather reflects the wealth, power, or fame of the clients whom lawyers serve (Katz, 1982)—in this, lawyers resemble the groupies of entertainment stars.

Consequently, unalienated work is the privilege of a few lawyers, not the hallmark of an entire profession. At both extremes of the professional hierarchy—sole practitioners barely scraping by and large-firm associates grasping for the pinnacle of success—law is a paycheck and work merely instrumental. Undergraduates and law students asked why they wish to become lawyers typically point to the promise of economic security. They have only the vaguest notion of what lawyers do, often based on the misleading stereotype of the courtroom performer (Erlanger & Klegon, 1978). Law is a refuge for those without sufficient scientific aptitude or the stomach for blood to become doctors (Carlin, 1962) and too risk-averse to be entrepreneurs—those devoid of any strong preferences (other than material comfort), who wanted to "keep their options open" (Stevens, 1973). And the work most lawyers actually do reflects this lack of emotional investment—whether as cause or effect. Much of it is thoroughly routine, requiring little or no intellectual effort (Carlin, 1962). Poor or even middle-class clients confer no significance on the lawyer who represents them—indeed, they taint the lawyer with their own insignificance; nor do they have the resources to allow the lawyer to make the work interesting (Bellow, 1977; Katz, 1982). Consequently, many lawyers operate at the lowest levels of incompetence they can get away with, rather than at the highest levels of skill they can attain (Hazard, 1978). Thus, the ethic of legal professionalism may assure quality representation for a few wealthy clients, but it has little effect on the services rendered to most.

Alienation in work, according to Marxist theory, is a function of capitalist relations of production. Lawyers, like other professionals, long have prided themselves on escaping those forms of exploitation and subordination. In some legal systems, this is definitional. The English barrister or Scottish advocate in private practice cannot employ another barrister or advocate or be employed and cannot even enter into a partnership (Abel, 1981b; Paterson, 1988). The German *Rechtsanwalt* and the French *avocat* lose their rights of audience if they

---

[3]Although precise figures are unavailable, the number of paralegals, clerical workers, and other support staff in lawyers' offices is several times greater than the number of lawyers (Abel, 1988a, 1988b). Many paralegals resent the tedium of the work they are given (Johnstone & Flood, 1982; Murphree, 1984).

accept employment with a company (Blankenburg & Schultz, 1988; Boigeol, 1988). Separate bars with similar restrictions have emerged in most Australian states (Weisbrot, 1988). Even in New Zealand, the barrister sole is a recognized status—a specialist in advocacy who practices alone—although this is not legally mandated (Murray, 1988). And a third of American lawyers still practice alone (Abel, 1988a). Yet the ideal of the independent practitioner always has been compromised in reality. The lawyers' freedom from the degradation of commerce has been bought at the expense of subordinates who handle the "dirty work" (Hughes, 1971), though this may be disguised by calling the subordinate an independent contractor—as in the case of the barrister's clerk (Abel, 1988b)—or justified by differences in class, gender, or race between legal professionals and their unadmitted employees.[4]

In any case, very few lawyers can indulge in the principled rejection of capitalist relations of production (Abel, 1985c; Harris, 1985). Privately practicing barristers, for instance, are less than a tenth of all English lawyers (Abel, 1988b). Most lawyers spend their entire professional careers as either employees or employers of other lawyers. Virtually all American lawyers now begin their careers as employees of judges, law firms, corporations, prosecutors, legal aid offices, and government departments. A majority remain employees until they retire. And the few who escape that status quickly become the employers of other lawyers. Furthermore, both employees and employers must operate within ever-larger organizations that inevitably adopt bureaucratic forms for supervising the quantity and quality of work performed. In such a setting it is hard for lawyers to maintain the pretense of autonomy, which is the core of the professional role. Certainly employees have little or no say in the major decisions affecting their working lives: whom they will represent, which cases they will handle, what strategies they will pursue, how many hours they will work, how much they will be paid, even whether they will remain employed (Spangler, 1986). As a result, clients do not benefit from the independent judgment of all the lawyers working for them, and, more important, society loses the moral balance of their professionalism. But perhaps lawyers—indeed, most professionals—never enjoy such autonomy in a market economy. Either they operate at the margin of survival, constantly hustling for clients, or they gain economic security through dependence on a few large clients—corporations, the ag-

---

[4]In 19th-century England and the United States, subordinates were working-class men. Women replaced men as clerical workers around the turn of the century. In the last 20 years, women also have begun to replace men as legal executives in English solicitors' firms (Abel, 1988a, 1998b).

gregated interests of individuals belonging to a group legal services plan, or the state. As the "conceptive ideologues" of capitalism, in Maureen Cain's striking phrase (1979), lawyers consistently extol free choice and condemn state intervention. Yet their own experience of becoming and being lawyers is characterized by profound constraint (although collective amnesia may repress this). Law students describe law school as infantilizing, narrowing, and desensitizing, invoking analogies to brainwashing and total institutions (D. Kennedy, 1982; Savoy, 1970). They find the range of intellectual inquiry limited by the structure of the socratic dialogue, the content of the curriculum, and the threat of the bar examination. Cutthroat competition—vividly depicted in *The Paper Chase*—thrives within the hothouse atmosphere of the law school. The need to find a job (since the days of hanging out a shingle are long gone) and the clear hierarchy of careers strongly shape student preferences. Although lawyers represent their profession as a means of realizing selfhood and attaining maturity as a productive adult, the institutional structures of practice greatly prolong subordination—often into the late 30s or early 40s. Indeed, an increasing number of firms are creating (or reviving) the status of permanent associate or salaried partner, who never will participate in decision making or profits. There is reason to fear that women disproportionately will be relegated to this subordinate status.

Idealism is intrinsic in the concept of a professional. It can emerge in strange and unpredictable ways. President Reagan sought to implement the conservative agenda on health by appointing as Surgeon General Dr. C. Everett Koop, an outspoken foe of abortion. But professional identification as a physician has led Koop to campaign vigorously against smoking (notwithstanding the tobacco industry's support for Reagan) and adopt a humane attitude toward the AIDs epidemic and its tragic impact on the gay community.[5] As professionals, all lawyers share some fidelity to the ideals that ground our legal system, such as equal protection or due process.[6] Justice Sandra Day O'Connor, not otherwise known as a social reformer, recently said about her pro bono activities as a private practitioner: "I don't think any legal service for

[5] Another example of the positive influence of the professional role is the decision by a group of Illinois pharmacists to refuse to sell a pain-killer that they believed endangered consumers, despite FDA approval and their own economic interest in making the sales (Rempel & Coleman, 1986).

[6] Howard Erlanger (1978a) found that legal aid lawyers were vigorous advocates of the interests of their poor clients not because they were red-diaper babies or politically active before entering practice but because the role itself produced such loyalty. Jack Katz (1978, 1982) eloquently describes how legal aid lawyers seek significance in their work and, in the process, become effective champions of their clients' interests.

which I was paid gave me as much satisfaction as helping someone who needed it" (Los Angeles Times, 1986). This altruism was more obvious 15 years ago, when a majority of law students publicly aspired to struggle for social justice (Erlanger, 1978b; Erlanger & Klegon, 1978; Stevens, 1973). Yet even today, when most law students seem attracted only by that New Grub Street known as Wall Street, they cannot disavow all concern for such fundamental values as fairness or evenhandedness.

If lawyers still aspire to play the role of Weber's honoratiores (1954, p. 230), however, they quickly encounter a fundamental dilemma: Under capitalism, legal services are just as commodified as any other form of labor. Lawyers serve only those who can afford their services and only to the extent of the client's ability to pay. Physicians have had to accept that the command "heal the sick" carries the implicit qualifier "if they have health insurance." Similarly, lawyers will heed the call to "represent the unrepresented" only if there is reasonable assurance of a contingent or court-awarded fee. What I find most distressing about this betrayal of professionalism is that so few professionals appear to notice it. Lawyers seem to experience no moral qualms about whom they represent—or whom they do not.[7] Nor is the problem resolved when a third party (public or private) subsidizes legal services for the unrepresented, for this inevitably leads to some measure of control by the paymaster as well as dilution or concealment of the political goals of representation.[8] Thus, the Legal Services Corporation has restricted its staff lawyers, the tax code limits the activities of public interest lawyers, and group legal service plans consciously are apolitical (Abel, 1979, 1985b).

Lawyers have sought to depoliticize the choice of whom to rep-

---

[7] That lawyers can and should represent any client who can pay is so widely accepted that few have studied the issue. Indeed, it is dignified as an ethical principle in England—the "cab-rank" rule that purportedly governs barristers. Robert Nelson (1983, 1985) and Eve Spangler (1986) found that American lawyers in large firms rarely questioned whom they represented. Indeed, questions are more likely to be directed at the rare lawyer who refuses to represent ethically objectionable clients. Only law students, who are incompletely socialized in professional norms, appear to be troubled about whom they will represent. In the fall of 1985, students at elite East Coast law schools boycotted interviews with a law firm that represented South African Airlines; the firm subsequently dropped the client. In the fall of 1986, Harvard law students boycotted labor law firms they accused of union-busting practices (Noble, 1986).

[8] Physicians feel constrained by Medicare reimbursement practices that are keyed to "diagnostic related groups" (Rahman, 1986). And accountants complain that "it is 'a farce' to think that CPAs fighting for government contracts each year don't 'do a little bending' in their client's favor. . . . A third CPA said he was threatened—unsuccessfully—by a Los Angeles official, told to write a favorable report or lose the next year's contract" (Goodman & Merina, 1984a).

resent by directing their idealistic or altruistic impulses elsewhere. Often this takes the form of pro bono services. But it is no more convincing for lawyers to say (to themselves or others), "Look at the two percent of our time we volunteer, not at the ninety-eight percent for which we are paid," than it is for a corporation that pollutes the environment, manufactures weapons, or supports repressive regimes to ask the public to remember it for sponsoring operas or donating scholarships. Lawyers also participate in bar association activities directed toward reforming the legal system by advancing our knowledge of law, codifying and unifying systems of rules, and improving the operation of courts, administrative agencies, local government, police, or prisons. Yet like all collective activity, this must find a lowest common political denominator in order to achieve the necessary consensus, which means that it typically avoids the controversial issues, such as civil liberties in the 1950s, civil rights in the 1960s, and the Vietnam War in the 1970s (Auerbach, 1976; Halliday, 1982; Powell, 1979). And bar associations inevitably become vehicles for pursuing the interests of the profession at the expense of those of the public. Consider, for instance, the opposition by the ABA to federal legal aid in the 1950s, the AMA to Medicare in the 1960s, and the American Trial Lawyers' Association to no-fault compensation schemes in the 1970s, or the contemporary struggles of English solicitors to defend their conveyancing monopoly and of English barristers to protect their exclusive rights of audience (Abel, 1985b, 1988a, 1988b).

These internal contradictions between professional idealism and economic realism undoubtedly cause pain to many lawyers and threaten their ability to achieve personal fulfillment through work. But other contradictions may have greater social consequences. Professions are a manifestation of the division of labor. Their favorite self-justification is the technical competence gained through specialization. "Would you want a plumber to perform brain surgery on you?" physicians triumphantly ask their critics. But I can concede I would not and still maintain that the markets that have been captured by professions, including law, are the products of historical accident and political struggles and far from isomorphic with the distribution of technical competence. English solicitors have been able to earn half their income from conveyancing for nearly 200 years because the English state happened to need their license fees to finance the Napoleonic wars and was willing to concede a monopoly in return—not because solicitors alone are technically capable of transferring property (Abel, 1988b). Furthermore, if specialization increases the skills of producers (thereby enhancing the satisfaction they derive from work), it necessarily undermines the competence of consumers, as Milton Friedman (an unlikely consumer advocate) has pointed out (1962, chap. 9). This de-skilling compels the consumer to depend on legal professionals and simultaneously reduces the client's ability to evaluate the lawyer's performance. We know that dependence breeds ambivalence, anxiety, and resentment in other contexts: between parent and child, teacher and student, or psychiatrist and patient, for instance. Therefore, it should not surprise us when clients complain bitterly that their law-yers fail to keep them informed, consult them, or answer their inquir-ies (Abel, 1981a).[9]

Like other professionals, lawyers respond to client ambivalence with protestations of total fidelity. When the client is paying for legal services (and especially when the client is paying handsomely), eco-nomic incentives and the prevailing ideology of consumer sovereignty both reinforce this assurance. Indeed, clients sometimes prefer to pay higher fees in the hope that price is a measure of quality. Of course, when the client is not paying, or is paying poorly, those same forces undermine trust (Casper, 1971; Hermann, Single & Boston, 1977). Yet the problems inherent in the fundamentally unequal relationship be-tween lawyer and client cannot be resolved by avowals of fealty.

First, lawyers should not be totally faithful to client interests. The preferred metaphor is the friend who sometimes says no, not the pros-titute who always says yes (Luban, 1983).[10] All legal systems impose countervailing obligations to legal institutions and processes and to the larger society. American lawyers cannot condone perjury by their clients or remain silent about future illegality (ABA Commission on the Evaluation of Professional Standards, 1981; Whiteside v. Nix, 1986). English barristers justify their exclusive rights of audience in part by arguing that solicitor intermediaries are necessary to protect the bar and the integrity of the judicial process from undue client pressure. And lawyers undermine their own declarations of loyalty by simulta-neously insisting that they cannot be held accountable for the actions or characteristics of their clients (Schwartz, 1978)—even though no one is fooled.[11]

---

[9]Differences in expertise also compel lawyers to translate between lay clients and the legal system (Cain, 1979; Sarat & Felstiner, 1986). And here, as elsewhere, *traduire, c'est trahir* (to translate is to betray).

[10]Compare Fried (1976) with F. Kennedy (1971). Marc Galanter (1983, p. 159) quotes a well-known Chicago practitioner as saying, "A good lawyer is like a good prostitute. . . . If the price is right, you warm up your client."

[11]Lawyers invariably *are* identified with clients about whom the public has strong feel-ings: those accused of heinous crimes, suspected communists during the McCarthy era in the United States, organized crime today, Klaus Barbie in France, or those charged with terrorism. The ACLU lost considerable support when it represented the

Second, although the battle model inherent in the adversary system fosters identification between the interests of lawyers and clients (Heinz & Laumann, 1982), this never can be total. Lawyers, like other professionals, pretend that money is just the incidental reward for a job well done.[12] But they often sacrifice client interests to enhance their own profits, running up the meter when the client is wealthy (Hoffman, 1982) or selling out the client in a settlement when repeat business is unlikely (Rosenthal, 1974; Schwartz & Mitchell, 1970). In extreme cases, they abuse their trust by mishandling client funds (the most frequent ground for discipline).

Third, the degree of sympathy and empathy lawyers express toward clients necessarily varies with the social distance between them (Simon, 1978, 1980). One justification for affirmative action programs is that only minority lawyers adequately can represent clients from their own ethnic group. And the discovery that women speak about moral issues in a different voice (Gilligan, 1982) strongly suggests that the virtual absence of women from the legal profession until the 1970s systematically distorted women's participation in the legal system (Menkel-Meadow, 1985). Finally, lawyer fidelity is meaningless to clients who cannot afford to buy it. And when third parties pay, they typically place limits on the fidelity that would be forthcoming were the client wealthier, influencing both who can be served and what services can be provided (Abel, 1979, 1985b).[13] Thus, by professionalizing and commodifying legal services, lawyers may have enhanced quality for the few but simultaneously reduced the ability of the many to participate in the legal system.

The division of labor not only renders the lay public dependent on lawyers, it also disables clients from evaluating the quality of legal services. The profession's response is to take responsibility for ensuring quality. But all too often this degenerates into efforts to prevent anyone from reviewing or controlling quality.[14] Professions stren-

---

American Nazi Party in Skokie. And sometimes identification and hostility are so extreme that the individual cannot obtain a lawyer.

[12] English barristers, for instance, still maintain that their fees are "gratuities." They leave the negotiation of fees to their clerks. They cannot sue solicitors or clients for nonpayment. And solicitors often delay many months before paying. But all this gradually is changing (Abel, 1988b).

[13] The most visible example of the limitations on state-subsidized services are the repeated attempts to prevent medical clinics from performing abortions for poor or adolescent women or even telling them where they can obtain abortions.

[14] For instance, Albert Shanker, president of the American Federation of Teachers, recently devoted his weekly New York Times advertisement to attacking the superintendent of schools of St. Louis for penalizing teachers whose students failed to reach

uously resist efforts to subject their members to civil or criminal liability for occupational behavior.[15] Although bar associations may coopt
laypersons onto disciplinary or governing bodies, they invariably are
dominated by the professional majority (Arthurs, 1982). Professional
associations even prohibit their members from disseminating evidence about ability or achievement, which would allow consumers to
make meaningful comparisons.[16] And law thus far has thwarted most
attempts to formalize specialization, even though consumers plausibly
could argue that, if professionalization enhances the quality of legal
services, specialization should make them even better.

Despite the profession's denials, however, legal services vary
enormously in quality (partly a function of the client's resources), and
far too often they fall below minimum standards of competence. Although professionals claim to care for the whole person through an
ongoing relationship,[17] most services actually are highly routinized
and perfunctory, and most contacts between lawyers and clients are
brief and transitory (Carlin, 1962; Rosenthal, 1974). But if patriotism
is the last refuge of the scoundrel in politics, the "free market" is his
last refuge in economics. Professions appeal to the shibboleth of "consumer sovereignty"—simply giving consumers what they want. But
this never has been true, since lawyers actively constructed consumer
dependence in the first place, and it is increasingly difficult to maintain as lawyers, like other professionals, energetically seek to stimulate demand through institutional and individual advertising.[18]

For all their failings, free markets undoubtedly do confer some

---

specified levels of performance or improve their performance on standardized tests
(Shanker, 1986).

[15] The conspiracy of silence by which doctors long prevented patients from suing for
malpractice is notorious. Since it has been broken, physicians have complained about
the "crisis" in malpractice insurance and have persuaded many state legislatures to
grant them special protection from tort liability.

[16] Despite the relaxation of restrictions on advertising (e.g., Bates v. State Bar of Arizona,
1977), most common law jurisdictions still prohibit lawyers from making comparative
statements about quality or expertise.

[17] For instance, with the liberalization of advertising rules, I have begun to get letters
like the following, from Adrian E. Kenney, D.D.S., M.S. (December 10, 1981): "Our
office is dedicated to providing the highest technical quality of dentistry. Special emphasis is placed both on esthetics and on the patient's comfort. We involve all of our
patients in a preventive dental program, and we believe in making everyone aware of
the many treatment alternatives. Many of our friends at UCLA appreciate the warmth
and personal care we give to each of our patients. This is often not the case in a larger
clinic-oriented dental practice."

[18] "Professional" driving schools persuaded the California legislature to require all those
under 18 to take 30 hours of classroom instruction from a "certified" instructor before
obtaining a permit and 6 hours of driving practice from the same instructor before
taking the road test. This costs $300 to $400.

benefits on consumers. But markets rarely are pleasant enviornments for producers. Those who win the competitive race may find that the rewards outweigh the costs, but there are few consolations for the losers. It is not surprising, therefore, that so many seek refuge from the vagaries of competition—through monopolies, cartels, and the numerous forms of state protection (such as patents, copyrights, trade marks, tariffs, zoning, price supports, and tax relief). Others seek to escape the market altogether, looking to the family as a haven in a heartless world (Lasch, 1979). And those who must sell their labor in order to live form guilds, trade unions, and professions.[19] These are three historically distinct embodiments of the same functional imperative. Professions are distinguished both by their aspirations (to income and status) and by the tactics they use to control their markets (at present, academic credentials).[20] They offer their members freedom from competition with nonprofessionals as well as curbs on intraprofessional competition. They justify these restrictions as both necessary and sufficient to allow professionals to concentrate on providing quality services without the distractions and temptations of commercialism.

Professions undoubtedly enhance the quality of life of their members, but the social costs are considerable.[21] American lawyers, for

---

[19] There may be tensions between the various forms of market control. Some commentators were troubled when physicians sought to supplement the monopoly they enjoy through licensing by patenting medical processes, such as human embryo transplants (Brotman, 1984).

[20] The following is an amusing example:

> To become a clown, "you just can't do what you did in the old days," said Kenneth J. Feld, president and producer of the Ringling Bros. and Barnum & Bailey Circus. These days, he said, potential clowns must get a degree from Clown College in Venice, Fla.
>
> Last year, the school, which is owned by the circus, admitted 60 people out of 3,000 applicants.
>
> "Today, the clowns are better trained and more skilled than in the 1930's and 40's," Mr. Feld said.
>
> "Don't get me wrong—they had great clowns back then," he added, ticking off names like Felix Adler, Lou Jacobs, Emmett Kelly and Otto Griebling. "It's just that it's more of a profession these days" ("Circus Work," 1986).

[21] Two examples should suffice. "A Federal Trade Commission study said today that state laws limiting the establishment of automobile dealerships in 36 states cost consumers $3.2 billion last year" (Molotsky, 1986).

> Consumers can save up to one-third on the cost of contact lenses—without compromising safety or quality—by buying their lenses from commercial vision centers rather than from private practitioners, according to a Federal Trade Commission study released Thursday. . . . The commission found that the average price for lenses, including examination, ranges from $119.21 to $183.85 for hard lenses and from $150.07 to $234.54 for soft lenses. The report said ophthalmologists are the

instance, have prohibited any layperson from selling a wide range of legal services, including advice (although few other legal professions claim so much territory) (Abel, 1985a). Lawyers have allowed laypersons to produce such services only in subordinated roles. Lawyers restrict entry into the profession by means of stringent barriers—typically academic credentials and state examinations—whose connection to assuring the quality of legal services is unproven and tenuous (Abel, 1988a).[22] These barriers inevitably have a disproportionate impact on lower-class and minority aspirants, whose underrepresentation within the profession further disadvantages their communities.

Once the profession has succeeded in limiting its numbers and repulsing incursions by outsiders, it turns to suppressing competition among its own members. Lawyers have established and policed minimum fee schedules. They have restricted interstate commerce by erecting barriers against lawyers admitted in other states. They have prohibited partnerships between lawyers and other professions. They sought to outlaw group legal service plans. And they have prohibited advertising and solicitation. These constraints inhibit innovation and discourage initiative among lawyers. They inevitably reduce efficiency, drive up prices, and obstruct access to legal services. They create a vice tax that those willing to run the (admittedly small) risk of punishment can extort from consumers. And ultimately they fail— competition cannot be suppressed indefinitely within a market economy and a liberal polity (Abel, 1988a).

Professions promise a refuge not only from the market but also from the state—a particularly attractive feature in an era when the state is seen more as adversary and oppressor than as ally and liberator. By contrast with both capital and labor, which are subjected to extensive state regulation and scrutiny, professions stave off government interference by claiming that they alone can regulate themselves effectively and promising to do so selflessly (Goodman & Merina,

---

most expensive, opticians and privately practicing optometrists next and commercial optometrists the least expensive. (Cimons, 1985)

[22] It cannot be mere coincidence that bar examination pass rates dropped dramatically in both the United States and England shortly after the Depression, when demand for lawyers' services declined, and dropped again in the United States in the mid-1980s, when voices were raised against the rapid increase in the production of lawyers (Abel, 1988a, 1988b). The medical profession is even more explicit about its attempt to limit numbers (Freudenheim, 1986). And teachers recently have become very interested in a national credential that would limit entry and upgrade status (Bernstein & Weinstein, 1985). The problem with such efforts is that they encourage evasion and fraud: Candidates try to improve their scores on standardized tests (Maeroff, 1985), they obtain credentials abroad and seek to have them recognized in the United States (Lyons, 1984a), or they simply buy falsified credentials (Hechinger, 1985; Lyons, 1984b).

1984b). But the record of professional self-regulation, particularly by lawyers, never lives up to these promises. Ethical rules are preoccupied with the concerns of lawyers (primarily competition and status), neglecting those of clients (delay, discourtesy, and incompetence). Whereas the state actively polices compliance with its criminal and regulatory codes, the professions passively wait for consumer complaints. Given the deskilling and dependence of the public, which are inherent in the emergence of professions, it should not be surprising that relatively few laypersons complain. Professional associations dismiss the vast majority of these complaints with little or no investigation, they punish an insignificant fraction of those accused, and punishments are mild (reprimands, fines, and brief suspensions rather than expulsions).[23] One reason for this self-restraint is that discipline inevitably exacerbates tensions among lawyers and creates opportunities for status competition (Carlin, 1966; Shuchman, 1968). Yet the inefficacy of self-regulation encourages clients to sue for malpractice, courts and agencies to discipline lawyers who appear before them, and politicians to seek publicity through lawyer-bashing and demands for external regulation.[24] Furthermore, the fundamental contradiction of self-regulation is that professions ultimately derive their powers from the state.[25]

Self-regulation is only one facet of the profession's larger claim to be self-governing. The bar association is the primary vehicle through which lawyers have sought to control entry, prescribe interaction among members, ensure minimum standards of competence and training,

---

[23] For data on the failure of lawyer discipline in the United States, see Abel (1981a, 1988a); for England and Wales, see Abel (1981b, 1988b). For descriptions of the failure of physician discipline, see Brinkley (1985a, 1985b) and Wolfe, Bergman, and Silver (1985).

[24] Public figures as diverse as U.S. President Jimmy Carter and Harvard University President Derek Bok have indulged in the sport. For the last few years, Robert Presley, a Republican state senator from Riverside, California, has made considerable political capital out of investigating the failure of lawyer discipline and introducing bills that would take that responsibility away from the State Bar Association. Sometimes two professions attack each other's privileges. When Los Angeles physicians created MD's Docket Search to disclose whether a prospective patient ever had filed suit for malpractice, the Los Angeles Trial Lawyers' Association responded with a threat to notify patients if a doctor they were thinking of consulting ever had been sued for malpractice ("Doctors and Lawyers," 1985). Christian fundamentalists recently challenged the authority of teachers to determine the content of public education, winning a federal district court judgment allowing them to withdraw their children from the offending classes (Clendinen, 1986). And federal regulatory agencies have started to make available to prospective patients the mortality rates of hospitals (Brinkley, 1986a, 1986b).

[25] In Norway, for instance, local advocates' associations can expel a member for misconduct, but since the state licenses lawyers, such explusion does not have any direct effect on the lawyer's right to practice (Johnsen, 1988).

preserve and advance the body of esoteric knowledge, and participate in public affairs. Yet lawyers have encountered major obstacles in organizing and acting collectively. First, they have had to overcome apathy, indifference, and individualism, which plague all voluntary associations (Olson, 1982). Paradoxically, many organizations have had to resort to state coercion in order to compel lawyers to join the very bodies that were supposed to express their innate collegiality and their independence from the state.[26] They have found, however, that involuntary membership incapacitates them from taking controversial political positions (Schneyer, 1983). Second, bar associations are no more exempt from the iron law of oligarchy than is any other organization. Part of the reason is the same apathy among the membership that initially frustrated and then impeded efforts to organize lawyers. But the failure of organizational democracy also reflects the profound stratification of the legal profession, the widely varying interests and resources that the different strata bring to the task of self-governance, and the growing heterogeneity of those entering the profession today (Halliday & Cappell, 1979). Third, the mere fact that all lawyers obtain the same credential does not ensure political consensus. The heated debate over the ABA Model Rules of Professional Conduct amply illustrates this (Abel, 1981a). Consequently, bar associations are confronted with the Hobson's choice between entering the political fray—thereby endangering their internal unity, stimulating protests from disaffected members, and risking secession—and the equally unattractive alternative of retreating into political passivity and economism—thereby encouraging membership apathy and betraying the professional ideal of public service (Halliday, 1982). Each course has stimulated the emergence of rival associations and accelerated the tendency toward syndicalism, which threaten both the unity and the status of the profession.

Lawyers defend their privileges of self-regulation and self-governance against charges of self-interest by maintaining that they represent an essential counterweight to the increasingly imperial state. Although all professions make such claims (Durkheim, 1957), lawyers can stress their fundamentally political role and portray themselves as institutional gadflies, constantly engaged in criticizing and curtailing overreaching and illegality by the state. The reality is more complex, however. The profession as a whole devotes an insignificant proportion of its energies to challenging state action on behalf of individuals (Heinz & Laumann, 1982), although it may glorify (often posthu-

[26] A large number of state bar associations made membership compulsory between 1920 and 1960 (Schneyer, 1983). Recently, the General Council of the Bar has compelled all privately practicing English barristers to join (Abel, 1988b).

mously) the few lawyers who dedicate their lives to opposition. When lawyers are not complicit with the state—seeking to mobilize its power on behalf of a client—they generally are indifferent to it. And as lawyers increasingly come to rely on the state to subsidize the delivery of services to less wealthy clients, their oppositional posture becomes even more difficult to maintain. Either they must mute their criticisms in order to placate their paymaster, or their intransigence may reveal selfish motives—as when physicians endanger the health of their patients by striking for higher pay.[27]

Professions promise an enclave within which the compulsions of the market and the state will be moderated, if not eliminated. But professionals do not just seek the quiet life through freedom from external constraints (Lees, 1966). They also wish to enrich their experience, particularly by strengthening their participation in a community of peers (Goode, 1957). This sense of community is fostered by commonalities of work and life history. Indeed, the traumatic rites of passage—professional school, state examinations, and apprenticeship— may serve more to engender solidarity than to ensure technical competence. Toward the same end, professions assert the equality of all their members, explicitly discouraging invidious comparisons. And when the myth of equality cannot be maintained, professions invoke a meritocratic ideology to explain differential reward. Yet once again professions pursue these goals with indifferent success and at considerable cost.

First, true community never is realized. Lawyers, like other professionals (Bucher & Strauss, 1961), always have been divided by function, structure, and strata. These divisions have widened in recent years as lawyers have become hyperspecialized, their practice environments have diverged, and the rewards of income, power, and status have become increasingly disparate (Heinz & Laumann, 1982). It is difficult to argue that senior partners must earn up to 50 times as much as sole practitioners in order for large firms to attract the most qualified lawyers and motivate them to work hard—and it is even more difficult to pretend that this is the best allocation of resources. The diffusion of capitalist relations of production within law also separates employers from employed lawyers—sometimes pitting them against each other as management and unionized labor. And in countries such as England and the Netherlands, where substantial amounts

---

[27] Ontario physicians recently struck for 3 weeks to protest the level of government payments ("Ontario Doctors," 1986). And when the English Lord Chancellor granted derisory increases in the level of legal aid payments in the spring of 1986, many barristers urged a boycott of prosecution briefs, which would have shut down the criminal justice system (Abel, 1988b).

of legal aid are delivered by private practitioners, a new division has emerged between those serving paying clients and those dependent on state funds (Abel, 1985b; 1988b). These antagonisms emerge and intensify in the very process of constructing and defending professionalism: Lower-stratum practitioners seek economic benefits by controlling entry and restricting competition from new entrants, while elite practitioners are preoccupied with enhancing the profession's image by defining the behavior of lower-stratum practitioners as misconduct and publicly punishing it. And the divergence has led to the proliferation of professional associations, which visibly belie the pretense of a single community.

Perhaps even more troubling than the structural impediments to community is the fact that professional collegiality has been constructed on a foundation of discrimination against those disadvantaged by religion, ethnicity, class, race, and gender.[28] Until the middle of the 20th century professions, like other elites, were unashamed of their prejudices. Most countries excluded women from law practice until the end of the 19th or the beginning of the 20th century—and Harvard Law School did not admit them until 1950. The American Bar Association excluded blacks until 1943. And state bars introduced character tests in the 1920s and 1930s explicitly to exclude recent immigrants from southern and eastern Europe. As each group overcame the barriers, its entry challenged the capacity of the profession to absorb diversity while remaining a single community. The prognosis is not good. The relatively universalistic portal of the academy admits Jews and Catholics above their proportions of the population, women at a little less than their proportion, and racial minorities at about half their proportion. But the more particularistic mechanisms for allocating newly qualified lawyers to roles within the professional hierarchy and advancing them throughout their careers have produced socioreligious, class, gender, and racial inequalities in the composition of the significant strata: large firms and small, partners and associates, private practitioners and lawyers employed in government and business. The prominent parallels between ascribed characteristics and rewards cast grave doubt on the meritocratic justification for the system of stratification. In response, the newer entrants

[28] It is typical of such communities that their members see nothing wrong in discrimination. Until recently, Rotary International excluded women, and it expelled the Duarte, California, chapter for admitting them. Wm. John Kennedy, the Los Angeles lawyer defending Rotary International, explained: "Well, the preference of Rotarians at their weekly meetings is to be with the boys. It's been that way for 75 years, and that's become the accepted standard. If you have to let in outsiders, it destroys the selectivity and prestige of the organization" (Savage, 1986). Rotary's "selectivity" extends to more than a million members.

frequently have formed their own professional associations to preserve and strengthen their distinct sense of community (cf. Glazer &
Moynihan, 1970).

Professions are a vehicle for enhancing the material interests of
members by suppressing competition. But they also represent aspirations to status and respect in a society that never has resolved the
contradictions between the ethos of egalitarianism and the reality of
extreme inequalities (Larson, 1977). Professions derive respect from
several sources: their unique technical competence, the gratitude of
clients and patients for help in moments of crisis, the apparent indifference of professionals to monetary gain, the altruism they display,
their dedication to widely shared ideals (such as justice and health),
their professed willingness to assist all those in need, and their exemplary public service.

Yet lawyers constantly complain about their poor image, apparently with good reason (Curran, 1977, pp. 227–259). Many lack distinctive skills—after all, law is just talk (Morris, Cooper, & Byles, 1973)—
and lawyers cannot mobilize the impressive technology of medicine.
The public often perceives legal skills as mystification or even deceit,
rather than expertise. Gratitude for help inevitably is mixed with ambivalence about dependence and uncertainty whether the professional
can be trusted. The pretense of indifference to money is hard to rec-
oncile with the conspicuous wealth of prominent lawyers and the high
fees they charge, both of which engender envy and resentment as well
as awe. The public correctly sees lawyers as two-faced: demanding
socialization of the costs of professional reproduction (society heavily
subsidizes all education) while simultaneously insisting on their exclusive right to consume the rewards commanded by their professional skills.[29] Avowals of dedication to the public good seem inconsistent with the extremely unequal distribution of lawyers' services
and the fact that they are consumed disproportionately by the wealthy,
the powerful, and the notoriously immoral or criminal. Nor does the
public accept the lawyers' claim that they are unaccountable for those
they serve so loyally. To the extent that the profession's reputation for
altruism depends on visible acts of charity, lawyers lose respect as
they accept state payment for what used to be pro bono services, and
especially as they become vigorous advocates of greater government
expenditure.[30] The social homogeneity of the profession, which elic-

[29] The profession vigorously opposed and successfully defeated recent proposals to compel
lawyers to make some return for the public's investment by rendering pro bono services (Abel, 1981a).

[30] The power of the public purse to corrupt is most visible in medical services. In one
recent scandal, 108 physicians were found to have earned an average of $348,672

ited respect when ascriptive inequality was widely accepted, now is seen, rightly, as illegitimate discrimination. But if lawyers seek to preserve their status by relegating newer entrants—women and minorities—to the lower strata, they will only invite further charges of sexism and racism. Finally, although a few lawyers engage in conspicuous short-term public service, the profession is deeply implicated in the impoverishment of the public sector that is inherent in capitalism. Most lawyers shun the public sector for the greater material rewards of private practice, and many of those who enter government service treat it as a revolving door, acquiring public expertise and contacts only to sell them at a profit to private enterprise (Spector, 1973).

Let me recapitulate the argument and conclude. I defined my topic as the contradictions of legal professionalism in order to disavow any suggestion that lawyers intentionally deceive either themselves or the lay public. We must not disparage the powerful ideals that attract entrants to the legal profession and inspire lawyers to seek meaning in their work. At the same time, we must acknowledge that most lawyers fail to attain these ideals and cannot do so without structural social change. Lawyers seek unalienated work—intrinsic rewards from the autonomous exercise of technical skill in the service of valued goals. Instead, they find economic pressures that make work merely instrumental, forcing them to sacrifice quality for profit; they enter capitalist relations of production that make them either bosses or bossed; and they become slaves to internal compulsions. Lawyers are motivated by dedication to justice, but they can operate only as hired guns, subordinate to an alien paymaster even when seeking to serve the unrepresented. Lawyers exalt the ideals of personal freedom and individual choice, but they find themselves ensnared in a social and economic web of careerism and competition. The very role of the lawyer manifests a division of labor that expands the technical competence of some, and thus the quality of their performance, while deskilling others and depriving them of any legal advice or representation. Lawyers respond to client fears of dependence by encouraging trust but often are unable to achieve either sympathy or identity of interest with their clients. Lawyers strive for and attain substantial protection

each during 1983 for examining applicants for social security disability benefits; 6 physicians earned more than a million dollars that year, and one earned about 3 million ("Panel Tells," 1986). In another, a group of 5 physicians and 3 pharmacists defrauded the government of $20 million ("11 Convicted," 1986). That no such scandals have emerged within the legal profession may be due more to the fact that legal aid is provided by salaried employees than to the superior morality of lawyers. French lawyers so feared the loss of "symbolic capital" that they initially opposed state payment for legally aided clients (Boigeol, 1988).

from the harsh winds of the competitive market, but only at the expense of other producers and all consumers. Lawyers claim exemption from state oversight, but their efforts at self-regulation and self-governance seem even less effective and less democratic. Lawyers justify that exemption by asserting their need for independence but rarely constitute a meaningful counterweight to state power. Lawyers seek the ideals of community and equality within the profession but pursue them by denying the personhood of outsiders, and they respond to growing diversity by reproducing illegitimate forms of stratification. Lawyers hope for public respect but confront ambivalence, envy, resentment, and mistrust. In order to remain faithful to the ideals of legal professionalism we must study its compromises and betrayals for clues to the kinds of structural social change that would be necessary to fulfill those promises.

References

Abel, R. (1973). A comparative theory of dispute institutions in society. *Law & Society Review, 8,* 217–347.

Abel, R. (1979). Socializing the legal profession: Can redistributing lawyers' services achieve social justice? *Law & Policy Quarterly, 1,* 5–51.

Abel, R. (1981a). Why does the American Bar Association promulgate ethical rules? *Texas Law Review, 59,* 639–688.

Abel, R. (1981b). Toward a political economy of lawyers. *Wisconsin Law Review, 1981,* 1117–1187.

Abel, R. (1984). Custom, rules, administration, community. *Journal of African Law, 28,* 6–19.

Abel, R. (1985a). Comparative sociology of legal professions: An exploratory essay. *American Bar Foundation Research Journal, 1985,* 1–85.

Abel, R. (1985b). Law without politics: Legal aid under advanced capitalism. *UCLA Law Review, 32,* 474–642.

Abel, R. (Ed.). (1985c). Lawyers and the power to change. *Law & Policy, 7*(1), 1–167.

Abel, R. (1988a). United States: The contradictions of professionalism. In R. Abel & P. S. C. Lewis (Eds.), *Lawyers in society: Vol. 1. The common law world.* Berkeley and Los Angeles: University of California Press.

Abel, R. (1988b). England and Wales: A comparison of the professional projects of barristers and solicitors. In R. Abel & P. S. C. Lewis (Eds.), *Lawyers in society: Vol. 1. The common law world.* Berkeley and Los Angeles: University of California Press.

Abel, R. (1988c). Lawyers in the civil law world. In R. Abel & P. S. C. Lewis (Eds.), *Lawyers in society: Vol. 2: The civil law world.* Berkeley and Los Angeles: University of California Press.

Abel, R., & Lewis, P. S. C. (Eds.). (1988a). *Lawyers in society: Vol. 1. The common law world.* Berkeley and Los Angeles: University of California Press.

Abel, R., & Lewis, P. S. C. (Eds.). (1988b). *Lawyers in society: Vol. 2. The civil law world.* Berkeley and Los Angeles: University of California Press.

American Bar Association Commission of the Evaluation of Professional Standards. (1981).

Model Rules of professional conduct (proposed final draft). Chicago: American Bar Association.

Applebome, P. (1986, October 19). Border people doubt bill will slow alien flow. *New York Times*, p. 1.

Arthurs, H. W. (1982). Public accountability of the legal profession. In P. A. Thomas (Ed.), *Law in the balance: Legal services in the eighties* (pp. 161–185). Oxford: Martin Robertson.

Auerbach, J. (1976). *Unequal justice: Lawyers and social change in modern America.* New York: Oxford University Press.

Bastard, B., & Cardia-Vonèche, L. (1988). The lawyers of Geneva: An analysis of change in the legal profession. In R. L. Abel & P. S. C. Lewis (Eds.), *Lawyers in society: Vol. 2. The civil law world.* Berkeley and Los Angeles: University of California Press.

Bates v. State Bar of Arizona, 433 U.S. 350 (1977).

Bellow, G. (1977, Spring). The legal aid puzzle: Turning solutions into problems (Working Papers for a New Society No. 52).

Bernstein, H., & Weinstein, W. (1985, November 1). Tests for new teachers get endorsement of AFL-CIO. *Los Angeles Times*, Sect. 1, p. 3.

Blankenburg, E., & Schultz, U. (1988). German advocates: A highly regulated profession. In R. Abel & P. S. C. Lewis (Eds.), *Lawyers in society: Vol. 2. The civil law world.* Berkeley and Los Angeles: University of California Press.

Boigeol, A. (1988). The French bar: The difficulties of unifying a divided profession. In R. Abel and P. S. C. Lewis (Eds.), *Lawyers in society: Vol. 2. The civil law world.* Berkeley and Los Angeles: University of California Press.

Brinkley, J. (1985a, September 2). U.S. industry and physicians attack medical malpractice. *New York Times*, p. 1.

Brinkley, J. (1985b, September 3). Medical discipline laws: Confusion reigns. *New York Times*, p. 1.

Brinkley, J. (1986a, March 3). U.S. distributing lists of hospitals with unusual death rates. *New York Times*, p. 8.

Brinkley, J. (1986b, November 4). Key hospital accrediting agency to start weighing mortality rates. *New York Times*, p. 1.

Brotman, H. (1984, January 9). Human embryo transplants. *New York Times Magazine*, p. 28.

Bucher, R., & Strauss, A. (1961). Professions in process. *American Journal of Sociology, 66*, 325–334.

Cain, M. (1979). The general practice lawyer and the client: Toward a radical conception. *International Journal of the Sociology of Law, 7*, 331–354.

Carlin, J. (1962). *Lawyers on their own: A study of individual practitioners in Chicago.* New Brunswick, NJ: Rutgers University Press.

Carlin, J. (1966). *Lawyers' ethics: A survey of the New York City bar.* New York: Russell Sage Foundation.

Casper, J. (1971). Did you have a lawyer when you went to court? No, I had a public defender. *Yale Review of Law and Social Action, 1*(4), 4–9.

Cimons, M. (1985, December 16). Vision centers provide good value, FTC says. *Los Angeles Times*, Sect. I, p. 4.

Circus work continues to draw the dreamers (1986, March 30). *New York Times*, p. 28.

Clendinen, D. (1986, October 25). Fundamentalists win a federal suit over schoolbooks. *New York Times*, p. 1.

Curran, B. A. (1977). *The legal needs of the public: The final report of the national survey.* Chicago: American Bar Foundation.

Curran, B. A. (1986). American lawyers in the 1980s: A profession in transition. *Law & Society Review, 20,* 19–52.

Doctors and lawyers square off on legal records (1985, December 16). *Los Angeles Times,* Sect. I, p. 11.

Durkheim, E. (1957). *Professional ethics and civic morals.* London: Routledge and Kegan Paul.

11 convicted of Medicare "fraud mill": 5 doctors, 3 pharmacists plead guilty. (1986, January 23). *Los Angeles Times,* Sect. I, p. 8.

Erlanger, H. (1978a). Lawyers and neighborhood legal services: Social background and the impetus for reform. *Law & Society Review, 12,* 253–274.

Erlanger, H. (1978b). Young lawyers and work in the public interest. *American Bar Foundation Research Journal, 1978,* 83–104.

Erlanger, H., & Klegon, D. (1978). Socialization effects of professional schools: The law school experience and student orientations to public interest concerns. *Law & Society Review, 13,* 11–35.

Freudenheim, M. (1986, June 14). Organized medicine considering defense against glut of doctors. *New York Times,* p. 1.

Fried, C. (1976). The lawyer as friend: the moral foundations of the lawyer–client relation. *Yale Law Journal, 85,* 1060–1089.

Friedman, M. (1962). *Capitalism and freedom.* Chicago: University of Chicago Press.

Galanter, M. (1983). Mega-law and mega-lawyering in the contemporary United States. In R. Dingwall & P. Lewis (Eds.), *The sociology of the professions: Lawyers, doctors, and others* (pp. 152–176). London: Macmillan.

Gilligan, C. (1982). *In a different voice: Psychological theory and women's development.* Cambridge: Harvard University Press.

Glazer, N., & Moynihan, D. (1970). *Beyond the melting pot: The Negroes, Puerto Ricans, Jews, Italians and Irish of New York City* (2nd rev. ed.). Cambridge, MA: M.I.T. Press.

Goode, W. J. (1957). Community within a community: The professions. *American Sociological Review, 22,* 194–200.

Goodman, M., & Merina, V. (1984a, June 11). Public auditing jobs: Lobbying smooths the way. *Los Angeles Times,* Sect. I, p. 1.

Goodman, M., & Merina, V. (1984b, June 12). Lobby stymies efforts to reform audit laws. *Los Angeles Times,* Sect. I, p. 3.

Haley, J. (1982). The politics of informal justice: The Japanese experience, 1922–1942. In R. Abel (Ed.), *The politics of informal justice: Vol. 2: Comparative studies* (pp. 125–148). New York: Academic Press.

Halliday, T. C. (1982). The idiom of legalism in bar politics: Lawyers, McCarthyism and the civil rights era. *American Bar Foundation Research Journal, 1982,* 913–988.

Halliday, T. C., & Cappell, C. L. (1979). Indicators of democracy in professional associations: Elite recruitment, turnover and decisionmaking in a metropolitan bar association. *American Bar Foundation Research Journal, 1979,* 697–767.

Harris, P. (1985). The San Francisco community law collective. *Law & Policy, 7,* 19–28.

Hazard, G. (1978). *Ethics in the practice of law.* New Haven, CT: Yale University Press.

Hechinger, F. (1985, August 6). Study finds "diploma mills" a booming industry. *New York Times,* p. 22.

Heinz, J. P., & Laumann, E. O. (1982). *Chicago lawyers: The social structure of the bar.* New York: Russell Sage, and Chicago: American Bar Foundation.

Hermann, R., Single, E., & Boston, J. (1977). *Counsel for the poor: Criminal defense in urban America.* Lexington, MA: Lexington Books.

Hoffman, P. (1982). *Lions of the eighties: The inside stories of the powerhouse law firms*. New York: E. P. Dutton.

Hughes, E. C. (1971). *The sociological eye* (2 vols.). Chicago: Aldine-Atherton.

Isaacman, B., & Isaacman, A. (1982). A socialist legal system in the making: Mozambique before and after independence. In R. Abel (Ed.), *The politics of informal justice: Vol. 2. Comparative studies* (pp. 281–324). New York: Academic Press.

Johnsen, J. T. (1988). The professionalization of legal counseling in Norway. In R. Abel & P. S. C. Lewis (Eds.), *Lawyers in society: Vol. 2. The civil law world*. Berkeley and Los Angeles: University of California Press.

Johnstone, Q., & Flood, J. (1982). Paralegals in English and American law offices. *Windsor Yearbook of Access to Justice, 2,* 152–190.

Katz, J. (1978). Lawyers for the poor in transition: Involvement, reform and the turnover problem in the legal services program. *Law & Society Review, 12,* 275–300.

Katz, J. (1982). *Poor people's lawyers in transition*. New Brunswick, NJ: Rutgers University Press.

Kennedy, D. (1982). Legal education as training for hierarchy. In D. Kairys (Ed.), *The politics of law* (pp. 40–61). New York: Pantheon.

Kennedy, F. (1971). The whorehouse theory of law. In R. Lefcourt (Ed.), *Law against the people: Essays to demystify law, order and the courts* (pp. 81–89). New York: Random House.

Larson, M. S. (1977). *The rise of professionalism: A sociological analysis*. Berkeley and Los Angeles: University of California Press.

Lasch, C. (1979). *Haven in a heartless world: The family besieged*. New York: Basic Books.

Lees, D. S. (1966). *Economic consequences of the professions*. London: Institute of Economic Affairs.

Los Angeles Times. (1986, May 5). Sect. I, p. 2.

Luban, D. (1983). The adversary system excuse. In D. Luban (Ed.), *The good lawyer* (pp. 83–122). Totowa, NJ: Rowman & Allanheld.

Lyons, R. (1984a, June 24). Foreign-trained doctors in for a thorough checkup. *New York Times*, Sect. IV, p. 24.

Lyons, R. (1984b, March 4). Investigators check on thousands for falsified degrees as doctors. *New York Times*, p. 1.

Maeroff, G. (1985, August 2). 2 coaching concerns barred from using S.A.T. materials. *New York Times*, p. 1.

May, L. (1986, November 4). ABA sees risk of fraud by people aiding illegal aliens. *Los Angeles Times*, Sect. I, p. 6.

Menkel-Meadow, C. (1985). Portia in a different voice: Speculations on a women's lawyering process. *Berkeley Women's Law Journal, 1,* 39–63.

Molotsky, I. (1986, March 14). State laws cost car buyers, U.S. study says. *New York Times*, p. 4.

Morris, P., Cooper, J., & Byles, A. (1973). Public attitudes to problem definition and problem solving: A pilot study. *British Journal of Social Work, 3,* 301–320.

Murphree, M. (1984). Brave new office: The changing world of the legal secretary. In K. Sacks & D. Remy (Eds.), *My troubles are going to have trouble with me: Everyday trials and triumphs of women workers*. New Brunswick, NJ: Rutgers University Press.

Murray, G. (1988). Lawyers in New Zealand: From colonial GPs to the servants of the capital. In R. Abel & P. S. C. Lewis (Eds.), *Lawyers in society: Vol. 1. The common law world*. Berkeley and Los Angeles: University of California Press.

Nelson, R. (1983). The changing structure of opportunity: Recruitment and careers in large law firms. *American Bar Foundation Research Journal, 1983*, 109–162.

Nelson, R. (1985). Ideology, practice and professional autonomy: Social values and client relationships in the large law firm. *Stanford Law Review, 37*, 503–552.

Noble, K. (1986, October 23). Law firms linked to "union-busting." *New York Times*, p. 14.

Olson, M., Jr. (1982). *The logic of collective action: Public goods and the theory of groups* (rev. ed.). Cambridge, MA: Harvard University Press.

Ontario doctors vote to end strike, stage rotating halts in services. (1986, July 5). *Los Angeles Times*, Sect. I, p. 6.

Panel tells social security agency waste. (1986, October 30). *Los Angeles Times*, Sect. I, p. 1.

Patterson, A. (1988). The legal profession in Scotland—An endangered species or a problem case for market theory? In R. Abel & P. S. C. Lewis (Eds.), *Lawyers in society: Vol. 1. The common law world*. Berkeley and Los Angeles: University of California Press.

Powell, M. (1979). Anatomy of a counter-bar association: The Chicago Council of Lawyers. *American Bar Foundation Research Journal, 1979*, 501–541.

Rahman, F. (1986, January 23). Medicare makes a wrong diagnosis. *New York Times*, p. 23.

Reifner, U. (1982). Individualistic and collective legalization: The theory and practice of legal advice for workers in prefascist Germany. In R. Abel (Ed.), *The politics of informal justice: Vol. 2. Comparative studies* (pp. 81–124). New York: Academic Press.

Rempel, W., & Coleman, E. (1986, July 6). Pharmacists curb sale of painkiller. *Los Angeles Times*, Sect. I, p. 1.

Report of a special task force to the Secretary, Department of Health, Education and Welfare. (1973). *Work in America*. Cambridge, MA: M.I.T. Press.

Riesman, D. (1951). Toward an anthropological science of law and the legal profession. *American Journal of Sociology, 57*, 121–135.

Riesman, D. (1957). Law and sociology: Recruitment, training and colleagueship. *Stanford Law Review, 8*, 643–673.

Rokumoto, K. (1988). The present state of Japanese practicing attorneys. In R. Abel & P. S. C. Lewis (Eds.), *Lawyers in society: Vol. 2. The civil law world*. Berkeley and Los Angeles: University of California Press.

Rosenthal, D. E. (1974). *Lawyer and client: Who's in charge?* New York: Russell Sage.

Sarat, A., & Felstiner, W. L. F. (1986). Law and strategy in the divorce lawyer's office. *Law & Society Review, 20*, 93–134.

Savage, D. (1986, November 4). Rotary's case for excluding women goes to Supreme Court. *Los Angeles Times*, Sect. I, p. 3.

Savoy, P. (1970). Toward a new politics of legal education. *Yale Law Journal, 79*, 444–504.

Schneyer, T. (1983). The incoherence of the unified bar concept: Generalizing from the Wisconsin case. *American Bar Foundation Research Journal, 1983*, 1–108.

Schwartz, M. (1978). The professionalism and accountability of lawyers. *California Law Review, 66*, 669–697.

Schwartz, M., & Mitchell, D. (1970). An economic analysis of the contingent fee in personal injury litigation. *Stanford Law Review, 22*, 1125–1162.

Shanker, A. (1986, October 26). Professionalism under fire: Power vs. knowledge in St. Louis. *New York Times*, Sect. IV, p. 7.

Shelley, L. (1984). *Lawyers in Soviet work life*. New Brunswick, NJ: Rutgers University Press.

Shuchman, P. (1968). Ethics and legal ethics: The propriety of the canons as a group moral code. *George Washington Law Review, 37*, 244–269.

Simon, W. (1978). The ideology of advocacy: Procedural justice and professional ethics. *Wisconsin Law Review, 1978*, 28–144.

Simon, W. (1980). Homo psychologicus: Notes on a new legal formalism. *Stanford Law Review, 32*, 487–559.

Spangler, E. (1986). *Lawyers for hire: Salaried professionals at work*. New Haven: Yale University Press.

Spector, M. (1973). Secrecy in job seeking among government attorneys: Two contingencies in the theory of subculture. *Urban Life and Culture, 2*, 211–229.

Stevens, R. (1973). Law schools and law students. *Virginia Law Review, 59*, 551–707.

Suit studies the wages of journalism. (1986, July 20). *New York Times*, p. 12.

Weber, M. (1954). *Law in economy and society*. Cambridge, MA: Harvard University Press.

Weisbrot, D. (1988). The Australian legal profession: From provincial family firms to multinationals. In R. Abel & P. S. C. Lewis (Eds.), *Lawyers in society: Vol. 1: The common law world*. Berkeley and Los Angeles: University of California Press.

Whiteside v. Nix, 105 S.Ct. 988. (1986).

Wolfe, S., Bergman, H., & Silver, G. (1985). *Medical malpractice: The need for disciplinary reform, not tort reform*. Washington, DC: Public Citizen.

Ziegler, D., & Hermann, M. (1972). The invisible litigant: An inside view of pro se actions in the federal courts. *New York University Law Review, 47*, 157–257.

CHAPTER 3

The Elementary Forms of Conflict Management

Donald Black

Conflict management is the handling of grievances, including litigation, mediation, arbitration, negotiation, beating, torture, assassination, feuding, warfare, strikes, boycotts, riots, banishment, resignation, running away, ridicule, scolding, gossip, witchcraft, witch-hunting, hostage-taking, fasting, confession, psychotherapy, and suicide.[1] Although diverse, its many varieties reduce to a smaller number, each arising under distinctive conditions.

The following pages describe five forms of conflict management—self-help, avoidance, negotiation, settlement, and toleration[2]—and propose the social fields[3] where their most extreme expressions occur. These fields and forms are isomorphic.

Self-Help

Self-help is the handling of a grievance by unilateral aggression (Black, 1983, p. 34, note 2). It ranges from quick and simple gestures

---

[1] This chapter could as well be called "The Elementary Forms of Social Control." For a discussion of this conceptual issue, see Black (1984b, p. 5, note 7).

[2] This typology was developed with M. P. Baumgartner and presented jointly in a talk entitled "Toward a Theory of Self-Help" at the Center for Criminal Justice, Harvard Law School, February 19, 1982. For related typologies, see Gulliver (1979, pp. 1–3) and Koch (1974, pp. 27–31).

[3] Related concepts of "field" are applied to this subject matter in Collier (1973, pp. 253–255), Goody (1957), and Moore (1973). In physics, a field is a "region of influence" (Whitrow, 1967/1973, p. 68).

DONALD BLACK • Department of Sociology, University of Virginia, Charlottesville, Viriginia 22903.

of disapproval, such as glares or frowns, to massive assaults resulting in numerous deaths. In simple societies, self-help occurs dramatically as blood revenge, feuding, and affairs of honor (see, e.g., Hasluck, 1954, pp. 219–260; Koch, 1974; Otterbein & Otterbein, 1965; Peristiany, 1966; Reid, 1970). It also includes cursing, sorcery, and the assassination of witches (see, e.g., Evans-Pritchard, 1937, Part 1, chap. 7; Knauft, 1985; Winans & Edgerton, 1964). In modern societies, it includes much fighting, beating, and killing among family members, friends, acquaintances, ethnic groups, and nations. Conduct regarded as criminal is often self-help (Black, 1983), as is virtually all so-called terrorism and insurrection. And, once begun, wars always involve the pursuit of justice by one or both sides.

What is the social structure of self-help? Where in social space is it most likely to occur? When, in particular, does it appear in its most extreme versions, with fatalities, severe injuries, or substantial property destruction?

The evidence indicates that self-help is not a unitary phenomenon in a single configuration of social relations. Rather, it arises in two drastically different situations. One produces vengeance, the other discipline and rebellion.

Vengeance

Pure vengeance is reciprocal. A grievance pursued aggressively begets aggression in return. The blood feud, for example, is a pattern of reciprocal homicide that may be nearly interminable (see Black-Michaud, 1975, pp. 63–85; Peters, 1975, pp. xxii–xxiii). Feuds are common in the Mediterranean region, such as among Bedouin nomads (Peters, 1967) and the shepherds of Albania, Greece, and Montenegro (Boehm, 1984; Campbell, 1964; Hasluck, 1954), among the Jalé of New Guinea (Koch, 1974, pp. 76–86), the Jívaro of Ecuador and Peru (Harner, 1972, pp. 170–193), the Yanomamö of Brazil and Venezuela (Chagnon, 1977, chap. 5), the Tausug of the Philippines (Kiefer, 1972, chap. 3), and the nomads of Tibet (Ekvall, 1964). In modern America, they develop among street gangs, Mafia families, neighbors, and ethnic groups (see, e.g., Ellickson, 1986; Rieder, 1985, pp. 171–202). International warfare also entails reciprocal vengeance.

Only groups can provide the continuous supply of victims needed for relatively permanent conditions of hostility. The famous Hatfield–McCoy feud of Kentucky and West Virginia, for example, lasted 12 years and included 12 deaths (see Waller, 1988). But extreme vengeance also arises among individuals, sometimes regulated by a "code of honor" specifying who should seek redress against whom, under what circumstances, and how (see generally Peristiany, 1966). Honor normally involves a defense of "manliness" (Pitt-Rivers, 1966, pp. 44–45) and was strongly emphasized among the nobility of Europe and the rural gentry of the American South, both famous for their fatal duels (see, e.g., Baldick, 1965; Wyatt-Brown, 1982). Gunfights in the frontier towns of the American West were similar (McGrath, 1984, chaps. 10–11). Today, honor is important among the young men of American slums and housing projects (see, e.g., Horowitz, 1983, chap. 5).[4] Individualized vengeance is also frequent and often fatal in American prisons (see, e.g., Abbott, 1981, pp. 85–90, 149–150).

What social characteristics do these cases of extreme vengefulness share? A few can be suggested: (1) *equality*, (2) *social distance*, (3) *immobility*, (4) *functional independence*, and (5) *organization*.

To elaborate: In simple societies, vengeance normally appears between structurally interchangeable groups comparable in size and resources, such as tribes, clans, or families. Individualized vengeance, including the defense of honor, also generally involves parties of equal standing:

> The power to impugn the honour of another man depends . . . on the relative status of the contestants. An inferior is not deemed to possess sufficient honour to resent the affront of a superior. A superior can ignore the affront of an inferior. . . . A man is answerable for his honour only to his social equals. (Pitt-Rivers, 1966, p. 31; see also p. 35; Berger, Berger, & Kellner, 1973, p. 86)

The Kabyles of Algeria regard challenging social inferiors as dishonorable (Bourdieu, 1966, p. 199). An insult from a black man, for example, should be ignored: "Let him bark until he grows weary of it" (Bourdieu, 1966, pp. 200, 207).[5] In slave societies, slaves have neither honor nor the ability to dishonor anyone else (Patterson, 1982, pp. 81–97). And when dueling flourished in the American South, "No gentleman ever accepted a challenge from one not considered his social equal" (Williams, 1980, p. 27). Codes of honor develop primarily in stratified societies but pertain to relations among peers, particularly elites such as aristocrats and slave owners (Berger et al., 1973, pp. 85–86; see also Gorn, 1985, pp. 41–42). Pure vengeance arises in egalitarian settings.

[4]Horowitz proposes that honor is more developed where men have little wealth and must achieve social status by violence and deference from others (1983, chap. 5). Ayers reports that honor was defended by all classes of the Old South (1984, chap. 1) and suggests that it migrated to northern cities with blacks (1984, p. 275).

[5]A Kabyle legend tells of a particular tribe that sent blacks against an opponent in war. The opponent capitulated rather than dishonor itself by fighting such a lowly foe. The losers thereby preserved their honor while the winners lost theirs (Bourdieu, 1966, p. 200).

Vengeance varies directly with relational distance[6]: "Feud is waged and vengeance taken when the parties live sufficiently far apart, or are too weakly related by diverse ties" (Gluckman, 1956/1969, p. 19; see also Cooney, 1988, chap. 3; Rieder, 1984, p. 154). Vengeance is therefore more frequent and severe between tribes than within them, between clans than within them, between families than within them. A survey of simple societies throughout the world indicates that homicidal vengeance fits this pattern (Cooney, 1988, chap. 3).[7] Also consistent is Colson's observation that cross-cutting ties such as marriages between members of different clans inhibit vengeance (1953; see also Boehm, 1984, pp. 172, 219; Cooney, 1988, chap. 3; Gluckman, 1956/1969, chap. 1; Otterbein & Otterbein, 1965; Thoden van Velzen & van Wetering, 1960). Vengeance develops most fully with horizontal segmentation, when people are separated by chasms in relational space, and social bridges across these chasms may reduce or terminate it. The headhunting Ilongot of the Philippines encourage intermarriage between feuding groups ("let their children marry") to restore peace (Rosaldo, 1980, pp. 65–66). The Yakan of the Philippines ritually establish blood ties ("blood brotherhood") to pacify feuding groups (Frake, 1980, p. 207), a practice followed by the Montenegrins of Yugoslavia as well (Boehm, 1984, pp. 136–137). Similarly, interracial ties inhibit race riots, and when a riot does occur, those with ties stay home (Senechal, 1990, chap. 4).

Cultural distance[8] encourages vengeance. Wide cultural differences accompany some of the most extreme cases: massacres of women and children, torture, mutilation, and genocide. Intertribal and international vengeance is more severe among those widely separated in cultural space, and the same applies to interethnic conflict within a society. So-called terrorism obeys the same principle.

But there is no vengeance where people live in different worlds. Those involved must be mutually accessible and share a social arena, however superficially. Their social arrangement is stable. The amount of violence in tribal societies thus varies inversely with the amount of spatial movement in their way of life (Thoden van Velzen & van Wet-

---

[6]Relational distance refers to "the degree to which [people] participate in one another's lives" and can be measured by "the scope, frequency, and length of interaction between people, the age of their relationship, and the nature and number of links between them in a social network" (Black, 1976, pp. 40–41).

[7]Homicidal vengeance between intimates such as married couples, lovers, and friends does not fit this model (see, e.g., Lundsgaarde, 1977, p. 230; Wolfgang, 1958/1966, p. 191). Perhaps the relationship is U-curvilinear (see Black, 1987, p. 574, note 11). Another exception is the killing of alleged witches, a practice that may involve neighbors, acquaintances, or even kinfolk (see, e.g., Knauft, 1985, chap. 7; 1987, pp. 462–472).

[8]"Cultural distance" refers to differences in the content of culture, such as differences in religion, language, and aesthetics (see Black, 1976, p. 74).

ering, 1960, p. 198). So do sorcery and the naming of witches (see, e.g., Baxter, 1972; M. Douglas, 1973, chap.7; Knauft, 1985; Winans & Edgerton, 1964). High rates of homicidal self-help in prisons, where the inmates are locked together, are similarly understandable (see A. Cohen, 1976). Nations are effectively locked into place as well. Rioters reside in the same city. Vengeance is inescapable.

Vengeance is also more likely among persons or groups independent of one another for their general well-being, economic or otherwise. Homicidal vengeance happens most frequently in societies with little division of labor, indicating little economic interdependence (Cooney, 1988, chap. 3; see also Durkheim, 1893/1964, Book 1). And nations lose their inclination for warfare in direct proportion to their interdependence.[9] People more readily kill those they can do without.

Finally, vengeance between organized groups is more extreme than vengeance between individuals. Simple societies with conflict between primordial collectivities such as clans produce the most. Egalitarian societies with "fraternal interest groups" (usually patrilineal clans) display a particularly high rate, and it typically occurs in the name of the groups themselves (Thoden van Velzen & van Wetering, 1960). Conflict between nations—also groups—has produced the most death and destruction throughout human history (see Cooney, 1988, chap. 5; Lee, 1979, pp. 398–399).

In sum, vengeance is most extreme in a social field combining several characteristics—equality, relational and cultural distance, immobility, independence, and organization—suggesting a collection of largely similar elements, separate yet frozen together in physical and social space. We might call this a *stable agglomeration*.[10]

Discipline and Rebellion

Self-help also appears under conditions radically unlike those associated with vengeance. A pure case is the master–slave relationship, where grievances in either direction—from master against slave (downward) or from slave against master (upward)—may have severe consequences, including death (see, e.g., Patterson, 1982; Wiedemann, 1981, chaps. 9–11). Downward self-help is discipline; the upward variety is rebellion (for similar usages, see, e.g., Foucault, 1975; Hobsbawm, 1959; Stinchcombe, 1964). They arise in the same settings and

[9]This pattern is consistent with Durkheim's (1893/1964) theory that functional interdependence (the "division of labor") increases compensation ("restitutive sanctions") at the expense of punishment ("repressive sanctions").

[10]In botany, an arrangement of plants is agglomerate if they are "crowded into a dense cluster, but not cohering" (*Random House Dictionary*, unabridged edition, 1967).

are complementary. Where discipline is most extreme—involving torture, mutilation, maiming, and homicide—so is rebellion. Where the former is mild, so is the latter. Both normally are penal in style and authoritarian in procedure (Baumgartner, 1984a, pp. 331–336).[11] Apart from slavery, illustrations include relations between guards and prisoners, lords and serfs, officers and enlisted men, parents and children, and husbands and wives in patriarchal families. States exercise self-help when they seize, imprison, torture, or execute individuals without using judicial procedures (e.g., Solzhenitsyn, 1973; Timerman, 1981). In fact, state discipline is often more severe than slave discipline (see generally Collins, 1974). And, like slaves, state-dominated individuals occasionally rebel.

The social structure of discipline and rebellion—in the extreme—has at least five characteristics: (1) *inequality*, (2) *vertical segmentation*, (3) *social distance*, (4) *functional unity*, and (5) *immobility*.

The greater the inequality, the more severe the discipline and rebellion. The master–slave relationship, a form of parasitism,[12] entails social inequalities of many kinds (Patterson, 1982, pp. 335–337), so it is understandable that slave discipline may be homicidal and often includes practices to intensify the suffering of those punished, even when the misbehavior seems trivial. In one Roman case, a slave who accidentally broke a crystal cup during a banquet was condemned to be thrown as food to lamprey eels (Wiedemann, 1981, p. 176).[13]

Whereas vengeance flows laterally (see Bateson's concept of "lateral sanctions"—1958, p. 98), discipline flows vertically (compare Rieder, 1984, pp. 140–144). Vengeance is heterarchical, and discipline is hierarchical (on the concept of "heterarchy," see Hofstadter, 1979, pp. 133–134).

Most discipline is applied to individuals who belong to a homogeneous class in a larger structure of social relations. A system of slavery extends beyond a slave's household, for example, and enlisted men, workers, students, and children belong to larger classes as well.[14] Moreover, a substantial distance separates them from their superiors in the system of inequality. Vertical segmentation corresponds to the relational segmentation associated with vengeance.

[11] Baumgartner remarks that "there is considerable isomorphism between upward and downward social control—so much, in fact, that there appears to be a greater affinity between the two than between either of these and the forms of social control found among equals" (1984a, p. 336).

[12] Biologist Edward O. Wilson defines parasitism as a kind of symbiosis "in which one partner benefits as the other suffers" (1971, p. 389).

[13] Slaves may be killed in nonpunitive circumstances as well, such as to satisfy the grief of a bereaved master, to accompany the burial of a deceased master, or for ritual purposes (see Patterson, 1982, p. 191).

[14] The same applies to women in patriarchal societies.

The least intimacy produces the most discipline.[15] Where slaves have little or no contact with their owners, for instance, such as in plantation-type farming and in mining, whipping and other corporal punishments increase (Patterson, 1982, pp. 198, 206). Even so, much discipline is found in relationships combining intimacy and distance, such as long-term relationships where shared activities and associates are limited. Slave masters, guards, and parents have many social involvements unknown to their charges. Their relational structure is jagged, close in some respects but not others. Cultural distance also increases discipline. Most master–slave relationships, for example, are interethnic (Patterson, 1982, p. 178).[16] And modern torture is often interethnic (Collins, 1974, p. 439, note 37).

Those involved in discipline are functionally unified: They participate in the same enterprise, whether production, warfare, imprisonment, or education. Their roles differ, but their lives intertwine. They are bound together for the long term.

Rebellion and discipline rise and fall together, even if the former may be less frequent.[17] The social field conducive to both is a *parasitical hierarchy*.

Avoidance

Avoidance is the handling of a grievance by the curtailment of interaction (Baumgartner, 1988, chap. 3). Either the aggrieved or offending party may initiate and accomplish it alone, unilaterally, or both may withdraw at the same time. Avoidance ranges from permanent flight to a temporary reduction in contact, begun and ended in a single encounter. It may be total or partial, and it may entail physical separation or only decreased communication. Examples include secession from a nation, migration from a region, desertion from an

[15] The incompatibility between discipline and intimacy seemingly explains why military organizations discourage fraternizing between officers and enlisted men.

[16] Patterson reports, however, that the treatment of slaves is not associated with ethnic differences (1982, p. 179).

[17] It is not clear that rebellion is less frequent than discipline. Social inferiors sometimes resist their superiors on a daily basis, such as by minimizing their labor, pilfering, and vandalizing property (see Baumgartner, 1984a; Scott, 1985, especially pp. 265–273). Discipline and rebellion may even tend toward a natural balance or equivalence (see Rieder, 1984, p. 142). Rebellion does not always involve direct action against superiors but may also be self-directed, such as when a slave mutilates himself or commits suicide. Technically speaking, this is property destruction. Durkheim calls such suicide "fatalistic" and explains it with "excessive regulation, that of persons with futures pitilessly blocked and passions violently choked by oppressive discipline" (1897/1951, p. 276, note 25). For a discussion of self-injury as a form of "social control from below," see Baumgartner (1984a, pp. 328–331).

army, resignation from an organization, running away, divorce, termination of a business relationship, the "cold shoulder," and suicide.
Because people also curtail interaction in the absence of grievances,
whether any given instance qualifies as conflict management may be
difficult or impossible to determine.

Without a visible complaint, avoidance eludes identification (see
Hirschman, 1970, p. 86). Its purest form is silent, and those avoiding
others may even explicitly deny that they harbor a grievance. Thus,
public officials resigning from office may deny the reason (such as
their involvement in a scandal) and cite "personal" concerns instead
(e.g., "to spend more time with my family"—Hirschman, 1970, p. 105).
Similar denials are common in everyday life ("No, I'm not avoiding
you. I've just been very busy").

Hunting and gathering societies often use avoidance (see, e.g., Lee,
1979, p. 372; Turnbull, 1965, pp. 100–109; von Fürer-Haimendorf, 1967,
pp. 17–24; Woodburn, 1979). Eskimos, for example, move from one
band to another when conflict arises and locate their dwellings to facilitate avoidance within a single village:

> Whenever a situation came up in which an individual disliked somebody
> or a group of people in the band, he often pitched his tent or built his
> igloo at the opposite extremity of the camp or moved to another settlement
> altogether. This is common practice even today. . . . People who like each
> other stay together; those who do not live apart. An additional detail is
> significant in this respect. If for any reason two families who are not on
> friendly terms have to camp close by, the openings of their dwellings will
> face in opposite directions, indicating that there is no intercourse between
> the two families. (Balikci, 1970, pp. 192–193; punctuation edited)

Shifting horticulturalists also favor avoidance (see, e.g., Carniero, 1970,
pp. 734–735; Stauder, 1972; Turner, 1957), as do gypsies (Grönfors,
1986, pp. 119–121), consumers in the modern marketplace (Hirschman, 1970), and suburbanites (Baumgartner, 1984b, 1988, chaps. 3–
4).

Temporary and partial avoidance is ubiquitous. But again the extremes are instructive. Although avoidance rarely has homicidal consequences apart from self-destruction, it may be fatal for relationships
(suggested by John Jarvis). Permanent and total avoidance is most likely
under the following conditions: (1) *absence of hierarchy,* (2) *social
fluidity,* (3) *social fragmentation,* (4) *functional independence,* and (5)
individuation.

Avoidance is uncommon in authority relationships, though slaves
sometimes flee their masters, serfs their lords, or soldiers their officers
(see Baumgartner, 1984a, pp. 320–324). But avoidance frequently occurs in nonhierarchical status systems without chains of authority.

The fluidity of social life, or the rate at which relationships begin and end (relational fertility and mortality rates), is a predictor of avoidance. The higher these rates, the more people use it (Baumgartner, 1984b, pp. 94–95; 1988, chap. 3). Since avoidance itself contributes to social fluidity, the association between the two may seem trivial or self-evident, but there is no necessary reason why people in fluid relationships should handle grievances with avoidance rather than confrontational modes such as vengeance or settlement by a third party.[18]

Hunters and gatherers have more fluid relationships than sedentary peoples, which partly explains their greater use of avoidance (Baumgartner, 1988, chap. 3; see also Cooney, 1988). Fluid relationships on the wagon trails to the American West in the 19th century meant that avoidance predominated over the brawling and gunfighting romanticized in books and movies (see Reid, 1980; compare Faragher, 1979, pp. 101–102). The highly unstable suburban world of modern America has so much avoidance that it has been called an "avoidance culture" (Baumgartner, 1988, chap. 3).

People may share many activities with their associates, or they may have more limited and focused interaction.[19] The latter produces avoidance. For example, commercial relationships today are highly fragmentary, often embracing only the business at hand, and avoidance is common (see Baumgartner, 1988, chap. 3). In traditional villages and families where people have many involvements with each other, however, confrontational modes are more likely. With modernization, relationships become increasingly emaciated, and avoidance proliferates (see Baumgartner, 1988, chap. 6).

Functionally independent people also use more avoidance (Baumgartner, 1988, chap. 3). Avoidance-prone hunters and gatherers have little division of labor and can subsist almost by themselves.[20] Similarly, as modern women become more independent, they increasingly use separation and divorce to resolve their problems with men. Business executives in relatively independent subdivisions use more

---

[18] Baumgartner distinguishes "confrontational" from "nonconfrontational" modes of social control, and classifies avoidance as a form of the latter (1984b).

[19] Gluckman calls the former "multiplex relationships" and contrasts them to "ephemeral relationships" that involve "single interests." He proposes the number of shared activities as a predictor of how disputes will be handled, arguing that those in multiplex relationships are more likely to be handled in a conciliatory fashion (1967, pp. 20–21).

[20] A division of labor usually occurs between men and women in hunting and gathering societies, but not between families. Individuals are generally not dependent on other individuals but rely on the multifamily band as a whole to share its food (Leacock, 1982, p. 159).

avoidance than those in more integrated and hierarchical companies (Morrill, 1986, chaps. 2–4). And all markets entail a degree of independence between the participants: Buyers and sellers can and do go elsewhere when dissatisfied (Hirschman, 1970). A business may be shunned by individuals for the rest of their lives, or by families for generations.[21]

When independent people disperse across physical space, avoidance increases (see Baumgartner, 1988, chap. 3). Hunters and gatherers again provide the prototypical case. At the opposite extreme are prisons and other "total institutions" (Goffman, 1961) where physical separation is impossible. Some even speculate that the state and law emerged when populations expanded in limited spaces and individuals could no longer avoid their enemies (Carniero, 1970; Mann, 1986, chaps. 3–4; Taylor, 1982, pp. 129–139).

A final factor conducive to avoidance is individuation, the capacity of individuals to act autonomously without implicating groups (see Baumgartner, 1988, chap. 3). Groups avoid each other, as when organizations terminate commercial relationships or nations sever diplomatic relations, but individuals do so more often. And individuals frequently avoid groups (Hirschman, 1970). For example, avoidance seems to be the primary means by which individuals express grievances against business organizations.

To summarize: An avoidance structure is generally not hierarchical, yet not necessarily egalitarian either, and tends to be fluid, fragmented, individuated, and composed of mutually independent participants. A social field with these characteristics might be called an *unstable aggregation.*[22]

Violence varies inversely with avoidance (see Baumgartner, 1984b, p. 97; 1988). For example, killings are more likely in settings where permanent and total avoidance is difficult or impossible: in agricultural societies, between contiguous groups such as street gangs, tribes, and nations, in maximum security prisons, and in families and households (see A. Cohen, 1976, p. 17). These settings differ markedly from the fluid, fragmented, and individuated settings where avoidance is

---

[21] Such avoidance does not necessarily relate to dissatisfaction with a product or service. In one American city, for instance, blacks in the 1970s were still avoiding businesses whose earlier owners had participated in an antiblack riot over 50 years earlier (Senechal, 1990, chap. 4).

[22] In biology, an aggregation is defined as "a group of organisms of the same or different species living closely together but less integrated than a society" (*Random House Dictionary,* unabridged edition, 1967). The social context of avoidance also resembles the phenomenon known in physics as "Brownian motion": the constant and irregular movement of tiny particles observable in a liquid such as a glass of water.

most common: among hunters and gatherers, in suburbia, in markets, wherever people daily swarm and disperse. Eliminate the conditions for avoidance, and violence increases. The nomadic Chenchu of India, for instance, traditionally handled conflict with avoidance, but after the British concentrated them in large settlements they became uncontrollably violent (von Fürer-Haimendorf, 1967, p. 22).

Like homicide, suicide often originates in human conflict (see, e.g., J. D. Douglas, 1967) and may be a form of avoidance (see Koch, 1974, pp. 74–75). Modern suicide occurs at a higher rate among relatively isolated individuals (Durkheim, 1897/1951, Book 2, chaps. 2, 3, 5), in societies that have high rates of marital separation and divorce (Durkheim, 1897/1951, pp. 259–262), and in urban rather than rural areas (Durkheim, 1899/1951, p. 353)—the same conditions as avoidance in general. And suicide varies inversely with homicide (Durkheim, 1897/1951, pp. 338–352; Henry & Short, 1954).[23] This is because the conditions associated with extreme avoidance are nearly opposite those associated with violent self-help (unstable aggregations versus stable agglomerations and parasitical hierarchies).

Negotiation

Negotiation is the handling of a grievance by joint decision:

> The decision is made by the disputing parties themselves. . . . Each party can only obtain what the other is in the end prepared to allow. Since the two parties necessarily began with some kind of difference between them . . . , the process of decision-making therefore involves a convergence. At least one party, but usually both, must move toward the other. (Gulliver, 1979, p. 5)

This may or may not include the intervention of a third party as a negotiator (see Black & Baumgartner, 1983, pp. 108–109).

Negotiation is the primary mode of handling major conflicts in many simple societies throughout the world. Often it involves haggling about compensation for a death or injury (see, e.g., Gulliver, 1963, 1969, 1971, chap. 5; Hasluck, 1954, chap. 15; Jones, 1974; Kroeber, 1926, pp. 514–515; Nader, 1965). Lawyers in modern societies also engage in much negotiation (known in the United States as "out-of-court settlement" in civil cases and "plea bargaining" in criminal cases—see, e.g., Black, 1984a; Galanter, 1983, for reviews of the evidence). The rapid growth of the legal profession in 20th-century Amer-

[23]One exception is Durkheim's "fatalistic suicide," which apparently occurs under some of the same conditions as violent rebellion. See footnote 17. Another exception would seem to be self-punishment by suicide (see J. D. Douglas, 1967, pp. 302–304).

ica (see, e.g., Curran, 1986, p. 20) may thus indicate an increased demand for negotiators.[24]

When do people bargain rather than use violence, avoidance, or
other forms of conflict management? When do they expend a great
deal of time and energy in this fashion? Extensive negotiations occur
most in social fields with the following characteristics: (1) *equality*,
(2) *cross-linkages*, (3) *organization*, (4) *homogeneity*, and (5) *accessibility*.

Negotiation is less likely among unequal parties. Superiors usually obtain what they want from their inferiors with little or no bargaining, while the latter may have trouble even initiating negotiations
with the former. Nevertheless, equality need not exist between the
adversaries themselves. Allies and other supporters on each side can
transform a conflict between unequal parties into one between equals.
In tribal societies, support typically arises from familial and residential affiliations (see, e.g., Frake, 1980; Gulliver, 1963, chap. 7; 1969).
Those serving as negotiators—usually status superiors of the adversaries—may also function as equalizers. For example, negotiators commonly equalize the adversaries in traditional Thailand: If A has a
grievance against a social superior (B), and B refuses to discuss the
matter with A, A may mobilize a superior (X) in his own hierarchy
acquainted with one of B's social superiors (Y). X and Y then negoti-
ate a settlement and urge A and B to accept it (Engel, 1978, pp. 76–
77). Negotiators can thereby flatten otherwise vertical conflicts:

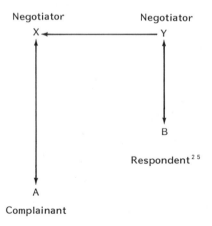

[24]This need not mean that negotiation itself is increasing but could also indicate that
   private individuals are increasingly unwilling or otherwise unavailable to act as negotiators.
[25]This diagram is adapted from Engel (1978, p. 77), whose version does not vary the
   positions of A and B to signify differing levels of social status.

Lawyers frequently have the same effect. Indeed, the structural transformation of cases in highly stratified societies such as the United States is one of their most significant functions. As familial and other primordial alliances decline, lawyers become the great equalizers of modern life. They offer equality as a commodity, for sale in the marketplace.[26]

The Thai practice described above illustrates another factor in negotiation: cross-linkages between the parties. Negotiation between A and B depends not only on equalization but also on A's connection to B through X and Y. Because of his link to Y, X provides a "crossover point" between A and B (Engel, 1978, p. 77). Indirect ties open communication, bridging social gulfs that might otherwise preclude discussion and bargaining. Vengeance structures generally lack linkages of this kind (see "Vengeance" above; see also Colson, 1953; Cooney, 1988, chap. 3; Nader, 1965; Peters, 1975, pp. xxiv–xxvii).

Cross-linking is another function (besides leveling) provided by lawyers. Even if they are not personally acquainted, the shared professional affiliation of opposing lawyers provides a social bridge between their clients. And once begun, negotiation increases intimacy between all concerned. On the other hand, adversaries already intimate, such as married couples, friends, or fellow employees, may find that the intervention of lawyers widens the social distance between them and compounds the fracture in their relationship. Their conflict may therefore escalate, increasing the likelihood of a permanent termination of their relationship (see, e.g., Griffiths, 1986; Macaulay, 1963).

A third factor: Negotiation is more extensive between corporate beings than between individuals. The conflict need not originate in groups as long as groups ultimately participate. The adversaries' allies may band together, or groups may customarily or contractually participate, such as where a traditional system of collective liability operates (see, e.g., Moore, 1972) or where insurance companies intervene (see, e.g., Ross, 1970). An outside negotiator also transforms the conflict into a corporate event. Homogeneity is relevant as well. Because negotiation requires communication, cultural closeness between the parties tends to facilitate it. A shared language obviously helps, as do other shared practices—another contrast with vengeance, where the most extreme cases frequently entail cultural cleavages.

Finally, negotiation requires mutual accessibility. Physical proximity and immobility are not necessary—as in vengeance—but only the possibility of communication, such as a telephone.

Negotiation structures resemble vengeance structures in their

---

[26]Programs providing legal services for the poor in societies such as modern America are presumably intended to remedy shortcomings of the marketplace in this respect.

equality, organization, and mutual accessibility, but not in their cross-linkages and cultural homogeneity. Negotiation can withstand the physical separation and mobility of its participants, though its ideal setting is less fluid than an avoidance structure. Neither a stable agglomeration nor an unstable aggregation, the social field most conducive to negotiation is a *tangled network*. It lies between the settings of vengeance and avoidance. Hence, the adversaries neither attack each other nor run away but do something between these extremes: They talk.

Settlement

Settlement is the handling of a grievance by a nonpartisan third party. Only a significantly nonpartisan third party can achieve the trilateral structure distinguishing this form of conflict management. The most familiar examples are mediation, arbitration, and adjudication. The mediator acts as a broker, helping the adversaries resolve their conflict without taking sides, the arbitrator decides how to resolve a conflict but cannot compel compliance, while the judge both makes a decision and, if necessary, enforces it. These roles appear in many societies and have received extensive scholarly attention (e.g., Black & Baumgartner, 1983; Eckhoff, 1966; Fuller, 1978; Galtung, 1965; Getman, 1979; Gulliver, 1977; Merry, 1982; Shapiro, 1980).

Mediation, arbitration, and adjudication differ in their degree of authoritativeness, including their decisiveness and coerciveness. Mediation entails neither a decision nor coercion by the third party, arbitration entails a decision but no coercion, and adjudication entails both. While mediation is the least authoritative of the three, still less so is friendly pacification, a mode of settlement in which the third party seeks merely to separate or distract the adversaries (Black & Baumgartner, 1983, pp. 99–100). The "camp clown" of the Mbuti Pygmies, for example, dampens conflicts by diverting attention to himself in a humorous fashion (Turnbull, 1965, pp. 182–183). Family members and other intimates often use friendly pacification in modern societies. Gossip is the least authoritative of all, a kind of trial in absentia unknown to the principals (see, e.g., E. Cohen, 1972; Gluckman, 1963; Merry, 1984).

Repressive pacification defines the other extreme. Here a third party handles the conflict as an offense in itself and seeks to crush it forcefully regardless of the concerns of the adversaries (Black & Baumgartner, 1983, pp. 106–107). Colonial administrators repressed vengeance and feuding in indigenous populations (see, e.g., Evans-Pritchard, 1940,

p. 152; Koch, 1974, p. 223; Reay, 1974, pp. 205, 209), and adults relate similarly to fighting among children (see Black & Baumgartner, 1983, p. 107).

Consider now the conditions associated with violent or otherwise highly authoritative settlement—adjudication and repressive pacification. Several variables seem relevant: (1) *inequality,* (2) *relational distance,* (3) *triangulation,* (4) *heterogeneity,* and (5) *organizational asymmetry.*

The authoritativeness of third parties varies directly with their social superiority (Black & Baumgartner, 1983, p. 113). Friendly peacemakers tend to be about equal to the adversaries, and mediators, arbitrators, and adjudicators tend to be (in the same order) increasingly elevated above them.[27] Repressive peacemakers are generally the most elevated of all, illustrated by the colonial administrators who once intervened in the tribal conflicts of Africa and Oceania. The tribesmen were effectively treated as "nonpersons" (Goffman, 1961, pp. 341–342)—like wildlife—and their disputes as "disturbances of the peace" (e.g., Koch, 1974, p. 223; Scheffler, 1964, p. 399). Conditions of great inequality also produce corporal punishment, such as whipping, torture, mutilation, and execution, but offenders of high status—closer to the third parties—may escape the harshest treatment. The Roman nobility, for example, were immune to crucifixion and to being thrown to wild beasts (Garnsey, 1968, p. 13).

Relational distance between the third party and the adversaries has the same effect as social superiority: The greater it is, the more violent the settlement (see Black & Baumgartner, 1983, p. 113). Friendly peacemakers tend to be very close to those they disentangle, mediators a bit less so, followed by arbitrators, judges, and repressive peacemakers.[28] Repressive pacification in colonial settings again defines the extreme: The administrators are usually unacquainted with the people they handle. So are judges who pronounce the death penalty.

The relational distance between a third party and each adversary must be approximately equal for the process to be significantly nonpartisan (see Simmel, 1908/1960, pp. 149–153). Imbalance breeds partisanship (see Black & Baumgartner, 1980, pp. 200–201). Third parties substantially closer to either adversary are likely to be disqualified

[27] Gossip is democratic, occurring in diverse locations in social space, including those socially beneath the offending parties.

[28] Where social superiority and intimacy occur together, third parties display a blend of warmth and repression, a pattern frequently seen when parents handle fighting between their children. This mixed form might be called paternalistic pacification. Therapy is a mode of third-party intervention defined by the participants as help, and not a form of conflict management at all (see Black & Baumgartner, 1983, pp. 109–111; see also Horwitz, 1982).

from handling the case (see, e.g., Ayoub, 1965, p. 13; Barton, 1919/ 1969, p. 87; Lewis, 1961, p. 229). The third party and the adversaries therefore tend to form an isosceles triangle of relational distance, with the former at the apex (Black & Baumgartner, 1983, p. 113; see also Black, 1984b, pp. 21–23). Settings lacking third parties equidistant from those in conflict generally have no settlement at all. A village completely bifurcated by kinship, for example, has no internal system of settlement for handling conflicts across family lines (see, e.g., Nader, 1965). Where third parties either considerably superior to the adversaries in social status or distant from them relationally are lacking, no settlement of an authoritative nature will occur. Hunters and gatherers, typically both egalitarian and intimate among themselves, often do not even have mediation, much less arbitration, adjudication, or repressive pacification (see, e.g., Lee, 1979; Turnbull, 1961, 1965; Woodburn, 1979).

Cultural distance has the same relevance as relational distance: The greater it is, the more authoritative the settlement procedure. Again the extreme example is the imposition of colonial authority by a foreign power, such as Europeans enforcing their conception of law and order in Africa and elsewhere. Cultural equidistance from the adversaries is also important, since cultural closeness, like intimacy, engenders partisanship (Black & Baumgartner, 1983, p. 114). In an intertribal conflict, for instance, a third party from either tribe—even if a stranger to all concerned—will normally not be acceptable to both sides. Culturally skewed procedures tend to create a system of alliance more than settlement (see, e.g., Beidelman, 1966, 1967).

Authoritative third parties usually represent a corporate entity, often a government. Capital punishment inflicted by legal officials is thus organizational behavior, but it virtually always applies to individuals and is therefore asymmetrical (see Coleman, 1982, pp. 19–30.). Most vengeance is symmetrical, whether between groups or between persons, and so is negotiation. Avoidance may be asymmetrical, but usually in the opposite direction: An individual is more likely to avoid an organization than vice versa.

The most authoritative settlement entails inequality between the third party and the adversaries, relational and cultural distance, triangulation, and organizational asymmetry—a social field we might term a *triangular hierarchy*.

Toleration

Toleration is inaction when a grievance might otherwise be handled. Although arguably not a form of conflict management at all, people sometimes consciously advocate or adopt toleration as the most effective response to deviant behavior, disagreement, or disruption (see, e.g., Lemert, 1967; Parsons, 1951, chap. 7). For example, members of organizations often use "unilateral peaceableness" to handle volatile situations (Boulding, 1964, pp. 47–48). Whether to forestall further conflict or not, people continually "lump it," "turn the other cheek," or "bite the bullet" (see, e.g., Baumgartner, 1984b; Felstiner, 1974, p. 81; Galanter, 1974, pp. 124–125; Merry, 1979; Yngvesson, 1976). Toleration is the most common response of aggrieved people everywhere.

A matter of degree, toleration is measurable by what might otherwise occur under the same circumstances. When a group exacts blood vengeance for one killing but does little or nothing after another, its behavior is extremely tolerant. The same applies when a case of inaction might otherwise result in police intervention, arrest, or prosecution. We can compare the degree of toleration across settings of all kinds, including societies and historical epochs. For instance, there is considerable variation in reactions to drunkenness, adultery, homosexuality, and homicide. Nothing is automatically subject to social control.

In principle, we can specify social conditions conducive to toleration—i.e., those least likely to provoke vengeance, avoidance, or anything else. One is social inferiority. Underlings such as slaves and students do not often violently rebel against their superiors, and when their superiors fight or victimize each other, they rarely do more than gossip.[29] Social inferiors may not be subjectively tolerant of their superiors, but behaviorally they are.

Another source of toleration is intimacy. People endure all manner of offenses by people close to them, including not only rudeness and insult of various kinds but also physical intimidation, beatings, and rape. In modern societies, criminal offenses between intimates are far less likely to be reported to the authorities (see, e.g., Block, 1974; Williams, 1984). In tribal societies where vengeance commonly follows homicide, within a family it is rare. The Bedouin of Cyrenaica, for instance, regard the killer of a fellow family member as "one who defecates in the tent" and, at most, temporarily exile him (Peters, 1967, p. 264; for other examples, see Goody, 1957, p. 97; Middleton, 1965, p. 51). And as people grow closer over time, they "normalize" conduct that earlier would have spurred them to action (Lemert, 1964, p. 86). Third parties intimate with those in conflict also tend to hang

[29] But social inferiors might be required to participate. For example, Roman law held that "if an owner was killed, all the slaves within earshot at the time had to be interrogated under torture and killed" (Wiedemann, 1981, p. 169). In 19th-century Mexico, servants were legally required to give their lives to protect their masters. Failure to do so was punishable by death (Romanucci-Ross, 1986, pp. 11–12.)

back or to employ the gentler modes of intervention, such as friendly pacification or mediation (Black, 1984b, pp. 22–23; Black & Baumgartner, 1983, p. 113).

Cultural closeness has the same effect as relational closeness. People who are vicious toward foreigners more readily forgive their own kind. Organization induces toleration as well. Conduct regarded as outrageous in an individual—lying, cheating, violence—may be countenanced in a group such as a government or corporation (see, e.g., Black, 1976, chap. 6; 1989, chap. 3). Toleration increases still more when the aggrieved party belongs to the offending group itself, a situation that combines several sources of toleration (inferiority, intimacy, homogeneity, and organization).

Much toleration also occurs in urban settings with masses of heterogeneous strangers, social atomization, and fluidity (Baumgartner, 1984b, 1988; Boswell, 1980, pp. 33–38). Toleration thus arises under opposite conditions, where social relations are either very tight or very loose: extremely close, homogeneous, stable, and possibly even oppressive *or* distant, heterogeneous, unstable, and free. Only in a *polarized field* of social life can all these conditions operate at once. Past populations never divided daily life between such drastically different worlds, but modern people increasingly do (see Black, 1976, chap. 7).

We can identify five modes of conflict management—self-help, avoidance, negotiation, settlement, and toleration—and the social fields associated with their most extreme versions. Vengeance, a form of self-help, reaches its highest level in *stable agglomerations*, where people are equal, independent, organized, socially separated, and yet frozen together in physical space. Two other forms of self-help, discipline and rebellion, flourish in *parasitical hierarchies*, where people are unequal, segmented into classes, socially distant, functionally unified, and bound together for the long term. Avoidance arises in *unstable aggregations*, without hierarchies of authority, where social relations are fluid and fragmented, and where people are mutually independent and individuated. Negotiation thrives in *tangled networks*, where people are equal, cross-linked, organized, homogeneous, and mutually accessible. Settlement develops to its highest level in *triangular hierarchies*, where people are unequal, socially distant, organizationally asymmetrical, and where their relational and cultural structure resembles an isosceles triangle. Lastly, toleration prevails at opposite extremes of social life, either very tight or very loose, which only a *polarized field* can contain in a single setting.

Conclusion

These models predict and explain the nature of conflict management. The more a social field resembles one of them, the more accurately we can anticipate its pattern of conflict management.[30] Where the fit is only partial, a less extreme version should occur. A stable agglomeration of individuals should have less extreme vengeance than a stable agglomeration of groups, for example, a parasitical hierarchy between intimates should have less extreme discipline than one spanning a greater distance in social space, and a triangular hierarchy with relatively little inequality should have less authoritative settlement than one with more inequality. Settings that mix characteristics of different models should mix these forms. Modern America's complex society contains all the social fields modeled here to some degree, and all the forms of conflict management appear. People everywhere participate in multiple fields of social relations—family, neighborhood, peer group, workplace, marketplace—each with its own pattern of conflict management. A modern adult may wield discipline at home, experience it at work, use avoidance in the neighborhood, seek third parties to handle strangers in the community, and demand vengeance against foreigners. Conflict management is as variable as social life.

But why? Why is each mode of conflict management associated with a particular configuration of social relations? Why is vengeance associated with stable agglomerations, avoidance with unstable aggregations, and so on? What is their affinity? A deeper pattern underlies them all: *Conflict management is isomorphic with its social field.*

Each mode of conflict management reproduces its social environment. Social settings with a high level of avoidance—unstable aggregations—exhibit much relational mortality apart from the handling of grievances. The Ndembu of Zambia, for example, have such a high level of relational mortality that their social life is described as "fissile" (Turner, 1957, p. xxiii). Villages, lineages, and families continually split apart, but not all this fission involves conflict. Spatial mobility is the Ndembu way of life, and their management of conflict reflects this larger tendency (see Turner, 1957, chaps. 5–7). A similar pattern appears in the suburbs of modern America: The constant fluctuation of relationships in neighborhoods, associations, and workplaces often has nothing to do with grievances, and avoidance only increases this fluidity (Baumgartner, 1984b, 1988). In markets, too,

[30] By the same logic, we could test these models by showing that social fields with completely opposite characteristics have the least conflict management predicted by each (suggested by Michael Musheno).

shopping for something better is how both business is conducted and conflict is handled (see Hirschman, 1970).

Discipline mirrors subordination. Business organizations with strict hierarchies, such as banking firms, have more discipline than decentralized and segmentary organizations, such as accounting firms and restaurant chains (Morrill, 1986, chaps. 2, 4). Grade schools have more than universities. Patriarchal families have more than egalitarian families. Where everyday life is dictated from above, so is the management of conflict.

Vengeance is an exchange. Its hallmark is balance: "an eye for an eye, a tooth for a tooth," one life for another (called "negative reciprocation" by Warner, 1958, p. 162; compare Sahlins, 1965, pp. 148–149). And it is most developed where wealth, armed forces and other resources are balanced as well. In herding societies, for example, livestock raids often equalize neighboring groups (Sweet, 1965). Negotiation arises where people are interlinked and continually bargain over their conditions of life. Settlement also reflects its social setting. A judge is to the parties in a case what a ruler is to the ruled. In many simpler societies, these are one and the same: the chief. Settlement expresses not only political hierarchies but also economic, religious, and domestic hierarchies.[31]

Conflict management is not a unique genus of behavior, then, but recapitulates and intensifies its larger environment.[32] It expresses and dramatizes its social field in a pure and concentrated fashion. Modern courts of law elevate the judge and require exaggerated etiquette, and similar rituals may accompany blood vengeance, duels, discipline, the termination of relationships,[33] and negotiations between tribes and nations. Because it resembles the whole of which it is a part,[34] conflict management serves diagnostically to identify various locations in social space. Ultimately it may reveal the elementary forms of social life.

---

[31] Lasswell observes that punitive child-rearing practices seem to occur in societies with punitive governments (1964, p. xii).

[32] It may therefore be difficult or impossible to transplant a mode of conflict management between socially different settings.

[33] For example, Jewish parents traditionally obey a 7-day period of mourning (shivah) when they disown a child for marrying a gentile. The Banyoro of Uganda may handle conflict between fellow clanmembers by "cutting kinship" (obwiko), a formal separation initiated when the aggrieved party utters a formula such as the following: "From now on, you shall not come to my place nor shall I come to yours, and your children shall not come to my place nor shall mine come to yours" (Beattie, 1971, p. 212, punctuation edited).

[34] Self-similarity is a basic organizing principle of nature, as when a branch resembles a tree or a leaf a branch. Self-similar structures, known as "fractals," are recognized in such fields as physics, chemistry, geology, and astronomy (see, e.g., La Brecque, 1987).

ACKNOWLEDGMENTS

This essay, prepared for the Distinguished Scholar Lecture Series, School of Justice Studies, Arizona State University, Tempe, February, 9, 1987, draws on a project supported by the National Science Foundation Program in Law and Social Science. I thank the following people for commenting on an earlier draft: M. P. Baumgartner, Albert Bergesen, Albert K. Cohen, Mark Cooney, Kathleen Ferraro, John Griffiths, John Hepburn, John Herrmann, Allan V. Horwitz, Pat Lauderdale, Calvin Morrill, Michael Musheno, Anna-Marie Oliverio, Roberta Senechal, and James Tucker.

References

Abbott, J. H. (1981). In the belly of the beast: Letters from prison. New York: Vintage Books.

Ayers, E. L. (1984). Vengeance and justice: Crime and punishment in the 19th-century American South. New York: Oxford University Press.

Ayoub, V. F. (1965). Conflict resolution and social reorganization in a Lebanese village. Human Organization, 24, 11–17.

Baldick, R. (1965). The duel: A history of duelling. London: Chapman and Hall.

Balikci, A. (1970). The Netsilik Eskimo. Garden City, NY: Natural History Press.

Barton, R. F. (1969). Ifugao law. Berkeley: University of California Press. (Original work published 1919)

Bateson, G. (1958). Naven: A survey of the problems suggested by a composite picture of the culture of a New Guinea tribe drawn from three points of view (2nd ed.). Stanford: Stanford University Press.

Baumgartner, M. P. (1984a). Social control from below. In D. Black (Ed.), Toward a general theory of social control, Vol. 1: Fundamentals (pp. 303–345). Orlando, FL: Academic Press.

Baumgartner, M. P. (1984b). Social control in suburbia. In D. Black (Ed.), Toward a general theory of social control, Vol. 2: Selected problems (pp. 79–103). Orlando, FL: Academic Press.

Baumgartner, M. P. (1988). The moral order of a suburb. New York: Oxford University Press.

Baxter, P. T. W. (1972). Absence makes the heart grow fonder: Some suggestions why witchcraft accusations are rare among East African pastoralists. In M. Gluckman (Ed.), The allocation of responsibility (pp. 163–191). Manchester: Manchester University Press.

Beattie, J. H. M. (1971). "Cutting kinship" in Bunyoro. Ethnology, 10, 211–214.

Beidelman, T. O. (1966). Intertribal tensions in some local government courts in colonial Tanganyika: I. Journal of Africa Law, 10, 118–130.

Beidelman, T. O. (1976). Intertribal tensions in some local government courts in colonial Tanganyika: II. Journal of African Law, 11, 27–45.

Berger, P., Berger, B., and Kellner, H. (1973). The homeless mind: Modernization and consciousness. New York: Random House.

Black, D. (1976). The behavior of law. New York: Academic Press.

Black, D. (1983). Crime as social control. American Sociological Review, 48, 34–45.

Black, D. (1984a). Jurocracy in America. *The Tocqueville Review—La Revue Tocqueville*, 6, 273–281.

Black, D. (1984b). Social control as a dependent variable. In D. Black (Ed.), *Toward a general theory of social control, Vol. 1: Fundamentals* (pp. 1–36). Orlando, FL: Academic Press.

Black, D. (1987). Compensation and the social structure of misfortune. *Law and Society Review*, 21, 563–584.

Black, D. (1989). *Sociological justice.* New York: Oxford University Press.

Black, D. & Baumgartner, M. P. (1980). On self-help in modern society. In D. Black, *The manners and customs of the police* (pp. 193–208). New York: Academic Press.

Black, D. & Baumgartner, M. P. (1983). Toward a theory of the third party. In K. O. Boyum & L. Mather (Eds.), *Empirical theories about courts* (pp. 84–114). New York: Longman.

Black-Michaud, J. (1975). *Cohesive force: Feud in the Mediterranean and the Middle East.* Oxford: Basil Blackwell.

Block, R. (1974). Why notify the police: The victim's decision to notify the police of an assault. *Criminology*, 11, 555–569.

Boehm, C. (1984). *Blood revenge: The enactment and management of conflict in Montenegro and other tribal societies.* Philadelphia: University of Pennsylvania Press.

Boswell, J. (1980). *Christianity, social tolerance, and homosexuality: Gay people in Western Europe from the beginning of the Christian era to the fourteenth century.* Chicago: University of Chicago Press.

Boulding, K. (1964). A pure theory of conflict applied to organizations. In G. Fisk (Ed.), *The frontiers of management* (pp. 41–49). New York: Harper & Row.

Bourdieu, P. (1966). The sentiment of honour in Kabyle society. In J. G. Peristiany (Ed.), *Honour and shame: The values of Mediterranean society* (pp. 191–241). Chicago: University of Chicago Press.

Campbell, J. K. (1964). *Honour, family and patronage: A study of institutions and moral values in a Greek mountain community.* Oxford: Clarendon Press.

Carniero, R. L. (1970). A theory of the origin of the state. *Science*, 169, 733–738.

Chagnon, N. A. (1977). *Yanomamö: The fierce people* (2nd ed.). New York: Holt, Rinehart & Winston.

Cohen, A. K. (1976). Prison violence: A sociological perspective. In A. K. Cohen, G. F. Cole, & R. G. Bailey (Eds.), *Prison violence* (pp. 3–22). Lexington, MA: D.C. Heath.

Cohen, E. (1972). Who stole the rabbits? Crime, dispute, and social control in an Italian village. *Anthropological Quarterly*, 45, 1–14.

Coleman, J. S. (1982). *The asymmetric society.* Syracuse: Syracuse University Press.

Collier, J. F. (1973). *Law and social change in Zinacantan.* Stanford: Stanford University Press.

Collins, R. (1974). Three faces of cruelty: Towards a comparative sociology of violence. *Theory and Society*, 1, 415–440.

Colson, E. (1953). Social control and vengeance in plateau Tonga society. *Africa*, 23, 199–212.

Cooney, M. (1988). *The social control of homicide: A cross-cultural study.* Unpublished doctoral dissertation, Harvard Law School.

Curran, B. A. (1986). American lawyers in the 1980s: A profession in transition. *Law and Society Review*, 20, 19–52.

Douglas, J. D. (1967). *The social meanings of suicide.* Princeton: Princeton University Press.

Douglas, M. (1973). *Natural symbols: Explorations in cosmology* (rev. ed.). New York: Vintage Books.

Durkheim, E. (1951). *Suicide: A study in sociology.* New York: Free Press. (Original work published 1897)

Durkheim, E. (1964). *The division of labor in society.* New York: Free Press. (Original work published 1893)

Eckhoff, T. (1966). The mediator, the judge and the administrator in conflict resolution. *Acta Sociologica, 10,* 148–172.

Ekvall, R. B. (1964). Peace and war among the Tibetan nomads. *American Anthropologist, 66,* 1119–1148.

Ellickson, R. C. (1986). Of Coase and cattle: Dispute resolution among neighbors in Shasta County. *Stanford Law Review, 38,* 623–687.

Engel, D. M. (1978). *Code and custom in a Thai provincial court: The interaction of formal and informal systems of justice.* Tucson: University of Arizona Press.

Evans-Pritchard, E. E. (1937). *Witchcraft, oracles and magic among the Azande.* London: Oxford University Press.

Evans-Pritchard, E. E. (1940). *The Nuer: A description of the modes of livelihood and political institutions of a Nilotic people.* London: Oxford University Press.

Faragher, J. M. (1979). *Women and men on the overland trail.* New Haven: Yale University Press.

Felstiner, W. L. F. (1974). Influences of social organization on dispute processing. *Law and Society Review, 9,* 63–94.

Foucault, M. (1975). *Discipline and punish: The birth of the prison.* New York: Pantheon.

Frake, C. O. (1980). Kin and supporters among the Yakan. In A. S. Dil (Ed.), *Language and cultural description: Essays by Charles O. Frake* (pp. 202–213). Stanford: Stanford University Press.

Fuller, L. L. (1978). The forms and functions of adjudication. *Harvard Law Review, 92,* 353–409.

Galanter, M. (1974). Why the "haves" come out ahead: Speculations on the limits of legal change. *Law and Society Review, 9,* 95–160.

Galanter, M. (1983). Reading the landscape of disputes: What we know and don't know (and think we know) about our allegedly contentious and litigious society. *UCLA Law Review, 31,* 4–71.

Galtung, J. (1965). Institutionalized conflict resolution: A theoretical paradigm. *Journal of Peace Research, 2,* 349–397.

Garnsey, P. (1968). Legal privilege in the Roman Empire. *Past and Present, 41,* 3–24.

Getman, J. G. (1979). Labor arbitration and dispute resolution. *Yale Law Journal, 88,* 916–949.

Gluckman, M. (1963). Gossip and scandal. *Current Anthropology, 4,* 307–316.

Gluckman, M. (1967). *The judicial process among the Barotse of northern Rhodesia* (2nd ed.). Manchester: Manchester University Press.

Gluckman, M. (1969). *Custom and conflict in Africa.* New York: Barnes and Noble. (Original work published 1956)

Goffman, E. (1961). *Asylums: Essays on the social situation of mental patients and other inmates.* Garden City, NY: Anchor Books.

Goody, J. (1957). Fields of social control among the LoDagaba. *Journal of the Royal Anthropological Institute of Great Britain and Ireland, 87,* 75–104.

Gorn, E. J. (1985). "Gouge and bite, pull hair and scratch": The social significance of fighting in the Southern backcountry. *American Historical Review, 90,* 18–43.

Griffiths, J. (1986). What do Dutch lawyers actually do in divorce cases? *Law and Society Review, 20,* 135–175.

Grönfors, M. (1986). Social control and law in the Finnish gypsy community. *Journal of Legal Pluralism, 24,* 101–125.

Gulliver, P. H. (1963). *Social control in an African society: A study of the Arusha, agricultural Masai of northern Tanganyika.* Boston: Boston University Press.

Gulliver, P. H. (1969). Dispute settlement without courts: The Ndendeuli of southern Tanzania. In L. Nader (Ed.), *Law in culture and society* (pp. 24–68). Chicago: Aldine.

Gulliver, P. H. (1971). *Neighbors and networks: The idiom of kinship in social action among the Ndendeuli of Tanzania.* Berkeley: University of California Press.

Gulliver, P. H. (1977). On mediators. In I. Hamnett (Ed.), *Social anthropology and law* (pp. 15–52). London: Academic Press.

Gulliver, P. H. (1979). *Disputes and negotiations: A cross-cultural perspective.* New York: Academic Press.

Harner, M. J. (1972). *The Jívaro: People of the sacred waterfalls.* Garden City, NY: Anchor Books.

Hasluck, M. (1954). *The unwritten law in Albania.* Cambridge: Cambridge University Press.

Henry, A. F., & Short, J. F., Jr. (1954). *Suicide and homicide: Some economic, sociological and psychological aspects of aggression.* New York: Free Press.

Hirschman, A. O. (1970). *Exit, voice, and loyalty: Responses to decline in firms, organizations, and states.* Cambridge: Harvard University Press.

Hobsbawm, E. (1959). *Primitive rebels: Studies in archaic forms of social movement in the 19th and 20th centuries.* New York: W. W. Norton.

Hofstadter, D. R. (1979). *Gödel, Escher, Bach: An eternal golden braid.* New York: Vintage Books.

Horowitz, R. (1983). *Honor and the American dream: Culture and identity in a Chicano community.* New Brunswick, NJ: Rutgers University Press.

Horwitz, A. V. (1982). *The social control of mental illness.* New York: Academic Press.

Jones, S. (1974). *Men of influence in Nuristan: A study of social control and dispute settlement in Waigal Valley, Afghanistan.* New York: Seminar Press.

Kiefer, T. M. (1972). *The Tausug: Violence and law in a Philippine Moslem society.* New York: Holt, Rinehart & Winston.

Knauft, B. M. (1985). *Good company and violence: Sorcery and social action in a lowland New Guinea society.* Berkeley: University of California Press.

Knauft, B. M. (1987). Reconsidering violence in simple human societies: Homicide among the Gebusi of New Guinea. *Current Anthropology, 28,* 457–500.

Koch, K.-F. (1974). *War and peace in Jalémó: The management of conflict in highland New Guinea.* Cambridge: Harvard University Press.

Kroeber, A. L. (1926). Law of the Yurok Indians. *Proceedings of the 22nd International Congress of Americanists, 2,* 511–516.

La Brecque, M. (1987). Fractal applications. *Mosaic, 17,* 35–48.

Lasswell, H. D. (1964). Preface. In S. Ranulf, *Moral indignation and middle class psychology: A sociological study* (pp. ix–xiii). New York: Schocken.

Leacock, E. (1982). Relations of production in band society. In E. Leacock & R. Lee (Eds.), *Politics and history in band societies* (pp. 159–170). Cambridge: Cambridge University Press.

Lee, R. (1979). *The !Kung San: Men, women, and work in a foraging society.* Cambridge: Cambridge University Press.

Lemert, E. W. (1964). Social structure, social control, and deviation. In M. B. Clinard (Ed.), *Anomie and deviant behavior: A discussion and critique* (pp. 57–97). New York: Free Press.

Lemert, E. W. (1967). The concept of secondary deviation. In *Human deviance, social problems, and social control* (pp. 40–64). Englewood Cliffs, NJ: Prentice-Hall.

Lewis, I. M. (1961). *A pastoral democracy: A study of pastoralism and politics among the northern Somali of the Horn of Africa.* London: Oxford University Press.

Lundsgaarde, H. P. (1977). *Murder in Space City: A cultural analysis of Houston homicide patterns.* New York: Oxford University Press.

Macaulay, S. (1963). Non-contractual relations in business: A preliminary study. *American Sociological Review, 28,* 55–67.

Mann, M. (1986). *The sources of social power, Vol. 1: A history of power from the beginning to A.D. 1760.* Cambridge: Cambridge University Press.

McGrath, R. D. (1984). *Gunfighters, highwaymen, and vigilantes: Violence on the frontier.* Berkeley: University of California Press.

Merry, S. E. (1979). Going to court: Strategies of dispute management in an American urban neighborhood. *Law and Society Review, 13,* 891–925.

Merry, S. E. (1982). The social organization of mediation in nonindustrial societies: Implications for informal community justice in America. In R. L. Abel (Ed.), *The politics of informal justice, Vol. 2: Comparative studies* (pp. 27–45). New York: Academic Press.

Merry, S. E. (1984). Rethinking gossip and scandal. In D. Black (Ed.), *Toward a general theory of social control, Vol. 1: Fundamentals* (pp. 271–302). Orlando, FL: Academic Press.

Middleton, J. (1965). *The Lugbara of Uganda.* New York: Holt, Rinehart & Winston.

Moore, S. F. (1972). Legal liability and evolutionary interpretation: Some aspects of strict liability, self-help and collective responsibility. In M. Gluckman (Ed.), *The allocation of responsibility* (pp. 51–107). Manchester: Manchester University Press.

Moore, S. F. (1973). Law and social change: The semi-autonomous social field as an appropriate subject of study. *Law and Society Review, 7,* 719–746.

Morrill, C. K. (1986). *Conflict management among corporate executives: A comparative study.* Unpublished doctoral dissertation, Department of Sociology, Harvard University.

Nader, L. (1965). Choices in legal procedure: Shia Moslem and Mexican Zapotec. *American Anthropologist, 67,* 394–399.

Otterbein, K. F., & Otterbein, C. S. (1965). An eye for an eye, a tooth for a tooth: A cross-cultural study of feuding. *American Anthropologist, 67,* 1470–1482.

Parsons, T. (1951). *The social system.* New York: Free Press.

Patterson, O. (1982). *Slavery and social death: A comparative study.* Cambridge: Harvard University Press.

Peristiany, J. G. (Ed.). (1966). *Honour and shame: The values of Mediterranean society.* Chicago: University of Chicago Press.

Peters, E. L. (1967). Some structural aspects of the feud among the camel-herding Bedouin of Cyrenaica. *Africa, 37,* 261–282.

Peters, E. L. (1975). Foreword. In J. Black-Michaud, *Cohesive force: Feud in the Mediterranean and the Middle East* (pp. ix–xxvii). New York: St. Martin's Press.

Pitt-Rivers, J. (1966). Honour and social status. In J. D. Peristiany (Ed.), *Honour and shame: The values of Mediterranean society* (pp. 19–77). Chicago: University of Chicago Press.

Reay, M. (1974). Changing conventions of dispute settlement in the Minj area. In A. L. Epstein (Ed.), *Contention and dispute: Aspects of law and social control in Melanesia* (pp. 198–239). Canberra: Australian National University Press.

Reid, J. P. (1970). *A law of blood: The primitive law of the Cherokee nation.* New York: New York University Press.

Reid, J. P. (1980). Law for the elephant: Property and social behavior on the overland trail. San Marino: Huntington Library.

Rieder, J. (1984). The social organization of vengeance. In D. Black (Ed.), Toward a general theory of social control, Vol. 1: Fundamentals (pp. 131–162). Orlando, FL: Academic Press.

Rieder, J. (1985). Canarsie: The Jews and Italians of Brooklyn against liberalism. Cambridge: Harvard University Press.

Romanucci-Ross, L. (1986). Conflict, violence, and morality in a Mexican village (2nd ed.). Chicago: University of Chicago Press.

Rosaldo, R. (1980). Ilongot headhunting, 1883–1974: A study in society and history. Stanford: Stanford University Press.

Ross, H. L. (1970). Settled out of court: The social process of insurance claims adjustments. Chicago: Aldine.

Sahlins, M. D. (1965). On the sociology of primitive exchange. In M. Banton (Ed.), The relevance of models for social anthropology (pp. 139–236). London: Tavistock.

Scheffler, H. W. (1964). The social consequences of peace on Choiseul Island. Ethnology, 3, 398–403.

Scott, J. C. (1985). Weapons of the weak: Everyday forms of peasant resistance. New Haven: Yale University Press.

Senechal, R. (1990). The sociogenesis of a race riot: Springfield, Illinois, in 1908. Urbana: University of Illinois Press.

Shapiro, M. (1980). Courts: A comparative and political analysis. Chicago: University of Chicago Press.

Simmel, G. (1960). The sociology of Georg Simmel (K. H. Wolff, Ed.). New York: Free Press. (Original work published 1908)

Solzhenitsyn, A. I. (1973). The Gulag Archipelago, 1918–1956: An experiment in literary investigation (Vols. 1–2). New York: Harper & Row.

Stauder, J. (1972). Anarchy and ecology: Political society among the Majangir. Southwestern Journal of Anthropology, 28, 153–168.

Stinchcombe, A. L. (1964). Rebellion in a high school. Chicago: Quadrangle Books.

Sweet, L. E. (1965). Camel raiding of North Arabian Bedouin: A mechanism of ecological adaptation. American Anthropologist, 67, 1132–1150.

Taylor, M. (1982). Community, anarchy and liberty. Cambridge: Cambridge University Press.

Thoden van Velzen, H. U. E., & van Wetering, W. (1960). Residence, power groups and intra-societal aggression: An enquiry into the conditions leading to peacefulness within non-stratified societies. International Archives of Ethnography, 49 (Part 2), 169–200.

Timerman, J. (1981). Prisoner without a name, cell without a number. New York: Vintage Books.

Turnbull, C. M. (1961). The forest people. New York: Simon & Schuster.

Turnbull, C. M. (1965). Wayward servants: The two worlds of the African Pygmies. Garden City, NY: Natural History Press.

Turner, V. W. (1957). Schism and continuity in an African society: A study of Ndembu village life. Manchester: Manchester University Press.

von Fürer-Haimendorf, C. (1967). Morals and merit: A study of values and social controls in South Asian societies. Chicago: University of Chicago Press.

Waller, A. L. (1988). Feud: Hatfields, McCoys, and social change in Appalachia, 1860–1900. Chapel Hill: University of North Carolina Press.

Warner, W. L. (1958). A black civilization: A social study of an Australian tribe (rev. ed.). New York: Harper and Brothers.

Whitrow, G. J. (Ed.). (1973). *Einstein: The man and his achievement.* New York: Dover. (Original work published 1967)

Wiedemann, T. (1981). *Greek and Roman slavery.* Baltimore: Johns Hopkins University Press.

Williams, J. K. (1980). *Dueling in the Old South: Vignettes of social history.* College Station: Texas A&M University Press.

Williams, L. S. (1984). The classic rape: When do victims report? *Social Problems, 31,* 459–467.

Wilson, E. O. (1971). *The insect societies.* Cambridge: Harvard University Press.

Winans, E. V., & Edgerton, R. B. (1964). Hehe magical justice. *American Anthropologist, 66,* 745–764.

Wolfgang, M. E. (1966). *Patterns in criminal homicide.* New York: Wiley. (Original work published 1958)

Woodburn, J. (1979). Minimal politics: The political organization of the Hadza of North Tanzania. In W. A. Shack & P. S. Cohen (Eds.), *Politics in leadership: A comparative perspective* (pp. 244–266). Oxford: Clarendon Press.

Wyatt-Brown, B. (1982). *Southern honor: Ethics and behavior in the Old South.* New York: Oxford University Press.

Yngvesson, B. (1976). Responses to grievance behavior: Extended cases in a fishing community. *American Ethnologist, 3,* 353–373.

CHAPTER 4

Why People Deviate in Different Ways

Richard A. Cloward and Frances Fox Piven

An Introductory Note on Justice and Deviant Behavior

The efforts of ordinary people to cope with the injustices that mark their lives often lead them to break the rules that otherwise regulate their behavior. But the rules they break on such occasions vary widely. Sometimes men and women try to cope with injustice by defying the rules on which economic and political power rests, and which are inextricably connected to the injustices they experience. On such occasions, rule violations have a transparent logic—as in the defiant struggles by blacks and women in contemporary American history. At other times, however, people turn to forms of rule-violating behavior—whether suicide, madness, addiction, theft—that leave intact the social legitimations and structures supporting injustice. This difference is obviously of great importance. Indeed, whether men and women break one rule or another has often determined the outcome of the perennial conflicts between poor and rich, between the powerless and the powerful, and has even changed history.

More generally, we think the most important victories for political freedom and economic decency have been won through periodic struggles by ordinary people against their rulers: by the risings of slaves against masters, serfs against nobles, peasants against princes, workers against industrialists. Here is the locus of justice. It wells up out of

RICHARD A. CLOWARD • School of Social Work, Columbia University, New York, New York 10025. FRANCES FOX PIVEN • Ph.D. Program in Political Science, Graduate School and University Center of the City University of New York, New York, New York 10036-8099.

the travails of ordinary people, and it acquires force as people resist
the various forms of exploitation and oppression imposed upon them
by their rulers.

None of this means that the oppressed are noble and their oppres-
sors not. The impulse to justice does not stem from the class distribution of moral virtue, but simply from location in the class structure
itself. Upend the hierarchy, make the underclass the overclass, and
the result would likely be the same, the same oppression and exploitation. Nor does it mean that all struggles mounted from the bottom
express values of justice, since they are sometime reactionary. Still,
the striving for justice has its roots in the aspirations of the subordinated, whoever they may be, to curb the power of their rulers. Our
preoccupation with the question of why people break the rules that
they do is therefore part of our larger concern with struggles by sub-
jugated people to influence the institutions that shape their lives.

The Theoretical Problem

The striking diversity of rule-violating behaviors presses the question upon us of why people deviate in the ways that they do. Revolutionary violence, madness, exotic movements of religious protest,
suicide, addiction, theft, and murder are clearly behaviors that exhibit
complex differences. Some are collective, others individualistic. Some
are directed against the society, and some against the self. And each
involves the violation of a different cluster of social norms. Surely the
differences among these behaviors demand theoretical attention. Yet
the question that has fascinated analysts is not *how* people deviate
but *why* they deviate at all.

There are no theories that cope adequately with the question of
why people violate different rules. Classical European "structural
malintegration" theories, with their twin emphases on stress and
weakened control as the preconditions of rule violation, are long-
standing examples of theories that generate utter confusion about the
question of why people deviate one way rather than another. Stress
and weakened control have been linked by one analyst or another to
virtually every form of rule-violating behavior. The same point can be
made about the "nonstress" schools of thought that developed in
American sociology, including the "cultural transmission," "differential association," "societal reaction," and "resource mobilization"
schools, as well as English "critical theory." While the adherents of
these schools have leveled a variety of criticisms against structural-
functional theories, none of these criticisms point to the failure to ex-

plain different forms of rule-violating behavior. Furthermore, the newer schools have not taken up this theoretical problem either; they have not given us a way of explaining different modes of rule-violating behavior.

Although the structural malintegration perspective claims roots in the classic works of European theorists, especially Tocqueville, Marx, and Durkheim, it was Durkheim's contribution that became ascendant, especially the propositions set forth in *Suicide* (1951), which provided a conceptual frame that dominated and distorted the sociological interpretation of other classical theorists. In Durkheim's paradigm (we will refer to it as the "classical paradigm"), deviant behavior is said to result when social conditions are so stressful as to impel people to act beyond the mores, or when social conditions are too disorganized to restrain them from doing so. People deviate because they "must" or because they "can."

Durkheim was preoccupied with the disruptive impact on social life of the spread of industrial capitalism, and it was in social disruption as such that he came to see the sources of suicide. His concepts of *egoism* and *anomie*, referring to the loosening of people from social bonds and collective sentiments, and to deregulation of social expectations, came to constitute the main repertoire of sociological thought on the sources of deviant behavior. Many more recent theories—for example, means/goals disjunctures, relative deprivation, rank disequilibrium, social disorganization—represent elaborations of one or the other of these arguments. And although Durkheim applied these notions principally to the explanation of suicide, they have since come to be employed as explanations of virtually all forms of social deviance. To cite one example, Harvey Brenner (1973) argued that mental illness results from "the impact of economic change on social disintegration" (p. 6). In subsequent work, Brenner (1977, 1978) went on to claim that economic fluctuations are correlated with crime rates, with a variety of pathologies indicated by overall mortality rates, and by specific cardiovascular disease mortality rates, cirrhosis of the liver mortality rates, suicide rates, homicide rates, and rates of imprisonment. In the same vein, Linsky and Straus (1986) maintain that higher rates of stressful life events (e.g., business failures, divorce rates, abortions, infant deaths, high school dropouts are associated with higher rates of crime, accidents, alcoholism, heavy smoking, and suicide, and higher mortality rates for 11 categories of disease.[1]

Structural malintegration theories also became dominant in efforts to explain widely different types of rule-violating behavior, such

[1] Francis T. Cullen (1984) reviewed a wide variety of theories of social deviance, and showed that the problem of explaining forms has been almost entirely neglected.

as religious movements and political protest. Bryan Wilson (1973, p. 3) makes this point in his review of the main theories being used to account for exotic religious cults and movements, whether thaumaturgical or millenarist:

> All structural-functional theories . . . necessarily see new religions of protest as evidence of "strain" in the social system. That strain is experienced by deviant religionists, is the condition for which they seek remedy, and is implicit (where it is not explicit) in most, if not all, explanations of new religious movements. Anomie, relative deprivation, frustration-aggression, compensation, are the sociological concepts most commonly employed in such explanations.

And the Tillys (Tilly, Tilly, & Tilly, 1975, p. 4) point to the way structural malintegration theories were used to explain the origins of political protest by noting that "collective violence appears as a by-product of processes of breakdown in a society. Large structural rearrangements in societies—such as urbanization and industrialization—in this view tend to dissolve existing social controls over antisocial behavior, just as the very fact of rearrangement is subjecting many men to uncertainty and strain. The strain in turn heightens the impulse toward antisocial behavior."

Our point is obvious: In the structural-functional tradition, the same general explanation is given for widely different forms of deviant behavior. Furthermore, this point holds whether a particular analyst emphasizes stress or weakened control, or both. On the stress side, Tocqueville (1947) thought that excessive expectations led to revolution and Durkheim thought they led to suicide. The most extreme examples of this tendency are found in the works of Parsons and Merton, each of whom made the untenable assumption that the same source of stress accounts for *all* forms of rule-violating action. Thus, Parsons (1954, chap. 7) asserted that all forms of deviance flow from ambiguous and conflicted normative expectations, and Merton (1968) asserted that all forms of deviance result from means–goals disjunctures.

Turning to the social disorganization side of the Durkheimian argument, Norman Cohn (1970) thought that the collapse of feudalism in the late medieval period, by creating "rootless masses," explained why people were caught up in the movements of "wild" millennialism that characterized that era. In a recent essay, Ben-Yehuda (1985, p. 210) claims that "the gradual dissolution of medieval societal boundaries created a witchcraze. . . ." And for Smelser (1959), the rootless masses cast up by the transition from feudalism to industrialism were susceptible to mobilization in extremist political movements. In the same vein, scholars associated with the "Chicago school" attributed various forms of criminal rule violation to the vast transformation produced by industrialization, urbanization, immigration, mobility, and secularization. Thrasher (1963, p. 338), for example, saw in these disorganizing forces the origins of "vice, crime, political corruption, and other social maladies." This is also the outlook of the latter-day social disorganization analysts who refer to themselves as "control" theorists (e.g., Hirschi, 1969; Kornhauser, 1978).

Nor do theoretical efforts to combine the effects of stress and weakened control produce a more satisfactory way of explaining why people deviate differently. Durkheim's account of egoistic suicide is of this genre: Low social cohesion is at once a source of strain and of weakened control. So is E. J. Hobsbawm's (1963) explanation of banditry among the Italian peasants in the 19th century, for he speaks of the way the "traditional equilibrium is upset . . . during the after periods of abnormal hardship, such as famines and wars, or at the moments when the jaws of the dynamic modern world seize the static communities in order to destroy and transform them" (p. 24). In the same terms, Barrington Moore (1969) says that "the main factors that create a revolutionary mass are a sudden increase in hardship coming on top of quite serious deprivations, together with the breakdown of the routines of daily life—getting food, going to work, etc.—that tie people to the prevailing order."

So, there it is. Structural malintegration is an all-purpose explanation of deviant actions as disparate as crime, suicide, millenarism, and revolution. What this amounts to saying is that the same thing causes everything, with the result that all forms of rule-violating behavior ostensibly vary together. This theoretical anomaly might have become evident long ago if analysts of religious movements read the literature on political protest, or if political analysts read the social deviance literature, and so forth. But academics tend to specialize in specific types of rule-violating behavior and to follow the literature mainly in their specialities, and so the anomaly continues to go largely unremarked upon.

It should also be emphasized that the problem of explaining why people deviate in different ways has not been given attention by analysts working in the "nonstress" traditions that developed in the United States. Theories of "deviant learning," for example, have been enormously important in American sociological approaches to the study of rule-violating behavior, beginning with the "cultural transmission" and "differential association" traditions (Shaw & McKay, 1929; Sutherland & Cressey, 1970). More recently, the societal reaction or "labeling" school, with its theoretical roots in George Herbert Mead, Herbert Blumer, Edwin Lemert, and Erving Goffman, has proposed another variant of deviant learning theory. Where the cultural transmission and differential association schools attributed the structural source of deviant learning to subcultures, societal reaction analysts attribute deviant learning to the formal agencies of social control. Thus, deviant behavior is acquired as a consequence of internalizing the invidious definitions imposed by agents of formal institutions of social control, such as criminal justice or psychiatric systems. Following Tannenbaum's (1938) initiating statement of the way processing by agencies of social control influences the individual's subsequent self-conception and behavior, Lemert (1951) called this outcome "secondary deviation," and an extensive literature on the socialization consequences of negative definitions soon developed (see, for example, Becker, 1963; Hawkins & Tiedman, 1975; Kitsuse, 1964; Pfuhl, 1980; Schur, 1965). According to citational studies of the major sociological journals, the labeling school had become the leading theoretical orientation in the study of social deviance toward the late 1960s and early 1970s (Cole, 1975), as contrasted to the study of political or religious deviance where this outlook has had much less impact.

But for our purposes, the important point about the deviant learning schools is that they assume rather than explain the existence of different forms of deviant behavior; what they explain is the persistence of these behaviors. The differential association school has never offered an explanation of why various forms of deviant activity are there to be learned in the first place. And the labeling school is well known for its explicit disavowal of the importance of "primary" deviation, as contrasted to "secondary" deviation, and thus sees no need to explain why the primary deviation that initiated the labeling process occurs, much less why it takes different forms.

The same point can be made about the development of "critical theory" in the 1970s (Taylor, Walton, & Young, 1973). Heavily influenced by the societal reaction school, critical theorists focused so exclusively on the role of the state in promulgating rules and definitions of rule violators that they ended by making the question of why people violate laws in the first place totally irrelevant. Young (1986), a major spokesman associated with that school, recently remarked that critical theorists created "a theory of crime without a criminology!" (p. 19). To remedy that defect, Young (writing this time with colleagues—Kinsey, Lea, & Young, 1986, p. 75) has reverted to an essentially Hobbesian version of crime causation and control, emphasizing "individual moral choice" and the relative "certainty of being detected" as the source of crime. But this only restores the problem of deciding why, when they can, people deviate one way rather than another. Indeed, critical theorists in particular would have benefited greatly from a focus on variations in rule violation. After all, their initial preoccupation with deviance as politics should have encouraged these theorists to ask, for example, when to expect defiance of criminal codes and when to expect insurgent challenges to political authority itself.

We should also mention the "resource mobilization" school, which developed in the 1970s to explain political movements (Gamson, 1975; McCarthy & Zald, 1973; Oberschall, 1973; Tilly et al., 1975). Theorists in this school maintain that collective action is best understood as an outcome of the availability of certain "resources"—solidarities in everyday life, for example. But precisely the same assertion can be made about religious movements, organized crime, juvenile gangs, and other forms of collective deviance that depend on the same or different sets of cohesive relationships in everyday life.

To put our point in general terms, theories of rule-violating behavior tend not to meet an essential requirement of the sociological method. They are not comparative. And not being comparative, they are unable to differentiate the conditions leading to one rather than another form of deviant behavior.

Toward a Theoretical Solution

In our opinion, there are three precepts that should guide an approach to explaining why people deviate as they do. One is that deviant behavior is social behavior, and should be explained by the same sociological variables employed to explain conforming behavior. Second, as social behavior, deviant behavior is necessarily complex behavior, and therefore requires complex explanations. Finally, it may be possible to construct these complex explanations by integrating features from a variety of different schools of thought about deviant behavior.

With respect to the first point, the most important yet unacknowledged feature of the stress and disorganization tradition is the assumption it shares with older presociological views that deviant behavior represents the primitive and bizarre, the breaking forth of irrational and unsocialized impulses, as when people are propelled by the boiling blood, furious bile, and mutinous liquors recounted by Foucalt, by the hypnotic force of LeBon's mob, or by the dynamics of frustration-aggression, reaction-formation, and compulsive modes of deviation that are at the center of the Parsonian scheme. With the erosion of the regulatory and integrative capacities of the society, stress intensifies, controls weaken, and a mindless aberrant behavior simply erupts—crime, suicide, madness, collective violence, and other less than social kinds of behavior. Consequently, the forms of deviant behavior seem to require no special attention, for the varying content is without social meaning. Only the sources of nonmeaning, or irrationality, call for explanation. This metaphorical portrait of deviance is deeply embedded, and it is surely part of the reason that it has appeared self-evident to so many analysts in the classical tradition that people who experience stress or weakened control will become mentally ill or, in an older terminology, bestial and wild. And if instead they kill themselves or rebel or become delinquent, then these distinctions are of little significance, for they are all essentially bizarre. In a word, by denying that deviant adaptations are forms of social and purposeful behavior, analysts working in the classical stress and disorganization tradition feel no need to bring sociological ideas to bear on the problem of explaining why deviant behavior takes different forms.

To put this point another way, many analysts working in the classical tradition fail to see that *rule-violating and rule-conforming behavior both belong to the same sociological universe.* Each is regulated by the same categories of social forces. If people's social ideas inform rule-abiding behavior, they should inform rule-violating behavior. If the types of social relationships in which people are enmeshed provide resources for conforming behavior, these same resources should structure deviant behavior. If the social norms governing such statuses as age, sex, and class pattern conventional roles, they should pattern deviant roles as well. And if reactions by others shape rule-abiding action, they should exert an influence on behavior that gravitates beyond the mores. In sum, what we know about the sociology of conventional behavior should be applicable to the sociology of deviant behavior.

This *social* perspective on deviant behavior is precisely the contribution of the American nonstress traditions. We noted earlier that these schools have not solved the problem of explaining why people violate different norms. Nevertheless, the American schools share the virtue of treating deviant behavior as social behavior. Rule violators are viewed, for example, as people acting on their social learning, or using their social resources. Consequently, we are oriented in the direction of thinking of deviant adaptations as essentially sociological in character, which is a major step forward.

If deviant behavior is social behavior, then it is necessarily complex behavior, shaped by a multifaceted social life. Generally speaking, however, prevailing theories tend to treat deviant behavior as if it transcends social context, except in the limited sense designated by particular theories. Thus, social conditions of one kind or another are said to generate stress and/or weakened control: Given frustrated aspirations, or relative deprivation, or disequilibrated social statuses, or diminished social integration, people turn to suicide. Or given some resource, such as solidarity, people revolt; or they respond to invidious definitions promulgated by agencies of social control by taking on criminal identities. In other words, deviant behavior is often conceived as if it springs full-blown from strain or weakened control alone, or from negative labels alone, or from the availability of some requisite resource, and all of this no matter the multifaceted historically specific social context in which people otherwise find themselves. In explaining deviant behavior, a theoretical understanding of the complex ways that social organization structures behavior may thus disappear from the analysis. Instead, deviant behavior is frequently treated as if it can occur largely independently of the limits and possibilities of any given social setting. It is as if, in the evolution of deviant behavior, people are more or less freed from the specific social context that otherwise molds action; as such, deviant behavior knows no limits except those defined by the source and intensity of stress, or by the decay of controls, or by exposure to particular kinds of learning, or by the availability of a given resource for action. Explanations of deviant behavior thus tend to ignore the one conclusion to which all of the study of social life has led: that the limits and possibilities for behavior are shaped in a social context that is intricate and multifaceted. In short, we will argue that the key to a comparative perspective on why people deviate, and why their violations take different forms, will be found in the cumulative interaction of a variety of sociological forces.

Indeed, the very multiplication of explanations of deviance gives reason to think that a more complete explanation of deviant behavior may be possible that would shed light on the circumstances leading to specific forms of rule violation. Those relatively few contemporary analysts who have tried to explain why people deviate in different ways have in fact been led in just this direction of developing more integrated explanations that take into account the cumulative interaction of different contextual variables. To explain why delinquent gangs take different forms, Cloward (1959) and Cloward and Ohlin (1960), for example, argued that it is necessary to go beyond stress:

> . . . the pressures that lead to deviant patterns do not necessarily determine the particular pattern of deviance that results. . . . In other words, we cannot predict the content of deviance simply from our knowledge of the problem of adjustment to which it is a response. In any situation, alternative responses are always possible. We must therefore explain each solution in its own right, identifying the new variables which arise to di-

rect impulses toward deviance toward one pattern rather than another. . . .
Failure to recognize the need for this task is, as we have noted, a major
weakness in many current theories. . . . All too often a theory that explains the origin of a problem of adjustment is erroneously assumed to
explain the resulting deviant adaptation as well. (pp. 40–41)

With this point made, Cloward (1959) said that it is necessary to identify "the distribution of illegitimate means," or to show how opportunities for deviant behavior of one kind or another are distributed
throughout the social structure, thus enabling us to speak of "differential illegitimate opportunity structures" as the crucial determinant
of the evolution and differentiation of deviant adaptations. Cloward
and Ohlin (1960) went on to draw upon a long tradition of research
on neighborhood social structures initiated by Kobrin (1951), Shaw
and McKay (1929), Sutherland and Cressey, (1970), and others in the
"Chicago school" to show that different types of slum social organization "intervened" to produce different types of delinquent subcultures (e.g., expressive violent gangs tend to grow up in highly disorganized slum communities, and instrumental criminalistic gangs tend
to grow up in highly integrated communities with stable structures of
adult-organized crime).

   Parallel multivariable formulations have been developed by several stress analysts preoccupied with political protest. In his well-known
"value-added" theory, Smelser (1962) suggested that the availability
or lack of availability of various "structural facilities" might make it
possible to explain why responses to strain take form in political protest rather than in panics, crazes, and fads. Later, Gurr (1968) distinguished between "instigating" and "mediating" variables, and introduced a host of "mediating" variables to explain why perceptions of
relative deprivation do not necessarily take form in civil violence, such
as the availability of religious mechanisms that facilitate millenarism
or the existence of electoral arrangements that facilitate the channeling of anger.[2] And Oberschall (1973, p. 32) asserts that in order to

---

[2]There is an important sense in which these theoretical developments essentially restore a sociological perspective that was explicit in the work of some earlier European
analysts, a perspective that was subsequently overtaken by the stress and disorganization paradigm, especially as it was framed by Durkheim. In explaining popular uprisings, for example, Tocqueville came to be remembered for the stress generated when
expectations rise beyond possibility of fulfillment, and Marx and Engels are said to
have emphasized the stress associated with "immiseration." But Tocqueville (1947)
also emphasized the way that divisions among elites may stimulate political unrest, as
well as the capacity of people to appraise the injustice of their situation in terms of
traditions of reciprocal rights and obligations governing the relations between the rulers and the ruled, and Marx and Engels (1948) emphasized such contextual dimensions as socially structured consciousness and socially structured solidarities. Such

understand the forms and outcomes of political struggle by "the groups
or collectivities that act upon grievances and react to provocations,"
it is necessary to introduce variables explaining why "conflict tends
to be violent or nonviolent, limited or large-scale, institutionalized or
unregulated."

In this chapter, we will proceed on the assumption that the various schools, which define themselves in opposition to one another,
are in fact each focusing on different aspects of the social context that
shape deviant action. If that is so, then an integrated analysis of deviant behavior could be within reach. Furthermore, a comparative ex-
ploration of why deviant behavior takes different forms suggests that
each of the schools may have implications for a broader range of deviant actions than is otherwise claimed. If, for example, political protest depends on particular social resources, then perhaps every form
of deviant behavior depends on distinctive resources. Moreover, our
effort to view different forms of deviance comparatively, from a common theoretical perspective, will enable us to identify similar or related explanatory ideas that have been used by analysts concerned
with different forms of deviant behavior, although often using a different nomenclature. This could make possible a fuller and more coherent statement of the unique contribution of the disparate schools
to an integrated theory. Thus, the societal reaction school could overcome its narrow preoccupation with stigma by incorporating the role
attributed to repressive force, or to conciliatory reforms, by analysts
who study the impact of such societal reactions on the course of protest movements.

In the pages to follow, we use an analytic scheme that draws upon
different perspectives now available in the literature, and we give illustrations of its applicability. As will become evident, we think the
main contributions of the various schools can usefully be considered
in four categories: those that refer to social ideas, to social resources,
to social norms, and to societal reactions. We can do little here except
sketch the main outlines of an integrated approach, and of necessity
many subtleties in the literature must be overlooked.

Social Ideas and Modes of Deviant Behavior

One thing we know about human collectivities is that they import
to their members a way of thinking about the world: a way of thinking
about their relationship to themselves, to others, to nature, to the past

---

perspectives, which incorporated complex features of social context, were more or less
extinguished by the spreading acceptance of the stress/disorganization paradigm.

and future, to space and time, to hierarchy and equality, and to all of the other complex aspects of social existence, including the causes of existence itself. Whether fully conscious and articulated or not, these conceptions constitute a cognitive and moral map. The resulting system of social ideas guides people in the routines of everyday behavior, and it provides the grounds for judgments as to how people should behave, including the grounds for obeying or defying rules. People's theories of causation tell them why their situation is as it is, and their moral ideas tell them how blame should be attributed—whether to self, social structure, chance, fate, or the gods. Their social ideas also enable them to assess their resources to act upon their situation, including resources for deviant actions. And they enable them to engage in a process of "anticipatory societal reaction"—that is, to think out what others will do to them if they try to change their situation by deviant means. All of this is to say that deviant behavior involves degrees of consciousness and intentionality, at least to the same extent as conforming behavior. As Oberschall (1973, p. 25) remarks in connection with collective protest, "there are emotional and nonrational components in collective behavior, but the same can be said for everyday behavior."

What we call social ideas, Berger and Luckman (1966) call the "social construction of reality." Their phrase correctly suggests that people's social ideas are never mainly a matter of individual construction. While individuals may invent or vary specific explanations of reality, they vary and invent within a body of socially inherited interpretations. It is in this sense that preexisting social ideas are part of a social context that influences behavior.

Although many of the grand sociological theorists, from Marx to Weber to Parsons, were preoccupied with the relationship of systems of meaning to social action, stress and disorganization analysts have nevertheless tended to ignore systems of meaning in explaining deviant behavior. The same point is true of many analysts in the non-stress schools. Thus, labeling theorists tend to diminish intentionality or meaning in the deviant act by insisting that "primary" deviance is itself insignificant, its causes ephemeral and accidental; what is significant is the actions of agencies of social control that inculcate deviant identities. And in explaining collective challenges to political authority, resource mobilization analysts (as well as "conflict theory" analysts who are preoccupied mainly with crime) also tend to ignore the ideological dimension of deviant behavior. Instead, such challenges may be treated simply as the reflection of ongoing processes of competition among contending groups. But to say of those instances when people are moved to demand the head of the king or to burn the ricks or to loot the granaries that they are merely participating in the normal politics of everyday life is to define away what needs to be explained. There is a very large difference between the black parishioners who one day sang "Swing Low, Sweet Chariot" in a southern black church and the blacks who sang "We Shall Overcome" in confrontation with armed police. To be sure, the solidarities underlying religious observance at one time may also make collective political action possible at another time. But in other ways, the transformation in behavior is extraordinary, and it demands explanation. We think the key to this transformation is in the changing interpretations people make of their reality.

Those strands of the American criminological tradition that emphasize social learning are, however, obviously about social ideas. Furthermore, there are striking parallels between this tradition in American criminology and a perspective on political protest that has emerged in scholarship on peasant movements and preindustrial protests. Studies of food riots and machine smashing (cf., for example, Rude, 1980; Thompson, 1963) emphasize popular social ideas in explaining why people sometimes challenge political authority. Similarly, some analysts of peasant movements (e.g., Scott, 1976; Wolf, 1969) base their explanations on traditional ideas about rights. In part, these analysts are reviving a Tocquevillian perspective on political protest. Tocqueville argued that violations by the nobility of the peasant's ideas about their traditional rights fueled popular uprisings during the French Revolution, and it is that theme that is, for example, expanded and elaborated in Thompson's thesis that violations of the "moral economy" of the English poor were a main cause of food riots.

At a more general level, the greater emphasis now being given in the study of deviant behavior to social constructionism—whether symbolic interactionism, phenomenology, or linguistic analysis—makes possible a convergence with the structural malintegration tradition. It is possible to ask how varying social conditions, such as rapid changes in economic circumstances, are variously perceived and defined by people depending on their social ideas, and how these meanings or evaluations predispose people toward different ways of acting, including deviant ways of acting of one kind or another. It is just this possibility that is implied by Scott (1976, p. 236) in his criticism of the relative deprivation explanation of collective protest:

> What is an intolerable gap between expectations and capabilities? Does the capacity for "toleration" vary from culture to culture, from individual to individual, or is it a panhuman constant? Does frustration always lead to solidarity or aggression or can it lead to an extinction of the original desires? . . . What is missing, quite simply, is society and shared values.

"Wants," as conceptualized in relative deprivation, have no necessary relation to learned standards of justice and equity; it is enough to have a
goal and be frustrated.

In this connection, we should note that although the literature on
the social ideas of deviants of different kinds remains very thin, theoretical developments on the significance of meaning systems has pro-
ceeded sufficiently to make research along these lines increasingly
feasible and useful. In the meantime, such studies as do exist that
describe world views—such as Maurer's (1955) linguistic study of the
relationship between the argot and behavior of pickpockets, and Rude's
(1980) study of protest ideology and mass mobilization—could be
reexamined from a comparative perspective.

We can illustrate the importance of social ideas by showing how
they help to explain two of the most vexing problems in the field of
deviant behavior—why women deviate so much less than men, and
why they tend to deviate differently from men (for example, their de-
viations are more likely to be individualistic rather than collective).
As to the first fact—that women deviate less—classical sociological
theory has nothing to say other than to maintain that women experience less stress and disorganization than men. Needless to say, the
characterization of women as somehow shielded from the effects of
social malintegration has never been empirically demonstrated, and
on reflection appears dubious. Durkheim dealt with the problem by
saying: "The two sexes do not share equally in social life. Man is
actively involved in it, while woman does little more than look on
from a distance." The notion here is evident enough: Women experience little stress because they are cloistered in the family system.
Moreover, Durkheim (1951) continued, "being a more instinctive crea-
ture than man, woman has only to follow her instincts to find calm-
ness and peace" (pp. 309–310). And Hirschi (1969), a vigorous advocate of disorganization or control theories as opposed to stress
explanations, having no way of explaining why adolescent girls are so
much less delinquent than adolescent boys, simply omitted girls from
the sample of high school students on which his well-known delinquency research was based with a footnote comment: "Since girls have
been neglected for too long by students of delinquency, the exclusion of them is difficult to justify. I hope to return to them soon" (pp.
35–36).

The social ideas associated with the caretaking role of women in
the traditional division of labor may go far toward explaining their
low rates of deviance. These social ideas emphasize obligations toward
others, or what is sometimes called the ethic of caring. Women may
thus be inhibited from many kinds of deviant behavior because their

values lead them to shun the destructive consequences in the lives of others. Conversely, males apparently feel freer to inflict these consequences. An inventory of the manifold ways that male deviance affects women makes this point vivid. When large numbers of men are imprisoned, become alcoholics or addicts, kill themselves, or desert during depressions or periods of chronic unemployment, it is women and children who are left to fend for themselves, just as they are left to live out the consequences of male sexual violence. But for women, the inflicting of physical harm upon others may be largely precluded by their social ideas. Thus, the fact that women commit suicide less than men may have nothing to do with Durkheim's assertion that they experience little stress; instead, it may have everything to do with the greater concern shown by women about the consequences that killing themselves would inevitably have for their children, husbands, and others who depend upon them.

As to the second fact—that women deviate differently from men—sociological theory also has had little instructive to say. Parsons (1954) merely said that women "express an undercurrent of aggression toward men with whom they are associated" (p. 345). By contrast, we have argued elsewhere (Cloward & Piven, 1979) that clues to the patterns of female deviance are provided by a cognitive and moral framework that ascribes women's problems to their biopsychological nature, an ideological definition that was most vivid in the 19th-century view of women, at least of middle-class women, as frail and decorative creatures whose temperamental excesses were presumably the result of their sexual organs (e.g., "wandering wombs") and whose delicate physical natures predisposed them to illness. Not surprisingly, given these ideas, women often resorted to "sick" roles—that is, to a variety of psychosomatic adaptations, such as conversion hysteria.

But women's ideas are more variegated and complicated, and under certain conditions lead to aggressive, collective modes of rule violation. Thus, Piven (1985) has recently been exploring what she calls the "moral economy of domesticity" as a way of explaining why women sometimes moved beyond the realm of the family and the politics of personal relations to do battle with the larger forces they perceived as threatening to destroy and transform their lives and the lives of family members. Women entered history when the traditional moral economy of domesticity, with its emphasis on the primacy of caretaking values, was violated. Thus, women joined and even led the food riots that swept across Europe in the 18th and 19th centuries in resistance to the "new-fangled" doctrine of the market—in England, women frequently took the lead in the food riots that broke out periodically in the 17th and 18th centuries (Thompson, 1963, p. 116). Women reformers in the United States and Europe at the end of the 19th century pioneered in the struggle for social welfare protections. In the United States during the 1960s, black women who could not feed and clothe their children joined in a protest movement to assert their right to welfare benefits as mothers. In each instance, we can see that it was the violation of the traditional caretaking values of the moral economy of the family that provoked the political action of women and also guided its forms, much as the "moral economy of subsistence" or the "moral economy of the English crowd" provoked and guided the political action of peasants.

Similar observations can be made about the contemporary anti-feminist movement. Much about this movement seems to fit the model suggested by the study of restorative peasant movements. The women participants in these movements may well have been activated by transgressions of the traditional moral economy of domesticity. The insular and patriarchal family is eroding, jeopardizing the old rights that had guaranteed women and their children a life and a livelihood within the family. The metaphor of family breakdown usually applied to these developments is somewhat misleading, for it suggests an evolutionary development beyond the control of human actors, and people do not oppose developments they do not attribute to human agents. But as some analysts have pointed out, the rate of marital dissolution has in fact not increased over the past century. What is different is that where once it was mainly through death that women or men were left alone to raise their children, now it is mainly through desertion and divorce or the failure to marry in the first place, and it is now mainly women who are abandoned. If ideas guide action and pattern the types of action people undertake, then we would expect these transgressions of the moral economy of domesticity to generate a restorative or reactionary protest politics among women. And there is ample evidence that this is just what has happened, with the rise of movements expressing indignation at the violation of older family norms and calling for the restoration of the traditional family order.

From our point of view, the importance of social ideas is that they help to solve the main problem in the study of deviance with which we began, the problem of why people deviate as they do. The ideas through which people perceive their world and interpret their own situations—its causes, its legitimacy, its potential mutability by one form of human action or another, including by deviant action—help to explain their actions. If people think their lot is fated, they are likely to do nothing more than endure. If they think their fate is decided by the gods, they may turn to magic or the invocation of ancestors to mediate with transcendental powers, or they may engage in extraordinary tests of faith in order to persuade the gods to restore their world as they knew it. And if they think their troubles are caused by the actions of other human beings, they may or may not take action, including deviant action, depending on still further factors, such as the resources for action available to them, as we shall now see.

Social Resources and Modes of Deviant Behavior

Another and obvious dimension of the social context that patterns the ways in which people respond to problematic situations has to do with the opportunities for action available to people in a given society at a given historical juncture at a given social location. Together with a number of other analysts, we call this dimension *social resources*. Deviant action requires resources; different forms of deviant action require different forms of resources. A singularly important theoretical task is to identify the types of resources that are requisite to various forms of rule-violating behavior.

Options for action are, of course, limited by biological capacities and by the natural environment. But even those capacities yielded by nature are further delimited and molded by social context. To put the matter most simply, options for action of any kind, rule-abiding or not, grow out of the social relationships in which people are enmeshed, and are structured and limited by those relationships. To identify the resources requisite to various forms of deviant behavior, in short, it is necessary to examine systems of social relationships.

This point has been most clearly recognized in some studies of crime and political protest. A half century ago, for example, Whyte (1943) pointed out that certain types of slum social structures are essential to the maintenance of organized racketeering. And in a paper prepared in 1944, Sutherland and Cressey (1973, pp. 32–32) observed:

> One factor in criminal behavior which is at least partly extraneous to differential association is opportunity. Criminal behavior is partly a function of opportunities to commit specific classes of crime, such as embezzlement, bank burglary or illicit heterosexual intercourse. . . . Criminal behavior is [also] sometimes limited by lack of opportunity. It is axiomatic that persons who commit a specific crime must have the opportunity to commit that crime.

And Sutherland pointed out that occupational positions of financial trust are requisite to the commission of crimes of financial trust. It is now widely recognized that different kinds of occupational positions determine access to crimes as diverse as pilfering, embezzlement, price-fixing, and graft.

A different but related contribution has emerged from the study of political movements. Smelser (1962) was the first to try to systematize the way in which what he variously calls "means" or "resources" or "structural facilities" conduce toward different kinds of collective behavior, including collective protest. In turn, Oberschall (1973, p. 26) notes that similar notions, although not spelled out systematically, can be found in Brinton's (1965) work on revolutions. (We think, in fact, that unacknowledged ideas about the relationship of resources to collective protest may permeate much of the historical and social science literature.) Furthermore, Smelser (1962) explicitly directs attention to the possibility that analyzing social resources might have broader implications, enabling us to determine why people violate different norms:

> In this volume, we excluded many other kinds of behavior, such as crime, suicide, drug addiction. . . . Having excluded them, we then erected an analytic framework for explaining collective outbursts and collective movements. May we conclude by suggesting that this analytic framework . . . can be brought to bear on many of these forms of behavior. . . . For suicide, then, we might ask: Given a certain type of strain, what conditions determine whether suicide or some other form of behavior arises? To answer this question, we would have to extend our consideration of variables such as conduciveness. . . . By such an extension . . . it should be possible to incorporate many related kinds of behavior into the same theoretical framework that we have used to analyze collective behavior alone. (p. 387)

More recently, the "resource mobilization" school has placed great emphasis on the idea that the social relationships to which people are bound influence whether collective action is possible. Their focus has been on the importance of solidarity to collective protest. People dispersed by their ordinary activities, their work, their family roles, their patterns of settlement, of worship, and of consumption are not likely to join together, even when they are motivated to break rules. Marx made this observation about peasants, whose mode of production he thought atomized them. A similar generalization can be made about women who remain in traditional family roles that tend to isolate them from one another, or about the unemployed who by virtue of their situation are not joined within an institutional context, and whose consequent dispersion atomizes them, at least until their numbers enlarge so that the neighborhood becomes a nexus for organization. Each of these are aggregations of people who experience life situations that might lead them to make common cause. In principle, they might even share a set of interpretations or social theory that predisposes them to

action, and to collective and rule-defying action, but their social relationships separate and disperse them, so that collective action is not
likely.

Conversely, people who are brought together by their work, their
pattern of settlement, worship, or consumption, have available the
possibility of collective action, including deviant collective action. Marx
characterized the proletariat this way when he argued that the mode
of production of industrial capitalism brought workers together and
thus created the collectivities out of which a revolutionary proletarian
movement would arise. Moore (1969), Skocpol (1979), the Tillys (1975),
Wolf (1969), and others have made the same point about the social
relationships underlying protests among peasants and preindustrial
people. They thus contradicted Marx's empirical observation about the
peasantry—an observation that probably owed too much to his concentration on the highly individualistic postrevolutionary French
peasantry—but did not contradict his theoretical insight into the significance of ongoing social relationships, and particularly production
relationships, in making rebellion possible. Peasants who are tied together by the manifold aspects of the organization of village life have
available the possibility of collective action, including collective rebellion. The Indians of Moreles who rose up under Zapata in the Mexican revolution were able to do so because, despite the incursions of
commercial agriculture, they continued to live within relatively intact
village social structures, in "cohesive social units, which possessed
the advantage of a social solidarity built up over long periods of time"
(Wolf, 1969, p. 27; Womack, 1968). And the successes of the civil
rights movement are attributed in part to the way church-related solidarities could become the basis for mobilizing both urban and rural
blacks for collective protest in the American South during the post-
World War II period (McAdam, 1982; Morris, 1984; Oberschall, 1973).
Putting the point most generally, people who are dispersed by their
ordinary activities are not likely to join together when they are motivated to break the rules.

Patterns of social relationships not only determine whether rule-
breaking action can take collective form but also help determine the
specific actions available once collectivities emerge. Thus, the solidarities of the working-class neighborhoods and the warrenlike street pattern of 18th-century Paris combined to account for the form of barri-
cade fighting that characterized the revolution of 1789, and persisted
in subsequent popular uprisings long after the street layout of Paris
had been redesigned to make barricades less than expedient (Cobb,
1970, pp. 170–171). In agrarian uprisings in the American South, merchants and landlords tended to become the targets of the farmers' ire

because it was merchants and landlords with whom the farmers had regular dealings, rather than with banks, speculators, and railroads that were in fact ultimately responsible for the farmers' plight. In a parallel way, tenants, when they are aroused, attack landlords with whom they are directly related, rather than the banks and speculators on whom the landlords themselves depend.

Or, to take a somewhat different example, the social relationships of welfare clients made welfare administrators both natural and accessible targets when clients became defiant in the 1960s; other and more influential targets in the political system were less accessible. More generally, the characteristic focus of urban protesters in the United States on neighborhood, housing, and educational issues would seem to be a reflection of the existence of a relatively vigorous system of local government with multiple points of access and relationships with local populations (Friedland, Piven, & Alford, 1977). Max Weber's (1946, p. 186) statement that "class antagonisms that are conditioned through the market situation are usually most bitter between those who actually and directly participate as opponents in price wars" can be extended to suggest precisely this: that whether individually or collectively, defiant people act in ways delineated by their social relationships.

A focus on social resources also contributes to an explanation of the lower rates and particular forms of deviant behavior among women. Because they have been traditionally confined largely to domestic roles, women have had much less access to many of the systems of social relationships that yield resources for various forms of deviant behavior. The underrepresentation of women in many occupations is a prime case in point, since occupational relationships make a considerable range of criminal adaptations possible. Such limitations on access to resources for different kinds of deviant behavior may help explain the historic pattern of lower rates of deviance among women, just as their traditional isolation from one another in household roles may explain their tendency to engage in more individualistic and privatized forms of deviant behavior (Cloward & Piven, 1979).

However, women have not been without resources, including resources for collective action. As Piven (1985) points out, the church has been an important nexus for organizing women, as in the case of both the suffragette movement and the contemporary antiabortion movement. In a parallel way, the women's movement has been greatly facilitated by the occupational relationships formed as women increasingly enter the labor market. And with enlarging occupational access, women are already beginning to show somewhat higher rates of many forms of crime.

Social Norms and Modes of Deviant Behavior

It is a sociological truism that human action is constrained by intricate sets of social rules or norms. But if it is axiomatic that social behavior is shaped by norms, that statement must apply to deviant action as well. Nevertheless, this axiom, which is treated as self-evident with regard to conforming behavior, is usually discarded when deviant behavior is considered. Parsons (1954) is representative of this way of thinking, for he defines deviance "as tendencies to depart from conformity with normative standards which have come to be set up as the common culture" (p. 206). This statement is true as far as it goes, but by not going further, it is misleading. The implication of this definition is that deviant behavior is nonsocial behavior in the sense that social norms no longer constrain behavior. It is as if to say that once a particular normative barrier has been breached, once the individual or group passes from the conventional to the deviant world, social norms no longer apply. Once on the other side of a particular normative barrier, there is a realm of behavior that lies beyond the social—and the sociological—pale.

To be sure, each form of deviant behavior entails the violation of a social rule. But when particular rules lose their controlling force, other rules remain in place, and they continue to exert influence over behavior. Put another way, people are subject to multiple and complex sets of social norms. When the individual is predisposed to violate one norm or a cluster of norms, that predisposition does not extend to other norms.

With this "obvious" sociological point made, we may ask what difference it makes that people who are predisposed to deviate do not escape the controlling force of most norms. The first implication is that they may not deviate at all if the deviant options open to them are inconsistent with other norms that continue to be compelling. Thus, men and women avoid modes of deviation that are inconsistent with gender norms. If, for example, women come to withdraw legitimacy from prevailing systems of political authority, they may nevertheless avoid collective violence, even when they possess the requisite solidarities. The reason may simply be that violence strains against prevailing gender norms (and may also be inconsistent with elements of their world views). For the same reason, women tend to avoid violent crimes, such as homicide. Similarly, the modes of deviant behavior that might be considered "age-appropriate" at one point in the life cycle may not be considered inappropriate at another age. Thus, when the members of juvenile gangs "spontaneously" abandon violence as they pass from adolescence to young adulthood, they are actually responding to age-graded normative expectations that gang fighting is not an "appropriate" form of deviant action for young adults, although safecracking might be. Were adolescent males to persist in participating in fighting gangs upon entering adulthood, they would be considered "deviant deviants." By thus deterring one or another type of deviation, multiple norms influence the rates of types of deviant behavior by age, sex, and other normatively defined social classifications.

The second implication is that multiple social norms also organize and structure deviant adaptations when they do in fact emerge. If, as a result of the interaction of social ideas and social resources, people violate one norm (e.g., a political, property, religious, sex, or age norm), they nevertheless continue to comply with other norms. Such compliance leads to an important structuring effect: When people deviate, they do so in ways that are normatively regulated—that is, in ways that are "age-appropriate," "class-appropriate," "sex-appropriate," and so forth. Lower-class males tend to support drug habits with aggressive behaviors: They push, pimp, rob, and burgle. Women are more likely to obtain funds through less aggressive behaviors, such as prostitution and shoplifting. This point is made even more vivid by examining the different ways men and women participate in the same broad form of deviance. In the commission of homicides, it is much less likely that women repeatedly shoot, stab, or beat the victims (Wolfgang, 1958, pp. 162–163, 328), since "violent offenses . . . do not appear to be easily reconciled with traditional conceptions of feminine behavior" (Smart, 1977, p. 16). Instead, violent crime is a "normal crime" for males (Swigert & Farrell, 1977). The most seemingly irrational behaviors reflect the same consistencies by gender. Females show higher rates of "neurosis and manic-depressive psychosis, with their possible common denominator of depressive symptomatology," while males show higher rates "of personality disorder with their possible common denominator of irresponsible and antisocial behavior" (Dohrenwend & Dohrenwend, 1976, p. 1453). Even in the act of suicide, women are less violent, choosing such means as gas and poison over jumping, hanging, or shooting.

This patterning process applies across the whole range of social norms. The force of religious norms emphasizing love and forgiveness of the oppressor that characterized southern black culture but not northern black culture made nonviolent civil rights protests possible in the South during the 1960s, but not in the North, where collective violence and riots were therefore more likely. Even the apparent exceptions to this generalization turn out on closer inspection to provide support for it. Thus, if women are inhibited from adopting aggressive, militant modes of deviation in most situations, they may regularly do so in some situations. For women, the socially defined role of feeding and caring for family members has historically shaped the terms of their participation in collective protest; it has tended to control the kinds of episodes in which they join, as well as the very concrete activities they undertake during those episodes. Women often participated in looting, and mainly looted food, clothing, and other household goods, because marketing and food riots were normatively congruent.

In sum, deviance cannot be defined, as it so typically is, as "tendencies to depart from conformity to normative standards." Every form of deviant behavior actually represents conformity with most norms even while one or several are violated. Behavior that breaches a given normative barrier is nevertheless social behavior in the sense that it continues to be governed by all of the other norms that regulate conforming behavior. When people commit rule violations, they do so in ways that remain largely consistent with social norms.

Another source of complexity arises from the fact that social norms do not influence behavior one at a time; they influence simultaneously and interactively, and the cumulative structuring effects are very strong. As these limiting conditions are aggregated, they progressively narrow the options for rule-violating behavior, and they progressively narrow the ways people can violate any given rule. Thus, the constraining influence of age, sex, and social class norms, taken together, is much greater than the constraints following from one or another of them, taken separately. As each additional limiting normative pattern is introduced, the deviant adaptations available at each point in the social matrix are drastically reduced, and the ways any given deviant adaptation can be played out is more sharply defined. In short, the more the normative patterns by which the individual or group is bound, the fewer the deviant alternatives that are available. In this sense, rates and forms of deviation are residual: They represent the exercise of those options remaining at each location in the social structure once the limiting effects of multiple social norms are taken into account.

We know of only one analysis in which multiple normative patterns were simultaneously introduced. The example is Cohen's *Delinquent Boys* (1955), in which he at first appears to attribute gang behavior to the experience of "status deprivation":

> The delinquent subculture, we suggest, is a way of dealing with the problems of adjustment we have described. These problems are chiefly status problems; certain children are denied status in the respectable society be-

cause they cannot meet the criteria of the respectable status system. The
delinquent subculture deals with these problems by providing criteria of
status which these children can meet. (p. 121)

Cohen could have left the matter at that, in which case his analysis
would have exemplified the classical perspective in which the stress
giving rise to deviation is also assumed to explain the specific form of
deviation. But he did not leave the matter there. Instead, he made a
series of further points, the first being that adolescent males, not females, are the ones likely to be gang participants, since gang involvement would be "sex-inappropriate" for females. Then he examines the
content of working-class and middle-class socialization patterns and
concludes that the use of violence as a problem-solving strategy is
more acceptable in working-class culture. Finally, he mentions age
but does little with it. He might have noted, for example, that gang
behavior appears in adolescence but not later, suggesting that the age
norms associated with latter phases in the life cycle preclude it. In
short, Cohen suggests that the content of the delinquent gang culture
is patterned by sex, class, and age norms.

Still other complications may be noted. One pertains to the relative influence of different norms. An adequate theory of the social
structuring of deviant behavior involves whether some norms are more
important than others—some analysts insist, for example, that sex is
a "master status." Furthermore, different normative patterns may work
at cross-purposes, conducing toward different deviant patterns. While
gender norms predispose males in a rather general way toward aggressive behaviors, that effect is modified by age norms; the aggressive
effect would be maximized in adolescence and minimized in later age
grades. Similarly, the psychiatric symptoms expressed by males who
are both of middle age and middle class will tend to veer closer to the
symptoms expressed by females than the structuring effect of sex norms
alone would suggest.

Another complexity is introduced when we consider the capacity
of people to identify with the norms of out-groups. A substantial body
of research has demonstrated the relevance of reference group orientations to an understanding of behavior, the general conclusion being
that nonmembership group norms can influence behavior in ways
comparable to membership norms. In other words, if people are in the
same objective status but are differentiated according to whether they
adopt the norms of another status, their modes of deviant behavior
ought to be different. This analysis of nonmembership reference orientations may explain such disparate phenomena as the (modestly)
rising rates of alcoholism among assimilating Jews or the distinctive

psychiatric symptoms of those in the lower class who identify with middle-class norms.

Perhaps one of the most important forces making for shifts in the rates of forms of deviant behavior are those stemming from fundamental changes in social institutions. As social institutions change, normative patterns are continually being eroded, transformed, destroyed. With such changes—whether the transformation of gender or family norms, the declining influence of religious norms, or drastic shifts in age norms—it is to be expected that the rates and forms of deviant behavior will also change. If, for example, gender norms are transformed so as to produce greater blurring in sex-role distinctions, then comparable blurring will be observed in the rates and forms of deviation by sex. Modes of psychiatric illness or crime previously reserved for men might become more readily available to women, and modes of crime and mental illness previously reserved for women might become more available to men. The same point can be made about changes in any normative pattern. In these terms, a central problem for the development of a theory of the structuring of deviant behavior is to identify the changes taking place in the content of normative patterns, and to trace their consequences in changing patterns of rule-violating behavior.

Progress toward a fuller understanding of the way in which social norms regulate deviant behavior depends, then, on a fuller understanding of how social norms regulate conventional behavior. As we said earlier, both modes of behavior belong to the same sociological universe; what regulates the one regulates the other. The problems posed for analysis, no matter their intricacy, are no different from those posed for the understanding of conforming behavior. The complexities and contradictions, the way that various normative patterns reinforce or oppose one another, or change over time, are puzzles to be solved for an understanding of both kinds of behavior. The point is that in sorting out the influence of various normative patterns in the structuring of conventional behavior, the question of how normative patterns also structure deviant behavior will be answered as well.

Social Reactions and Modes of Deviant Behavior

When people act against rules, agencies of social control may respond. In turn, these responses have consequences for the course of an ongoing deviant pattern. This important point has long been recognized in the study of many different forms of rule-violating behavior. A more comprehensive understanding of rule-violating behavior might be developed if the materials on disparate social reactions, and disparate consequences, were brought together and subjected to comparative analysis.

The "societal reaction" school that emerged in American criminology after World War II focused especially on stigmatizing processes. Even the most cursory overview of the broader literature on societal reactions to rule-violating behavior suggests, however, that these reactions are quite varied, including all forms of force and coercion. Furthermore, concessions are also societal reactions: Food rioters sometimes won price concessions, for example, or southern civil rights protestors won some political rights. And studies of protest widely point to complex forms of cooptation.

Similarly, the societal reaction school has emphasized the persistence of deviance as the outcome of societal reactions. But deterrence is probably the historically most common result of societal reaction; people simply shift from deviant to conforming patterns. If that were not so, we would be in the awkward position of arguing that social control never works, that it is perverse in the sense that efforts at social control always sustain rather than deter deviance. On the other hand, there is clear evidence that societal reactions sometimes do lead to the persistence of deviant actions. Finally, shifts from one form of deviant behavior to another also occur (e.g., gang delinquents in the American cities of the 1950s who shifted to heroin use, or third world millenarian movements that gradually evolved into secular revolutionary movements).

To begin to untangle the relationships between different societal reactions and different deviant outcomes, we think it might be useful to relate societal reactions to the three sets of variables that we think explain the initiation and forms of rule-violating behavior: ideas, resources, and norms. How do specific societal reactions alter, augment, or stabilize the social ideas, the social resources, and the social norms that entered into the production and structuring of deviant action in the first place?

Societal reactions alter people's social ideas. Thus, negative labeling may influence people's ideas about themselves, encouraging people to persist in deviant action. This is the essence of the claim by labeling theorists that invidious definitions are self-fulfilling, such that the offender incorporates a deviant self-image and becomes, in Lemert's (1951) terms, a "secondary deviant." By contrast, when national political leaders finally responded to civil rights protestors with concessions rather than repression, including especially granting the right to vote, they reinforced the social idea that influence can be effectively exercised through the franchise (Piven & Cloward, 1977, chap. 4). As a result, southern blacks did not persist in protesting (despite vexing economic grievances) but instead turned to conventional electoral activity. Similarly, some analysts of third world religious and revolutionary movements claim that the repressive measures employed by colonial authorities against third world millenarian movements sometimes converted them into revolutionary movements because the experience of repression undermined people's ideas about the effectiveness of appeals to the gods, and gave greater legitimacy to the view that change could be won only through secular action against colonial authorities (cf., for example, Wilson, 1973). Repression, in other words, changed people's ideas about the viability of different strategies of social change and helped to convert religious movements into revolutionary protests.

Societal reactions can increase or decrease the resources available to a group, and this too produces variable outcomes. For example, in the late 1950s, a police crackdown on violent juvenile gangs in some of the big urban centers took the form of arresting and sentencing leaders to reformatory terms, and of forcibly dispersing gang members whenever they were seen to assemble in the streets. These and related measures eroded the solidarity resource on which gang existence depended, and the gang atrophied. Similarly, uprooting and resettling peasant populations is a standard method of depriving guerilla movements of the resource base on which they depend. Conversely, much has always been made in the literature on crime and mental illness of the way the resources associated with incarceration stabilize careers in crime and mental illness by enabling inmates to acquire additional learning and skills.

Societal reactions may also affect norms, buttressing or changing them, or bringing new norms into being. Thus, protests by homosexuals won legislative and other legal concessions enlarging the range of permissible sexual relations between consenting adults. In this instance, a normative change promotes the persistence of the original action, which becomes, by virtue of this response, at least somewhat less deviant. But societal reactions can also reinforce norms, with definite consequences for deviant outcomes. Thus, it has been true historically that when women "acted-out"—that is, when they become assaultive, engaged in collective protest—they were often responded to as if they were physically or mentally "ill." Showalter's book, *Women, Madness, and English Culture, 1930–1980*, contains pictures of suffragettes on a hunger strike being treated as hysterics and forcibly fed in London jails in 1912. This kind of societal reaction, in turn, tends to exert pressure on women to adopt modes of deviance more in keeping with gender norms, such as mental depression. The point is that a given societal reaction, by reinforcing norms (in this case, gender norms), can produce a sequence of changing deviant adaptations (in this case, from aggressive to passive ones).

In conclusion, we should note that in our examples so far we have tended to treat the influence of the variables in our theoretical scheme more or less one at a time. But ideas, resources, norms, and reactions interact in complex ways. Because of changing ideas, resources may be utilized that would otherwise remain latent; or, because of the availability of new resources, ideas may change. Thus, we think we have developed only the barest outlines of a solution to a problem that has for too long been neglected in the sociology of deviant behavior. No explanation of rule-violating behavior can be complete that fails to account for the concrete modes of deviation in which people engage.

References

Becker, H. (1963). Outsiders: Studies in the sociology of deviance. Glencoe, Il: Free Press.

Ben-Yehuda, 1985.

Berger, P. L., & Luckman, T. (1966). The social construction of reality. Garden City, NY: Anchor Books.

Blumer, H. (1969). Symbolic interactionism: Perspective and method. Englewood Cliffs, NJ: Prentice-Hall.

Brenner, H. (1973). Mental illness and the economy. Cambridge: Harvard University Press.

Brenner, H. (1977). Health costs and benefits of economic policy. International Journal of Health Services, 7, 4.

Brenner, H. (1978).

Brinton, C. (1965). The anatomy of revolution (rev. and exp. ed.). New York: Vintage Books.

Cloward, R. A. (1959). Illegitimate means, anomie and deviant behavior. American Sociological Review, 24(April), 164–176.

Cloward, R. A., & Ohlin, L. E. (1960). Delinquency and opportunity: A theory of delinquent gangs. New York: Free Press.

Cloward, R., & Piven, F. F. (1979). Hidden protest: The channeling of female innovation and resistance. Signs, 4(Summer), 651–669.

Cobb, R. C. (1970). The police and the people: French popular protest movements 1789–1820. London: Oxford University Press.

Cohen, A. K. (1955). Delinquent boys: The culture of the gang. New York: Free Press.

Cohn, N. (1970). The pursuit of the millennium. New York: Oxford University Press.

Cole, S. (1975). The growth of scientific knowledge: Theories of deviance as a case study. In L. A. Coser (Ed.), The idea of social structure: Papers in honor of Robert K. Merton (pp. 175–220). New York: Harcourt Brace Jovanovich.

Cullen, F. T. (1984). Rethinking crime and deviancy theory: The emergence of a structuring tradition. Totowa, NJ: Rowman & Allanheld.

Dohrenwend, B. P., & Dohrenwend, B. S. (1976). Sex differences and psychiatric disorders. American Journal of Sociology, 81(May).

Durkheim, E. (1938). The rules of the sociological method (8th ed.). New York: Free Press.

Durkheim, E. (1951). Suicide: A study in sociology. New York: Free Press.

Ehrenreich, B., & English, D. (1978). For her own good. Garden City, NY: Anchor Press.

Friedland, R., Piven, F. F., & Alford, R. (1977). Political conflict, urban structure, and the fiscal crisis. International Journal of Urban and Regional Research, 1, 3.

Galtung, J. (1964). A structural theory of aggression. Journal of Peace Research, 2, 2.

Gamson, W. (1975). A strategy of social protest. Homewood, IL: Dorsey Press.

Gove, W. R., & Tudor, J. R. (1973). Adult sex roles and mental illness. American Journal of Sociology, 78(January), 812–835.

Gurr, T. R. (1968). Psychological factors in civil violence. World Politics, 20(January). Princeton: Princeton University Press.

Hawkins, R., & Tiedman, G. (1975). The creation of deviance: Interpersonal and organizational determinants. Columbus, OH: Charles E. Merrill.

Hirschi, T. (1969). Causes of delinquency. Berkeley: University of California Press.

Hobsbawm, E. J. (1963). Bandits. New York: Pantheon.

Ianni, F. A. J. (1974). Black mafia: Ethnic succession in organized crime. New York: Simon & Schuster.

Kinsey, R., Lea, J., & Young, J. (1986). Losing the fight against crime. Oxford: Basil Blackwell.

Kitsuse, J. I. (1964). Societal reaction to deviant behavior: Problems of theory and method. In H. Becker (Ed.), The other side. New York: Free Press.

Kobrin, S. (1951). The conflict of values in delinquency areas. American Sociological Review, 16(October), 653–661.

Kornhauser, R. R. (1978). Social sources of delinquency: An appraisal of analytic models. Chicago: University of Chicago Press.

Lemert, E. M. (1951). Social pathology. New York: McGraw-Hill.

Linsky, A. S., & Straus, M. A. (1986). Social stress in the United States: Links to regional patterns in crime and illness. Dover, MA: Auburn House.

Marx, K. & Engels, F. (1948). Manifesto of the Communist party. New York: International Publishers.

Maurer, D. (1955). Whiz mob: A correlation of the technical argot of pick-pockets with their behavior pattern. Gainesville, FL: American Dialect Society.

McAdam, D. (1982). Political process and the development of black insurgency 1930–1970. Chicago: University of Chicago Press.

McCarthy, J. D., & Zald, M. (1973). The trend of social movements in America. Morristown, NJ: General Learning Corporation.

Mead, G. H. (1934). Mind self and society. Chicago: University of Chicago Press.

Merton, R. K. (1968). Social structure and anomie. In Social theory and social structure (enl. ed., pp. 185–214). New York: Free Press.

Moore, B., Jr. (1969). Revolution in America? New York Review of Books, January 30.

Morris, A. D. (1984). The origins of the civil rights movement. New York: Free Press.

Oberschall, A. (1973). Social conflict and social movements. Englewood Cliffs, NJ: Prentice-Hall.

Parsons, T. (1954). Certain primary sources and patterns of aggression in the western world. In Essays on sociological theory (rev. ed.). New York: Free Press.

Pfuhl, E. H., Jr. (1980). The deviance process. New York: D. Van Nostrand.

Piven, F. F. (1985). Women and the state: Ideology, power and the welfare state. In A. Rossi (Ed.), Gender and the life course. Chicago: Aldine.

Piven, F. F., & Cloward, R. A. (1977). Poor people's movements. New York: Pantheon.

Rude, G. (1980). Ideology and popular protest. London: Lawrence & Wishart.

Schur, E. M. (1965). Labelling deviant behavior: Its sociological implications. New York: Harper & Row.

Scott, J. C. (1976). The moral economy of the peasant: Rebellion and subsistence in Southeast Asia. New Haven: Yale University Press.

Shaw, C. R., & McKay, H. D. (1929). Delinquency areas. Chicago: University of Chicago Press.

Showalter, E. (1985). The female malady: Women, madness and English culture, 1930–1980. New York: Pantheon.

Skocpol, T. (1979). States and social revolutions. Cambridge: Cambridge University Press.

Smart, C. (1977). Women, crime and criminology: A feminist critique. Boston: Routledge and Kegan Paul.

Smelser, N. J. (1959). Social change in the industrial revolution. Chicago: University of Chicago Press.

Smelser, N. J. (1962). Theory of collective behavior. New York: Free Press.

Sutherland, E. H., & Cressey, D. R. (1970). Criminology (8th ed.). Philadelphia: J. B. Lippincott.

Sutherland, E. H., & Cressey, D. R. (1973). Critique of the theory. In K. Schuessler (Ed.), On analyzing crime. Chicago: University of Chicago Press.

Swigert, V., & Farrell, R. A. (1977). Normal homicides and the law. American Sociological Review, 42(February).

Tannenbaum, F. (1938). Crime and the community. New York: Columbia University Press.

Taylor, I., Walton, P., & Young, J. (1973). The new criminology: For a social theory of deviance. London: Routledge and Kegan Paul.

Thompson, E. P. (1963). The making of the English working class. New York: Vintage Books.

Thrasher, F. M. (1963). The gang: A study of 1,313 gangs in Chicago. Chicago: University of Chicago Press.

Tilly, C., Tilly, L., & Tilly, R. (1975). The rebellious century. Cambridge: Harvard University Press.

Tocqueville, A., de (1947). L'ancien regime (M. W. Patterson, Trans.). Oxford: Basil Blackwell.

Weber, M. (1946). Essays in sociological theory (H. H. Gerth & C. W. Mills, Trans.). New York: Oxford University Press.

Whyte, W. F. (1943). Street corner society: The social structure of an Italian slum. Chicago: University of Chicago Press.

Wilson, B. (1973). Magic and the millennium. New York: Harper & Row.

Wolf, E. (1969). Peasant wars of the twentieth century. New York: Harper & Row.

Wolfgang, M. E. (1958). Patterns of criminal homicide. Philadelphia: University of Pennsylvania Press.

Womack, J., Jr. (1968). Zapata and the Mexican revolution. New York: Knopf.

Young, J. (1986). The failure of criminology: The need for radical realism. In R. Mathews & J. Young (Eds.), Confronting crime. London: Sage.

CHAPTER 5

Criminal Actors: Natural Persons and Collectivities

Albert K. Cohen

Introduction

This chapter deals with the theoretical issues that are raised by the fact that collectivities are actors and produce criminal and deviant acts. They are those actors to which individual human beings or "natural persons" are related as "members"; the members are seen to "belong to" the collectivities. Like other actors, collectivities have names and reputations. We love them, hate them, admire them, and resent them. They range from families and ball teams to nation-states. Some of the things they do are deviant. Some of the things some of them do are crimes. (Some of them cannot commit crimes for the same reason that some natural persons—e.g., idiots, infants, and the insane—cannot commit crimes: The law says they can't, and crime is what the law says it is. The law can, of course, change its mind in these matters, and may be of a different mind in different jurisdictions.)

Collectivities are outstanding contributors to the gross national criminal product. Criminologists themselves are fond of describing the staggering costs of the crimes of business corporations, one species of collectivity. Legislation creating new crimes or increasing penalties for established crimes—e.g., legislation to protect the consumer, the

ALBERT K. COHEN • Department of Sociology, University of Connecticut, Storrs, Connecticut 062680
*With the permission of the editors of *Crime and Social Deviance*, published at Bar Ilan University, I have incorporated most of the substance of a paper published (in Hebrew) in *Crime and Social Deviance*, 9 (1981), 18–26.

natural environment, and the health and safety of workers—is increasingly directed at collective actors, and collective actors are increasingly the targets of criminal prosecutions. In the forums of everyday life, away from the criminal courts, we pronounce judgments of crime or deviance on almost all the collectivities we do business with: the electric company—not just the clerk—for overcharging us; the university—not just the dean—for underpaying us; the hospital—not just the doctors or the nurses—for neglecting us; the FBI and CIA—not just their agents—for breaking and entering, opening other people's letters, tapping phones, and telling lies. In light of all this, it is remarkable—and it would be an intriguing topic for the sociology of sociology—that very few students of crime and deviance have addressed themselves systematically to questions like these: What sort of an actor is a collectivity anyway? What does it mean to say that a collectivity "does" something—anything, but especially deviant things like bribery, theft, slander, racial discrimination, and murder? What is entailed in explaining what a collectivity does? What is the relevance of existing deviance theory to the criminality and deviance of collectivities, and what, in turn, do the latter imply for our theories? Do collectivities call for a theory of their own? Will one theory do for both collectivities and natural persons? And, if so, what would it look like? (Hereafter, for simplicity and economy of expression, I shall speak mostly of "crime" and "criminology," but most of what I have to say will apply equally well to noncriminal deviance.)

Collectivities, Corporations, and White-Collar Crime

From the literature of criminology one could easily form the impression that criminal collectivities are all business corporations, that the crimes of business corporations and white-collar crime are more or less the same thing, and that when one sets about explaining white-collar crime, it boils down to explaining the crimes of natural persons, usually company officers. Even Edwin H. Sutherland (1949), who introduced white-collar crime to criminology, failed to appreciate the theoretical implications of the fact that the subjects of his research, his white-collar criminals, were mostly corporations. The conclusion that he drew from his research was that traditional criminological theory was deficient because it could not explain the crimes of rich, intelligent, capable, and respectable businessmen. He failed to draw the additional conclusion that a theory capable of explaining the crimes of businessmen might still be inadequate to the crimes of corporations because corporations are not natural persons and their crimes cannot be reduced to those of their officers. At this point I will mention only one consideration that should have given Sutherland pause.

As Sutherland himself was fond of pointing out with his own data, corporations may be criminal recidivists and usually are. However, although the corporation that commits an offense at one time is the same corporation that repeats the offense some years later, the people who occupy the boxes in its table of organization may be a very different, indeed an entirely new, set of people. But if the crimes of corporations are those of their officers, and the officers at Time One were a different set of people from those at Time Two, then the officers could not have been recidivists, still less the corporation. Was Sutherland deceived, then, in believing that his corporations were recidivists? I believe that Sutherland was right. Corporations can be recidivists because, according to the law's criteria of sameness, as distinguished from those applied by some nominalist philosopher or criminologist, the corporation at Time Two may be the same as at Time One. It may be an actor and a recidivist "in its own right," which means that it is defined in the law in terms of properties that do not translate into a list of people.[1]

[1] There is by now a substantial literature that recognizes that business corporations can be criminal actors at law and deviant at the bar of public opinion and that their offenses raise troubling questions of explanation and control. Perez (1978) very straightforwardly announces his intention to construct a theory to account for "law violations attributable to the corporate entity" as distinguished from "those that can be traced back or constructively attributed to individual directors." I do not intend to review this literature, which is both considerable and diverse, but I think it fair to say that there are few efforts in this literature to deal systematically with the range of questions raised in the second paragraph of this essay. I have the feeling that a lot of writers find it hard to take seriously the notion that corporations are really as much actors, for purposes of theory, as are natural persons. Sometimes they substitute their own definitions for the legal definitions, which they would not do in dealing with the crimes of individuals. Few of them use the term *collectivities* in speaking of corporations and prefer the term *organizations*, which is perfectly legitimate, but they often seem to be more concerned with organization as a context of action for individuals who play roles in the corporation than with the organization as an actor. Much of the literature is mainly descriptive; much of it is concerned with practical questions of how to control the corporate animal. At any rate, it is the literature of a field in ferment, and I believe that, as it continues to grow, it will lead to a profound transformation of criminological theory. A few of the more important items are Coleman (1974), Cullen et al. (1987), Ermann and Lundman (1982), Hochstedler (1984), Schrager and Short (1978), Stone (1976), and Vaughan (1983). The Coleman book does not deal directly with crime, but is a very important work on the nature of corporate actors, not limited to business firms.

In contrast to the foregoing and calculated to disturb the equilibrium and compla-

Granting that the business corporation is an actor in its own right, it is still important to recognize that it is scarcely representative of the universe of collectivities. This universe includes voluntary associations with political, religious, recreational, or charitable goals, ball teams, universities, hospitals, and revolutionary and reformist political organizations. Governments and their agencies do not commit crimes, but only because the criminal law does not take cognizance of them as criminal actors. They do, however, produce lots of noncriminal deviance, especially those agencies whose job it is to prevent and punish deviance. Theoretical work that is based on business corporations is likely to be preoccupied with organizational characteristics that are salient in that kind of collectivity, such as distinctions between ownership, management, and workers, a strongly hierarchical organization, success and survival determined by profit expressed in monetary terms, or revenues derived from the sale of goods or services in a market. A focus on the CIA or trade unions or civil rights organizations or the Provisional IRA or sports organizations would invite attention to different sets of organizational characteristics and result in corresponding alterations in our theories. Furthermore, if we attend to a wide spectrum of collectivities, we are likely to find that the distinctive and conspicuous characteristics of each represent extreme values of variables that are present in some degree, albeit less conspicuously, in most other collectivities, and that are, therefore, candidates for representation in a general theory.

Interaction Process and Common Sense

For some thousands of years now people have been debating the reality of collectivities. These debates have been heavily philosophi-

cency of those who, like me, believe that corporations and other collective actors are more than fictions, metaphors, and abbreviations, is a paper by two prominent crimonologists, Travis Hirschi and Michael Gottfredson (1987). The paper is primarily concerned with rebutting the notion that white-collar crime is different, in ways that are important for theory, from ordinary crime and that established theories, therefore, cannot handle white-collar crime. They argue, on the contrary, that "control theory," originally developed to explain juvenile delinquency and ordinary crime, is quite adequate to white-collar crime as well. It is a cogent argument for a unified and comprehensive theory of crime. To be unified and comprehensive, however, it must deny that "unit-of-analysis issues"—for example, "Do organizations commit crime?"— are consequential for criminological theory. Crimes committed by organizations, they say, are really crimes committed by people in leading positions in the organizations; at least, they can be explained by attending only to those people. Control theory can explain all crime by reducing collectivity crime to ordinary crime. I believe that the reductionist argument is wrong but that a vigorous statement of that position is good for criminology.

cal. In the remainder of this chapter I propose to develop a position on this issue that is adequate for criminological and, more generally, for sociological purposes, and does not require us to decide whether collectivities are more or less real than natural persons in some philosophical sense.

Let us put aside, for the moment, our concern about collectivity crime versus individual crime. Let us take as our starting point the platitudinous proposition that *all* crimes are the outcomes of interaction processes that take place over a period of time rather than all at once, and see if it leads us to conclusions that are not so platitudinous. The proposition implies that a plurality of participants are involved in the production of the criminal product. These participants may be conspirators, provocateurs, audiences hissing, booing, egging on, or turning the blind eye, kinsmen and friends "covering up." They may be victims, some of whom manifestly precipitate their own victimization (Wolfgang, 1958). Some victims may never even learn that they have been victimized. All victims, however, help to bring about the event, if only by providing, in their person or property, an attractive target at the right time and the right place. But participants include also the milling crowd, unaware of pickpockets in their midst but providing nonetheless the cover and distraction that the pickpockets need; the people who sell the burglars or forgers the hardware they need; the customers who unknowingly provide the market for hot goods and therefore the incentive to steal them. They include also the people who can be counted on to maintain the lawful, workaday routines of our banks, postal system, telephone companies, airlines, and even police departments and courts, because they provide services and resources that are preconditions for the consummation of crimes. For example, the faithful clerks and couriers of the postal system are indispensable to the crime of mail fraud. Who knows how many criminal projects (not limited to mail fraud) were frustrated in Ireland by the 6-month mail strike in 1979?[2]

---

[2]There is an "interactionist" literature in criminology that emphasizes the following ideas: that the thing to be explained is mainly the crime, not the guilty conduct of one of the contributors to the event; that the event is produced by interaction among two or more parties; and that this interaction takes time to work itself through. This research is typically based on research on homicide. There are usually only two or three parties participating directly in the interaction process over the span of time over which it is studied. Each case is a single sequence of face-to-face interactions. A conceptual scheme is developed for coding the actions and responses of participants, usually as challenges to one's identity and responses to such challenges, including withdrawing and retaliatory attacks on the identity of the other party. Homicide, or criminal violence short of homicide, is the culmination of an escalating sequence, or series of stages, of attack and counterattack. The task of research is to discover the characteristics of the sequences that lead to the different possible outcomes. The task of theory is

All of these people, circumstances, and relationships affect the outcome of the interaction process; all figure in the answer to the question "What made it happen?" Therefore, all must figure somehow in a general theory of crime. The criterion for inclusion in such a general theory is not wickedness, reprehensibility, or fault on the part of the person we designate as the offender (or the victim who "precipitates" the offense); it is participation in the production of the criminal offense. (It does not follow, of course, that theory must consist of or contain an endless list of people, circumstances, and relationships. It is the office of theory to "reduce" such a list, not by throwing away information but by identifying a manageable set of variables that abstract, from the profusion and concreteness of these "multiple factors," whatever it is about them that is relevant to the production of criminal outcomes.)

The approach from the side of the law and, more often than not, the perspectives of everyday life, or common sense, is different. It does not begin by asking, "What made it happen?" but rather, "Who did it?" and "Why did he do it?" The law is mainly interested in justice, not explanation. It wants to know whom to hold responsible. It explores motives not primarily in order to explain but in order to determine guilt. In the complex matrix of interaction it seeks out the *actus reus* and the *mens rea*; the person in whom these lodge is the guilty party, the one who "did it." This approach is likely to leave out most of what happened and most of the people who helped make it happen. Of course, sophisticated common sense will take cognizance of some other parties, like particularly provocative victims or people who are witness to murder or rape but "refuse to become involved." It is noteworthy, however, that even witnesses and victims will not usually figure in the explanation unless their contribution is dramatic and reprehensible in its own right, which is consistent with the thesis that much of what passes for explanation in law and everyday life is really concerned with the assignment of blame (Cohen, 1988).

I think that the interaction process perspective, as I have described it, is mundane, commonplace sociology. But for many criminologists this perspective exists as an abstract idea that seldom comes down to earth. When they get around to doing research and explaining crimes, they adopt, unconsciously and uncritically, the commonsense approach. First you find out who did it. Then you try to figure

---

to explain them. These studies are completely compatible with my position in this chapter. They are, however, limited in several ways: the exceedingly narrow range of offenses with which they deal, the space and time limitations, the small number of participants, the focus on natural persons. See Felson and Steadman (1983), Hepburn (1973), Luckenbill (1977), and Shoham, Ben-David, and Rahav (1974).

out why they would do a think like that. Let us explore further some less commonplace implications of the interaction process approach.

In the commonsense view, deciding "who did it" is not theoretically problematical; anybody who has access to "the facts" and who has eyes in his head can literally see who did it. In point of fact, however, deciding who did it—the attribution of agency—is never merely a matter of getting at "the facts." Most events can be seen in different ways: as an act of this natural person, that natural person, some set of natural persons, some collectivity—or as an act of God. It may even be seen as a symptom of a disease—that is to say, not as something somebody did but as something that happened to somebody. The origin or authorship of the same event may be read off in different ways by different people. These differences cannot ordinarily be ascribed to ignorance and error. If A paid B to administer poison to C and C died in consequence thereof, did A kill C? Different legal systems produce different answers to such questions, according to their conceptions of causation, agency, and responsibility—that is, according to their respective rules for locating the authorship of an act. The attribution of agency, whether to natural persons or collectivities, is an example of the social construction of reality by bringing the data of experience under these rules. Criminologists need not worry about whether these rules are right or reasonable, nor need they waste time trying to improve upon them. What they do have to do is to find out what they are—that is to say, what are the criteria by which members of the system under investigation construct the realities they recognize and respond to?

Not only is agency an example of the social construction of reality. So, for that matter, is the actor to whom agency is attributed. In a suit before a Massachusetts court, some Indians claiming to be representatives of the Mashpee tribe sued the town of Mashpee on behalf of the tribe. But the court had first to decide whether the Indians of Mashpee were really a tribe or just a bunch of Indians. The legal issue was: What does it take to be a tribe? The court decided that the Indians of Mashpee were not a tribe. Because they were not, they could not sue or do anything else because they did not exist as a tribe (Brodeur, 1978). I would add, parenthetically, that one could also ask, "What does it take to be an Indian?" and the answer would be a recipe for the social construction of another reality—in this case, a certain kind of "natural person." (As the United States struggles with the abortion issue and the question of the status of the fetus—or even the fertilized egg—it is becoming increasingly obvious that the natural person is no less a social construction than, say, the corporation or tribe.)

A social object that is a collectivity of a certain sort—or no collec-

tivity at all—according to a particular legal system may be something
else according to the perspectives of everyday life, the perspectives of
the celebrated man in the street. That ornament of English jurisprudence, Frederick W. Maitland, lecturing in 1903 on The Natural Person and the Corporation (Maitland, 1936), said: "Lately in the House
of Commons the Prime Minister [Mr. Balfour] spoke of trade unions
as corporations. Perhaps, as he is an accomplished debator, he anticipated an interruption. At any rate, a distinguished lawyer on the Opposition benches interrupted him with 'The Trade Unions are not corporations.' 'I know that,' retorted Mr. Balfour, 'I am talking English,
not law.' A long story was packed into that admirable reply."

"Socially constructed realities" are not, of course, necessarily nor
as a rule fictions or figments of the imagination. Their existence can
be empirically verified. The test is: Is there something observable "out
there" with characteristics that can be matched to the cognitive maps
or schemata that define objects of the kind in question—say, corporations, Indian tribes, or ball games? If there is, they are as real for sociological purposes as office managers, older brothers, and third base-
man. On the other hand, some socially constructed objects that are, in
the words of W. I. Thomas, real in their consequences, like witches,
phlogiston, and many of the conspiracies by which we explain our
misfortunes, turn out to be fables or fictions by this same test of reality, or just plain errors. It is important to note, moreover, that, in the
social construction of reality, cognitive maps function in two ways.
First, they enable us to locate, identify, and draw boundaries around
objects "out there." But some things are "out there" only because there
were cognitive maps in our heads first. Cognitive maps are also blueprints. We dispose and arrange ourselves, our actions, and our environments according to the blueprint and we become or create the thing
the blueprint describes. So there really are things going on out there
that match our definition of the corporation, but these things are going
on because we have this definition; in the beginning was the word.

Interaction Process and Structural Frames

I have, in effect, proposed that there are two analytically distinct
kinds of questions: (1) How does the interaction process unfold and
make things happen? (2) How do members conceptualize that process,
describe the participants, and assign agency? The two questions do
not, however, refer to two stages of a chronological sequence. Conceptualization and attribution are not things that happen only after the
interaction process has run its course. On the contrary, *the course that*

it runs is itself shaped by the way in which members represent to themselves what is happening and who is doing it. Different members contribute bits and pieces to the construction of the larger units of interaction. What those bits and pieces will be will depend on members' answers to "What is going on here?" "What is the name of the game?" "Am I an independent operator or part of something bigger?" "If, as a result of what I and others are doing here, something happens, who will be seen to have done it?" Given the name of the game, the answers to the remaining questions are provided, for the most part, by the rules of the game. For example, in football or basketball, the rules of the game generate "teams" and "players," and they provide a code for translating mere motion into "plays" and individual and team accomplishments. Let us call these rules "structural frames." The flow of action in families, firms, universities, and persons is shaped in exactly the same way by the structural frames that generate these actors and contain the action.

It would follow that the crimes of collectivities do not "reduce to" the acts of individuals, but neither do those of natural persons. Both are—or, if you will, reduce to—the outcomes of interaction processes interpreted in the light of structural frames that govern the processes themselves. In both cases, the criminologist is engaged in analyzing the interaction process and in constructing theory about the relationship between interaction process, the structural frames employed by the participants and their audiences, and the outcomes that are socially defined as crimes of this or that kind of actor. On the most general level, therefore, such a theory would be a theory about both collectivity crime and individual crime. Neither would reduce to the other, but neither would they exist in theoretically discrete worlds.

For that matter, collectivity crime and individual crime do not exist in empirically discrete worlds either. The same interaction process can generate crimes of the collectivity and of individuals acting for the collectivity. Or the victim can be a collectivity and the offender an individual inside or outside the collectivity. Or members of the collectivity may see themselves as victims of a criminal or deviant act, but have to pause and consider whether the offender was the collectivity acting through another member of the collectivity or the collectivity member acting on his own but exploiting the power that goes with his role in the collectivity. For example, employees may ask, "Is the foreman an S.O.B. in his own right, so to speak, or is the company, acting through the foreman, an S.O.B.?" How the interaction runs off from that point on—e.g., whether the employees will respond with deviance of their own and whom the retaliation will be directed at— will depend on how they answer the question (Kemper, 1966).

I have set forth some notions that, if they are sound, should provide a basis for the reconstruction of criminological and deviance theory so that they can cope more effectively with the social reality of
the behavior of collective actors and, for that matter, of natural persons as well. I do not have such a theory. I cannot even offer a strategy
or an agenda for the construction of such a theory. However, in the
pages that follow, I will explore, in a less abstract way, some of the
theoretical implications of this kind of interaction process approach.
In particular, I will show how some considerations that figure promi-
nently in current, individually oriented, criminological theory continue to be relevant and fruitful, in hiterto unappreciated ways, in this
kind of an approach.

The Ecology of Identities

I begin with a longish example, what I will call the "ecology of
identities," which is one component of the "ecology of interests." All
criminal behavior occurs in some context of interests. That is to say,
all participants in the interaction process have something to gain or
lose by the way it develops. What each contributes to the flow of action is his response to the opportunity or threat, in light of his interests, in what is going on. Action flows, as it were, through a terrain
whose topography is defined by this ecology of interests. This would
be equally true of the confidence man and his mark and of the much
larger cast of characters in the dramas of Watergate and Irangate.

But what are our interests? We have no interests more vital than
our interests in recognizing in ourselves, and having others recognize
in us, a certain sort of person—the sort of person we claim to be or
would like to be able to claim to be. In short, our interest in establish-
ing and validating an identity. Other things acquire the status of interests as they serve the realization of this identity. Personal qualities,
possessions, performances—our own and others'—take on meaning as
threats and opportunities as they thwart or facilitate the expression
and validation of this identity. Any field of interaction can, then, be
charted as an ecology of identities, and the flow of action, to criminal
or to conforming ends, will be shaped by interaction among these
identities.

One of the effects of the collectivity frame—indeed, implicit in its
definition—is a transformation of the ecology of identities. To be a
member of a collectivity is to have, as part of one's identity, the role
of collectivity member. This means that the status, reputation, honor,
and stigma that attach to the name of the collectivity attach also, to

some degree, to its members. Those members who are in this way affected have therefore an interest in preventing those events that will be socially defined as criminal or deviant acts of the collectivity, or in any way—to use the felicitous expression coined by Goffman for talking about natural persons—spoil its identity.

Events so defined are not necessarily limited to those that are clearly definable, according to technical legal criteria, as acts of the collectivity. Things that members do "on their own" (as far as the law is concerned) may nonetheless be socially defined as expressions or manifestations of the moral character of the collectivity, even as something the collectivity "did." The arrest of a college professor for doing or dealing in drugs or the scandalous conduct of a soldier "off duty" and out in town, but wearing the uniform and insignia of his unit, may damage the good name of the respective collectivities and therefore embarrass and hurt their fellow collectivity members. Each member, therefore, acquires a stake in the conduct of all other members; each becomes accountable to a greatly expanded panel of monitors and censors, each of whom has an interest in shaping the conduct of his fellows so that it does not spoil the identity of the common collectivity. At the same time, each has an interest in concealing the discreditable conduct of his fellows.

This ecology of identities creates a characteristic dilemma of collectivities: how publicly to emphasize the fusion of identities in order to maximize the general profit from the good deeds of members and, at the same time, to avoid the contamination from their bad deeds resulting from the same fusion. I would think the FBI and the CIA would provide classic instances of this dilemma. A different sort of example is provided by the citizens of a nation-state. When their highest officials, exercising the authority of their offices, perform or direct actions that excite widespread admiration and respect outside the country, citizens swell with pride at what they collectively ("we") have done. When, on the other hand, the actions are generally perceived as base, criminal, or barbaric (e.g., "genocide"), citizens tend to deny that what their leaders have done or caused to be done can be legitimately defined as acts of the collectivity and therefore as acts of which all citizens are joint authors. The doctrine of collective guilt is always odious. Collective merit, on the other hand, is usually taken for granted.

How people regulate their own conduct and how they try to regulate that of their fellows depends, of course, on the criteria for attributing action to the collectivity, for that, in turn, will determine the repercussions of conduct in the ecology of identities. It depends also on the extent to which the identities of various categories of members take on the coloration of the common collectivity identity. In some collectivities, the community of identity is general and uniform. In others, there may be a clear distinction between members with prominent representative roles, and therefore quickly and profoundly enhanced or tainted by conduct attributed to the collectivity, and other members who may be only slightly affected. American citizens in New Jersey and Oklahoma, far from the firing line in Vietnam, were shamed by the conduct of "their" troops at My Lai. They had always believed that "we" do not do that sort of thing. Workers in the Ford Motor Company's assembly line, on the other hand, probably did not feel personally tainted by the scandal of the Pinto's gasoline tanks, whose propensity to burst into flames led to an indictment of Ford for criminal homicide (Cullen, Maakestad, & Cavender, 1987; Swigert & Farrell, 1980–1981).

We started with some large and loose generalizations about the transformation of the ecology of identities under collectivity conditions. Now it becomes apparent that the nature of the transformation and its qualititative dimensions will vary with different sorts of collectivities. Apart from this, it is apparent also that no simple function will capture the relationship between variation in the ecology of identities and criminal and deviant outcomes. For example, the common interest in the good name of the collectivity will tend to inhibit conduct that will likely lead to attributions of crime or deviance to the collectivity. At the same time it may also provide the motivation for the "cover-up," a species of deviance often attributed to collectivities. However, the main point should be clear: The interaction process and its outcome depend very much on the ecology of identities, and the ecology of identities varies with the structural frame.

The Ecology of Identities
in the United States and Japan

Since the mechanisms of control that are activated by the collectivity frame depend on properties that are variable across systems, this approach should have implications for the explanation of intersocietal differences in criminality and deviance. Let us, for illustrative purposes, consider the differences between Japan and the United States. Almost everybody who writes on Japan speaks of the law-abidingness of the Japanese, of their attachment to conventionality and respectability generally, and of the part played by their powerful "group orientation" and "informal group pressures" in producing all this conformity. But why is group pressure so much stronger in Japan than in the United States, and how exactly does group pressure work to make the Japanese so well-behaved? (Because I am trying to illustrate a mode of analysis and not trying to prove a thesis, I will oversimplify and forgo documentation, but I think the following two propositions about Japanese society will be generally supported by the literature.) First, the crucial feature of the Japanese "group orientation" is the centrality and importance of collectivity membership in the constitution of individual identity, a centrality and importance that can probably not be matched in any Western society. Second, the identity of the collectivity—the imagery that it evokes, its reputation, its standing in a community of collectivities—are affected by an exceptionally wide range of conduct on the part of its members. Much conduct that, in the United States, discredits only the individuals who produce it may in Japan stigmatize and embarrass the collectivities to which they belong. Because of the high degree of fusion of individual and collectivity identity and because of the breadth and scope of the collectivity's responsibility for the conduct of its members, Japanese collectivities, through the mechanisms I have described, are extraordinarily effective in disciplining the conduct of their members, including a great deal of conduct that would elsehwere, and notably in the United States, be considered "none of their business."[3]

   This Japanese immersion in the collectivity may be contrasted to American individualism. By individualism I do not mean egocentrism, self-indulgence, indifference to the welfare of others, or even reluctance to subordinate one's interests to those of the group. I mean, rather, the centrality and importance, in the constitution of the self, of individual performances, achievements, and personal qualities, in contrast to affiliation with collectivities. Such selves may be compatible with, or even demand, dedication and self-sacrifice in the service of others, if the specific standards by which the self is judged demand such "altruistic" behavior. They may or may not include such behavior. My point is that if (1) collectivity membership weighs little in the constitution and therefore the evaluation of the self, and (2) the boundary between what one does as a representative of a collectivity and what one does in a "private" capacity is sharply drawn and narrowly limits the representative role, an important set of mechanisms

[3] Ames (1981, p. 84) mentions an event that occurred during the annual national high school baseball tournament in 1975. "This tournament is the most popular sports event in Japan, except perhaps for the periodic sumo wrestling tournaments. One of the teams competing in the finals was disqualified because two students of the high school (not members of the team) were arrested for kidnapping a child and assaulting its mother. . . . The peer and teacher pressure on students not to commit acts that would bring disgrace on the school harks back to the Edo period . . . notion of collective responsibility for crimes."

for the exercise of "external" control and discipline of the actor is absent or weak. Of course, whatever I have described here as "Japanese" can be found in abundance in the United States, and what is characteristically American can be found in Japan. The differences are differences of degree, but they are differences that make a large difference.

The logic of my argument would seem to require that in Japan collectivity members not only will bring pressure to bear on one another as individuals but also will bring pressure to bear on officials to manage the affairs of the organization in such a way that the organization as a collective actor will not commit criminal and deviant acts, according to the Japanese rules for assigning authorship and guilt to collectivities. Rates of collectivity crime and deviance should be lower than in the United States. On these matters I have little information, partly because there is little published on the subject. At any rate, there are two problems that systematic comparative research will have to deal with. One is that Japanese law derives largely from continental European models, and continental legal systems are reluctant to recognize collectivities as criminal actors. (This does not mean that in such systems collectivities cannot be legal actors and even subject to penalties in a variety of noncriminal, civil actions.) Another is that there are probably significant differences between Japan and the United States in the seriousness with which certain kinds of illegal behavior are regarded. For example, it is reported that Japanese laws on insider trading are frequently violated and infrequently enforced, both resulting from the fact that the conduct in question is simply not considered very reprehensible, at least by comparison to the United States. I have identified here two issues of comparability that apply not only to comparisons between Japan and the United States but to comparative criminological research in general.

There is another distinction bearing upon the nature of the collectivity as a social object and actor that seems to me now rather obvious but did not occur to me until I began comparing Japan and the United States. In the United States what are known as "hostile takeovers" of business corporations result, very often, in the dismemberment of the organization and the closing down of some of its operations and the sale of others, partly to finance the purchase itself, partly to maximize profitability. The decisions concerning the disposition of the parts of the organization tend to be based on cool, rational, unsentimental assessments of their financial yield. It is in spirit rather like the purchase by a carpenter or a mechanic of a box of tools at an auction, each of which he then decides to keep or sell depending on its use-

fulness to him in his work, weighted against the money he can realize
by its sale.

Such takeovers are rare in Japan. Why? I suggest—these are speculations that I have not been able to test, but they seem plausible—
that Japanese and American attitudes toward collectivities tend to be
located at widely separated points along a continuum (but not at the
poles). At one pole is the view of the collectivity as a structure con-
trived, like a material object, to facilitate the accomplishment of some
purpose, to be manipulated, altered, taken apart, given away, or sold
depending on the relative utility of the respective courses of action.
At the other pole is the view of the collectivity as a living entity with
an intrinsic—not merely instrumental—value, and invested with a kind
of sanctity. Toward such entities people feel respect, loyalty, even re-
verence. Such collectivities do not merely serve the purposes of natural persons; they make claims upon natural persons, who may acquire merit by serving the purposes of the organization. Collectivities
viewed in the first light are utilities; those viewed in the second light
are intrinsically valued objects (IVOs). The first attitude is more characteristic of the United States, the latter of Japan. Both exist, however,
in both societies. Americans may relate, mildly or passionately, to
churches, colleges, political organizations, and all sorts of voluntary
organizations as IVOs. Generally speaking, however, they find it difficult to comprehend or even believe that people can feel the same way
about Great Eastern Plumbing Supply, Incorporated, or Archipelago
Power and Light Company. Japanese can relate more readily and more
intensely to any kind of a collectivity as an IVO.[4]

I think it obvious that these two orientations to collectivities are
not equally compatible with deliberate dismemberment of organizations, the buying, selling, or trading of parts, or closing down the organization or some of its components in the name of practicality, ex-
pediency, or profit. More generally, collectivities perceived as utilities
are not so likely to be endowed with a moral character that suffuses
the identities of its members; members tend to be weakly bonded to

[4] According to an article in the New York Times (May 23, 1989, pp. D1, D10) some
Japanese firms are now sending members of their staffs to the United States to be
taught by American securities professionals "the rough and tumble acquisitions [not
necessarily hostile] game, a uniquely American business and an activity that until
recently barely existed in Japan." Japan is described as "a country that regards corporations as surrogate families for their employees," and where "the idea of buying or
selling a company is fraught with negative implications." The article quotes the head
of a Japanese mergers and acquisitions department: "You don't have so many deals
traditionally because to put a company up for sale generally means there has been
some kind of failure. . . . It is very shameful."

the organization and to fellow members, and the bonds to be based on self-interest. Collectivities perceived as IVOs tend, like natural persons, to have colorful and morally toned identities in whose preservation and enhancement members have a stake. Because of the fusion of collectivity and member identities, members tend to be strongly bonded to the collectivity and other members. To protect their stake in the reputation of the collectivity, members tend to exercise surveillance over, and attempt to influence the conduct of, the collectivity itself and of other members insofar as their conduct reflects on the identity of the collectivity.

Legitimation

Traditional criminological and deviance theory consists largely of solutions to the problem of legitimacy: How do actors deal with moral impediments to forbidden conduct and what sort of actors are they? Among the answers we have moral imbeciles; psychopathic, sociopathic, and affectionless personalities; moral lacunae; repression and other mechanisms of defense; delinquent superegos; delinquent subcultures; the learning of attitudes, values, and rationalizations through differential association; and techniques of neutralization. Some of these refer to an inability, for reasons of biology or of learning, to experience moral sentiments, some to specific defects or omissions in the formation of the conscience, some to investment of criminal conduct with positive moral affect, and some to denial or evasion of the conscience. They have in common that they all seek to explain why such-and-such a person committed a crime, and to explain this in part by saying something about *that* person's moral state. We have seen, however, that, from an interaction process perspective, the task is to explain the event, *what made it happen*. To understand the murder of Kitty Genovese we must understand not only "the mind of the murderer" and his conscience but also the minds of the "thirty-eight witnesses" (Rosenthal, 1964) and *their* consciences. How was it possible for those mainly law-abiding and respectable citizens to stand by and "not get involved" while their neighbor was being stabbed to death? To take another example, we are used to asking how the prostitute copes with the moral impediments to the practice of her profession. We do not typically ask how the customer copes with the moral impediments to *his* part in the crime. In short, as in the matter of interest and identity, the legitimation that is to be explained is not to be located at a single point in a social field. It is the *ecology* of legitimation that we have to explore.

Again we may ask: What difference does it make when we move from a natural person to a collectivity frame? We might start by identifying four mechanisms affecting the moral composition of an ecological field. The first is recruitment—that is, the drawing together and affiliation of people who are already "morally prepared" for the activity in question. The second is socialization: Individuals who are already in the network of association but who do not have the "right" moral attitudes are "educated" to accept the deviant activity in which the structure engages. Third is allocation (or mobility) within the field. The commission of the interdicted activity may require different moral attitudes at different positions; the appropriate distribution of attitudes may be accomplished by moving the recruits or the resocialized members about within the field. Fourth is extrusion or disposal—that is, getting rid of people who do not have the right moral attitudes and are likely to make trouble. Some examples: If a pickpocket is looking for a confederate or if somebody is trying to assemble a task force to commit a complex burglary, that person will typically shop around for somebody who already has the right moral attitudes, somebody who has already undergone the necessary socialization. This is recruitment. The employees of a business firm may acquire the attitudes and vocabularies that enable them to participate in the firm's criminal activities only after joining the firm and through their experiences in the firm. This is socialization. In addition, the firm may take pains to promote to certain management or other "sensitive" positions only persons who have been screened, so to speak, for the moral perspectives necessary for the corporate acts of deviance, and to move others who are not trusted to where they can do no harm. This is allocation. Finally, there is the hypothetical spy, a citizen of country A, selling that country's secrets to his employer, country B, and suspected by his employer of a bad conscience and therefore of unreliability. His employer in one way or another terminates his services. This would be extrusion.

I will make a few tentative observations to open up the large and complex subject of the relationship between the structural frame and the use of these mechanisms.

Structures for accomplishing criminal acts that are not held together by a collectivity frame—that is, structures whose participants are seen and who see themselves as independent actors doing business with other independent actors—are likely to be small and their cohesion and effectiveness likely to depend on the compatibility of a particular set of personalities. When such persons contemplate a criminal enterprise and need partners or collaborators, they are likely to seek them out on the basis of an existing affinity, including affinity between their respective moral outlooks. Pickpockets find partners, prostitutes find customers, thieves find fences, and the people they find are typically people who are already morally prepared for the activity in question; they do not have to be converted or persuaded. If any member's motivation to participate in the criminal activity is overcome by moral doubts, the activity does not go forward and the structure is likely to be dissolved.

In short, the predominant mechanism under natural-person conditions is recruitment, or importation into the structure of persons who have already been morally processed to accept the legitimacy of the criminal activity in question. (Of course, this presumes an environment—a market, if you will—that contains such persons, and it leaves open the question of where, when, and how they became such persons. Although I do not intend to pursue these questions here, they obviously need to be answered. I note, however, that the object of analysis here is the criminal act, not the criminal actor. From the perspective of the criminal act—or the relational structure that produces it—it may make sense and be sufficient to say that the legitimation problem is solved through importation of the necessary moral attitudes from the environment. How they come to be present in the environment is another question.) However, I must also emphasize that, although recruitment is the predominant mechanism in the natural-person frame, it is not the exclusive mechanism. For example, when one party to a friendship succeeds in sexually seducing the other party by convincing that party that sexual intercourse under the given circumstances is morally acceptable, legitimation has been accomplished within the relationship; the mechanism is socialization.

When we turn to collectitities, we must make a distinction. First we have collectivities that exist primarily to pursue some perfectly legitimate objective. They take the collectivity form in order to realize economies of scale, to obtain certain legal advantages, to minimize risk to individual participants, to maximize their effectiveness by harnessing the energies and talents of many individuals to a single objective. In recruiting people for such a collectivity, primacy tends to be given to the possession of technical skills and other qualities relevant to the organization's primary (and legitimate) goals. Individuals recruited on such criteria, however, are likely not to have the moral attitudes appropriate to the illicit activities for which they are destined or to which they may become privy. The legitimation job, if it is to be done, must be done after these individuals have joined the organization through on-the-job socialization, so to speak. Some, however, will absorb their moral education more rapidly and completely than others; some will cling obdurately to the ideals and ethics they

acquired before entry into the organization and become troublemakers. In such organizations we would also expect to find, therefore, allocation and extrusion in the service of legitimation.

Collectivities engaged in criminal behavior tend to be of the sort
just discussed: organizations devoted primarily to lawful aims. When
criminal activity is the *primary* objective and *raison d'être*, people
tend to avoid the collectivity frame because it tends to increase their
visibility and also, because of mechanisms discussed above under
"ecology of identity," to facilitate the attribution of agency and liability to all participants and therefore to increase their vulnerability to
sanctions. An exception is organizations, like the Provisional IRA,
whose primary object is the pursuit of political objectives through activities that are illegal but that nonetheless enjoy a certain legitimacy
among a large constituency outside their own membership. Their ability to obtain the inputs they need from that constituency is enhanced
by being able to present themselves as a coherent entity, an army, the
constituency's army fighting its war. In such collectivities an appropriate moral climate is assured by recruitment of new members who
have already been molded into true believers while growing up in the
organization's environment; there is correspondingly less to be accomplished by socialization, allocation, and extrusion mechanisms within
the organization.

I should mention a possible fifth mechanism: subcultural change.
When individuals, relating to one another as natural persons or as
members of an organization, confront common problems to which there
are no manifest legitimate solutions or opportunities that cannot be
seized because there are no manifest justifications, they may, through
an interaction process I have described elsewhere (Cohen, 1955), generate new, jointly supported beliefs and values that will give moral
sanction to previously interdicted conduct. This is subcultural innovation. It may take the form of a *folie à deux*, a set of ideas confined
to an elite insider group or beliefs shared by the mass of the members
of a large-scale organization. It is not immediately apparent that this
mechanism has any special affinity for the natural person or collectivity frame, but it does seem to be conceptually distinct from the others,
and it would be worth exploring whether it might not work somewhat
differently within the different frames. By way of example, the collectivity mode of harnessing human energies is likely to create among its
participants a high degree of interdependency, related to the division
of labor necessary for the accomplishment of collectivity tasks and to
a common stake in a shared identity. Because of this interdependency,
parochial subcultures that run the risk of alienating individuals who
do not embrace them may not work for those who do embrace them.

This may be especially true for those collectivities that depend heavily on voluntarism and idealism for the loyalty and cooperation of their members. It may be, then, that under certain collectivity conditions, subcultural legitimations may be adopted only if the subcultural community—those who carry the subculture—is nearly coextensive with the collectivity's membership. This strain toward moral and ideological convergence throughout the collectivity may be less characteristic of collectivities in which membership and performance are based on coercion or exchange (cf. Etzioni, 1961).

Visibility Control

The accomplishment of any crime requires that information be available to those with a "need to know"—e.g., confederates or customers—although they will not all need to know the same information. At the same time, it is in the nature of crime that, if the "wrong" people know, it can get you in trouble. The accomplishment of the crime also requires, therefore, the denial of information to potential troublemakers. For example, the different forms of prostitution—call girl, streetwalker, brothel inhabitant—represent, from one point of view, different ways of coping with this dilemma. Call girls minimize their visibility to the police and are seldom arrested, but, by the same token, they also reduce their visibility to potential customers. Streetwalkers are visible to both police and customers but reduce their vulnerability to arrest by the artful use of ambiguity in dealing with potential customers and by early-warning arrangements. They still have to reckon on occasional arrests and fines, which are viewed as business expenses. Whorehouses maximize their visibility to all parties and purchase immunity from arrest by paying off the police.

Again, one would then ask how the form, the severity, and the possible ways of coping with this dilemma are affected by the structural frame. For example, when operating within the natural-person frame, there might be only one person with a "need to know" and, indeed, only one knowing participant. There may, on the other hand, be several participants who are knowledgeable, but theirs is likely to be "guilty knowledge," and therefore all share an interest in keeping that knowledge confined to their own circle. On the other hand, the kind of aggregation and coordination of effort that is the special virtue of the collectivity frame makes it difficult to limit the spread of information among insiders, and each insider who knows is a potential leak to troublemakers outside the collectivity. However, members of collectivities are typically dependent upon the collectivity in a variety of ways and therefore easily persuaded or coerced to silence, as we have learned from the literature about "whistle-blowers" in the United States (Westin, 1981). Most collectivities are fairly successful at controlling whistle-blowers and other ways of leaking information to the "wrong" people. Some, however, leak badly. Again, it is clear that we are exploring a fairly complex scene and are a long way from genuinely theoretical propositions. It is also clear, however, that this "dilemma of visibility control" is something that a theory of criminal behavior must somehow take account of, that it is equally relevant to individual and collectivity crime, and that the terms of the dilemma change, although not always in the same way, as we move from "natural" frames to collectivity frames.

System Impacts of Punishment

Among the considerations affecting the production of criminal behavior are the nature and severity of anticipated sanctions. These in turn depend upon the policy of sanctioning agents. One of the factors that bear upon such policy is the sanctioning agent's assessment of the costs that proposed sanctions will inflict upon parties other than the offender at whom the sanctions are in the first instance directed (Mann, Wheeler, & Sarat, 1980). For example, judges' sentences may take into account the costs that imprisoning the offender may inflict upon a workingman's family, a doctor's patients, a small businessman's employees, if the continuation of the business depends upon his being there to run it. In seeking some alternative to imprisonment, judges may be moved by humanitarian concern for innocent parties or by a self-interested concern for their own positions and prospects. For example, the regard in which they are held and therefore their prospects for reelection or reappointment may be affected by the policy they are seen to pursue.

These secondary effects of sanctions are strongly related to the nature of the actor upon whom they are inflicted. You can impose ruinous fines upon natural persons, put them in jail, or even snuff out their lives. The effects upon families, employees, patients, and clients may be disastrous. Still, the radius over which these effects spread is usually limited. In the life of the larger community—the city, state, or nation—these disasters are not disasters. A certain number of them is normal and expectable, and they attract little notice.

What I have just said may be true also of smaller collectivities. However, collectivity frames, such as the concept of the corporation, make it possible to bring together very large numbers of people, aggregate their resources, and focus their energies on the mass production of goods and services. Not only may such collectivities produce a large volume of goods and services; they may produce most or all of the total available in the city, state, or nation. They may also be large consumers of other people's goods and services, large employers of labor, and large taxpayers. What criminal penalties are available against such collectivities that would be comparable, in terms of deterrence or satisfaction of the popular sense of justice, to those that are available against natural persons? You cannot put them in jail, but you could close them down or hit them with enormous fines—in the hundreds of millions of dollars or more, depending on the wealth of the particular collectivity—or do various other things to increase greatly their costs of doing business, impair their capacity to produce, or drastically reduce the value of their assets.

I need not dwell on the wide-ranging system impacts that could result from such sanctions. These ramifying costs need not be deliberately induced by the offending collectivity. I am speaking of effects, tripped by the imposition of the criminal sanction, over which the collectivity may have no control. In short, the collectivity format makes possible a many-fold multiplication of the disruptive system impacts of criminal sanctions. Since modern governments are increasingly held accountable for the state of economy and society—unemployment, the gross national product, the cost of living, public health—governments have an interest in minimizing these disruptive impacts. Therefore, prosecutors are reluctant to seek and courts reluctant to impose on the collectivity criminal sanctions or, at any rate, sanctions severe enough to deter or to satisfy the sense of justice.[5]

Government hesitates to punish offenders when by so doing it punishes itself. The same principle is at work when the government confronts illegal strikes by trade unions and professional associations. By concerting together within the collectivity frame, people can inflict

[5] To illustrate, the Pennsylvania Department of Environmental Resources assessed $39.8 million in fines against the Wheeling-Pittsburgh Steel Company for delays in cleaning up pollution from its blast furnaces and coke ovens at its Monessen, Pennsylvania, plant. In meetings involving the company, the Department of Environmental Resources, and local leaders from the United Steelworkers of America, an agreement was worked out giving the company 3 years in which to complete the cleanup and dropping all but $100,000 of the $39.8 million fine, in order to make the company more eligible for $100 million in government-guaranteed loans to help it survive. Like other companies in the steel industry, Wheeling was in severe financial straits. These loans were under the control of the federal government's Economic Development Administration; their purpose was to help retain and create jobs in areas with high unemployment. It was more important to the state government to help the company get the loans than to punish it for past transgressions. (See the New York Times, March 21, 1978, and also Meditations, March 23, 1978, and May 22, 1979, for related stories.)

far more damage than they could otherwise; that is why unions are effective. That is also why laws are passed making some strikes illegal, and why governments are more interested in settling such illegal strikes—by garbagemen, policemen, teachers, bus drivers, doctors, firemen—than they are in punishing the crime. If the collectivity's solidarity and morale are at a high pitch and its members are sufficiently inspired by their own sense of virtue, severe criminal sanctions are likely to protract the conflict, aggravate the damage, and make still more trouble for government.

Of course, there are measures open to government other than the imposition of criminal penalties on the collective body. Governments may prosecute individual members for their part in the collectivity crime. They may also engage the collectivity in the civil courts, and they may have available to them a variety of extrajudicial "conflict-resolution" and "regulatory" mechanisms. This is not the place for an extended discussion of the feasibility, from the point of view of government, of the alternatives. The purposes of this example has been to point out another set of considerations that bear upon crime in general, to show how the specific content of those considerations changes under collectivity conditions, to propose that those changes account in large part for the relatively sparing use of the criminal sanction against collectivities, and to suggest that this, in turn, may tend to encourage crime by those same collectivities.

Conclusion

To repeat, this is neither a theory nor the beginning of a theory. I do think, however, that it deserves to be characterized by that tired expression, a prolegomenon to a theory. I have argued that criminological theory should be able to handle both the crimes of natural persons and the crimes of collectivities without reducing either one to the other. I have also argued that the kind of theory that can do this will look rather different from the theory that we are used to and that it will entail quite important changes in the way we think about individual crime, not just collectivity crime. I have suggested, by way of example, four phenomena whose systematic investigation might get us started on the construction of such a theory. In my discussion of interaction process I may have given the impression of indiscriminate eclecticism, of a kind of mutliple-factorial imperialism. What I was proposing there, however, was the problem, not the solution. I repeat that the task of theory consists precisely in confronting a discouraging, seemingly limitless list of things, ill-defined and overlapping, that almost certainly have "something to do" with what we are trying to explain, and reducing this to a relatively short but highly abstract set of concepts that lends itself to the discovering of genuine theoretical propositions. I am convinced that the four examples I have given stake out some of the ground that a definitive theory will have to cover.

References

Ames, W. (1981). Police and community in Japan. Berkeley: University of California Press.

Brodeur, P. (1978, November 6). A reporter at large: The Mashpees. New Yorker, p. 62ff.

Cohen, A. K. (1955). Delinquent boys: The culture of the gang. Glencoe, IL: Free Press.

Cohen, A. K. (1988). An offense-centered approach to criminological theory. In Z. P. Separovic (Ed.), Victimology: International action and study of victims (Vol. 1) (Papers given at the Fifth International Symposium on Victimology, Zagreb, Yugoslavia, 1985).

Coleman, J. S. (1974). Power and the structure of society. New York: Norton.

Cullen, F. T., Maakestad, W. J., & Cavender, G. (1987). Corporate crime under attack: The Ford Pinto case and beyond. Cincinnati: Anderson.

Ermann, M. D., & Lundman, R. J. (1982). Corporate deviance. New York: CBS College Publishing.

Etzioni, A. (1961). A comparative analysis of complex organizations. New York: Free Press of Glencoe.

Felson, R. B., & Steadman, H. J. (1983). Situational factors in disputes leading to criminal violence. Criminology, 21(1).

Hepburn, J. R. (1973). Violent behavior in interpersonal relationships. Sociological Quarterly, 14(Summer), 419–429.

Hirschi, T., & Gottfredson, M. (1987). Causes of white-collar crime. Criminology, 25, 949–974.

Hochstedler, E. (Ed.). (1984). Corporations as criminals. Beverly Hills, CA: Sage.

Kemper, T. (1966). Representative roles and the legitimation of deviance. Social Problems, 13, 288–298.

Luckenbill, D. F. (1977). Criminal homicide as a situated transaction. Social Problems, 25, 176–186.

Maitland, F. W. (1936). Moral personality and legal personality. In H. D. Hazeltyne, G. Lapsley, & P. H. Winfield (Eds.), Selected essays (pp. 222–239). Cambridge: Cambridge University Press.

Mann, K., Wheeler, S., & Sarat, A. (1980). Sentencing the white-collar offender. American Criminal Law Review, 17.

Perez, J. (1978). Corporate criminality: A study of the 100 largest industrial corporations in the U.S.A. Doctoral dissertation, University of Pennsylvania.

Rosenthal, A. M. (1964). Thirty-eight witnesses. New York: McGraw-Hill.

Schraeger, L. S., & Short, J. F., Jr. (1978). Toward a sociology of organizational crime. Social Problems, 25, 405–419.

Shoham, S. G., Ben-David, S., & Rahav, G. (1974). Interaction in violence. Human Relations, 27(5), 417–430.

Stone, C. D. (1976). Where the law ends: The social control of corporate behavior. New York: Harper.

Sutherland, E. H. (1949). White collar crime. New York: Dryden.

Swigert, V. L., & Farrell, R. A. (1980–1981). Corporate homicide: Definitional processes in the creation of deviance. *Law and Society Review, 15,* 161–182.

Vaughan, D. (1983). *Controlling unlawful organizational behavior: Social structure and corporate misconduct.* Chicago: University of Chicago Press.

Westin, A. F. (1981). *Whistle-blowing: Loyalty and dissent in the corporation.* New York: McGraw-Hill.

Wolfgang, M. E. (1958). *Patterns in criminal homicide.* Philadelphia: University of Pennsylvania Press.

CHAPTER 6

Social Movements

Andre Gunder Frank and Marta Fuentes

This chapter will develop the following theses:

1. The "new" social movements are not new, even if they have some new features and the "classical" ones are relatively new and perhaps temporary.

2. Social movements display much variety and changeability but have in common individual mobilization through a sense of morality and injustice and social power through social mobilization against deprivation and for survival and identity.

3. The strength and importance of social movements is cyclical and related to long political economic and (perhaps associated) ideological cycles. When the conditions that give rise to the movements change (through the action of the movements themselves and/or more usually because of changing circumstances), the movements tend to disappear.

4. It is important to distinguish the class composition of social movements, which are mostly middle class in the West, popular/working class in the South, and some of each in the East.

5. There are many different kinds of social movements. The majority seek more autonomy rather than state power and the latter tend to negate themselves as social movements.

6. Although most social movements are more defensive than offensive and tend to be temporary, they are important (today and tomorrow perhaps the most important) agents of social transformation.

7. In particular, social movements appear as the agents and reinterpreters of "delinking" from contemporary capitalism and "transition to socialism."

8. Some social movements are likely to overlap in membership or

ANDRE GUNDER FRANK and MARTA FUENTES • H. Bosmansstraat 57, 1077 XG Amsterdam, Netherlands.

be more compatible and permit coalition with others and some are likely to conflict and compete with others. It may be useful to inquire into these relations.

9. However, since social movements, like street theater, write their own scripts—if any—as they go along, any prescription of agendas or strategies, let alone tactics, by outsiders—not to mention intellectuals—is likely to be irrelevant at best and counterproductive at worst.

The "New" Social Movements Are Old

The many social movements in the West, South, and East that are now commonly called "new" are with few exceptions new forms of social movements that have existed through the ages. Ironically, the "classical" working-class and union movements date mostly only from the last century, and they increasingly appear to be only a passing phenomenon related to the development of industrial capitalism. On the other hand, peasant movements, localist community movements, ethnic and nationalist movements, religious movements, and even feminist or women's movements have existed for centuries and even millennia in many parts of the world. Yet many of these are now commonly called "new," although European history records countless social movements like the Spartacist slave revolts in Rome, countless religious wars, the peasant movements, or wars, of 16th-century Germany, historic ethnic and nationalist conflicts throughout the continent, and women's movements that unleashed backlashes of witch hunts and more recent forms of repression. In Asia, the Arab world and the expansion of Islam, Africa, and Latin America, of course, multiple forms of social movements have been the agents of social resistance and transformation throughout history.

Only ecological or green movements and peace movements can more legitimately be termed *new,* and that is because they respond to social needs that have been more recently generated by world development. Generalized environmental degradation as a threat to livelihood and welfare is the product of recent industrial development and now calls forth largely defensive new ecological, or green, social movements. Recent technological developments in warfare threaten the lives of masses of people and generate new defensive peace movements. Yet even these are not altogether new. World, colonialist, or imperialist capitalist development has caused, or been based on, severe environmental degradation in many parts of the third world before (as after the conquest of the Americas, the slave wars and trade in Africa, the rape of Bengal, for example) and has aroused defensive social movements, which included, but were not confined to, environmental issues. Of course, war has also decimated and threatened large populations before and has elicited defensive social movements from them as well. Foreshadowing our times, Aristophanes described a classical Greek women's and peace movement in his play *Lysistrata*.

Whether new or old, the "new social movements" today are by far what mobilizes most people in pursuit of common concerns. Far more than "classical" class movements, the social movements motivate and mobilize hundreds of millions of people in all parts of the world—mostly outside established political and social institutions that people find inadequate to serve their needs—which is why they have recourse to "new," largely noninstitutionalized social movements. This popular movement to social movements is manifest even in responsive behavior outside of membership in the social movements themselves: Millions of people around the world have spontaneously responded to visits by the Pope (beyond the Catholic Church as an institution) and there was massive spontaneous response to Bob Geldof's extrapolitical institutional Band Aid, Live Aid, and Sport Aid appeals against hunger in Africa. The latter was an appeal and a response not only to compassion but also to the injustice of it all.

The Appeal to Justice and Injustice in Social Movements

Varied as these social movements have been and are, if there is a single characteristic that they have in common, it is probably their defensive concern with justice or their offensive defense against a shared sense of the injustice, as analyzed in Barrington Moore's *Injustice: The Social Bases of Obedience and Revolt* (1978). This felt concern with (in)justice, perhaps more than the deprivation of livelihood and/or identity through exploitation and oppression through which this sense of (in)justice manifests itself, has probably been the essential motivating and driving force of social movements both past and present. However, this concern with (in)justice refers largely to "us," and the social group perceived as "we" was, and is, very variable as between the family, tribe, village, ethnic group, nation, country, first, second, or third world, or humanity, and gender, class, stratification, caste, race, and other groupings, or combinations, of these. What mobilizes us is this deprivation, oppression, or injustice to "us," however "we" define and perceive ourselves. Each social movement then serves not only to combat against deprivation but in doing so also to reaffirm the identity of those active in the movement and perhaps also those "we" for whom the movement is active. Thus, such social movements, far from being new, have characterized human social life in many times and places.

The "classical" working-class and labor union movements can now be seen to be particular social movements, which have arisen and continue to arise in particular times and places. Capitalist industrialization in the West gave rise to the industrial working class and to its grievances, which were expressed through working-class and unionization movements. However, these movements have been defined and circumscribed by the particular circumstances of their place and time—in each region and sector during the period of industrialization and as a function of the deprivation and identity that it generated. "Workers of the world unite" and "proletarian revolution" have never been more than largely empty slogans. With the changing international division of labor, even the slogans have become meaningless. Working-class and union movements are eroding in the West, while they are rising in those parts of the South and East where local industrialization and global development are generating analogous conditions and grievances. Therefore, the mistakenly "classical" working-class social movements must be regarded as both recent and temporary, not to mention that they have always been local or regional and at best national or state-oriented movements. We will examine their role in the demand for state power when we discuss the latter below.

So what is new in the "new" social movements is perhaps that they now tend to be more single class or stratum movements—middle class in the West and popular working class in the South—than many of them were through the centuries. However, by that criterion of newness, the "classical" old working-class movements are also new and some contemporary ethnic, national, and religious movements are old, as we will observe when we discuss the class composition of social movements below.

Social Movements Are Cyclical

Social movements are cyclical in two senses. First, they respond to circumstances that change as a result of political economic cycles. Second, social movements, their membership, mobilization, and strength tend to be cyclical because the movements usually mobilize most people to respond negatively to circumstances that are themselves cyclical. Political-economic cycles—which one is more determinant is under dispute—generate changing circumstances that affect people detrimentally, or at least more so, particularly during the "downward" economic and "upward" political phases of the cycles. Although it is not beyond dispute, there is growing evidence of long political-economic cycles, often associated with the name of Kondratieff. This long cycle was in an upward phase at the beginning of this century. Then came a long downward "crisis" interwar phase (where the two world wars belong in the cycle is also under dispute), a renewed postwar recovery, and again a new downward "crisis" phase beginning in the mid-1960s and becoming more visible since 1973. Social movements appear to have become more numerous and stronger in the downward phase from 1873 to 1896 in the preceding century, during the war and interwar crisis period of this century, and again during the contemporary period of economic, political, social, cultural, ideological, and other crises.

It is useful to examine the historical context, if not determination, of past and contemporary social movements, although many of their members regard themselves as moving autonomously in pursuit of timeless and sometimes universal-seeming ideals, like the true religion, the essential nation, or the real community. The development of the present world political-economic crisis and its multiple ramifications in different parts of the world is generating or aggravating feelings of economic, political, cultural, and identity deprivation and is an affront to the sense of justice for hundreds of millions of people around the world. In many cases, particularly among middle-class people, newly deteriorating circumstances contradict their previously rising aspirations and expectations. More and more people feel increasingly powerless themselves and/or see that their hallowed political, social, and cultural institutions are less and less able to protect and support them. Therefore—and in part paradoxically—they seek renewed or greater empowerment through social movements that are mostly defensive of livelihood and/or identity, like rural and urban local community, ethnic, nationalist, and some religious movements, or often are escapist like the mushrooming religious cult, spiritualist, and some fundamentalist movements. Ecological, peace, and women's movements—separately or in combination with the other social movements—also seem to respond to the same crisis-generated deprivation and powerlessness that they seek defensively to stem or redress. Only marginally are these movements offensively in pursuit of betterment, like the women's movement that seeks to improve women's position in society and society itself—albeit at a time when the economic crisis is undermining women's economic opportunities.

As social movements come and grow cyclically in response to changing circumstances, so do they go again. Of course, if the demands of a particular social movement are met, it tends to lose force as its *raison d'être* disappears or when it is institutionalized and ceases to be a social movement. More usually, however, the circumstances themselves change—only in part, if at all, thanks to the social movement itself—and the movement looses its appeal and force through irrelevance or it is transformed or its members move to another movement with new demands. Moreover—as movements that mobilize *people* rather than institutionalizing action—even when they are unsuccessful or still relevant to existing circumstances, social movements tend to lose their force as their capacity to mobilize wanes. This susceptibility to aging and death is particularly true of social movements that are dependent on a charismatic leader to mobilize its members. The various 1968 movements—and most revolutionary and peasant movements—are dramatic examples of this cyclical life cycle of social movements.

Social Movements' Class Composition

The new social movements in the West are predominantly middle-class-based. This class composition of the social movements, of course, reflects in the first instance the changing stratification of Western society from more to less bipolar forms. The relative and now often absolute reduction of the industrial labor force, like the agricultural one before it, and the growth of tertiary service sector employment (even if much of it is low-waged) and self-employment increased the relative and absolute pool of middle-class people. The decline in industrial working-class employment has reduced not only the size of this social sector but also its organizational strength, militancy, and consciousness in "classical" working-class and labor union movements. The grievances about ecology, peace, women's rights, community organization, and identity—including ethnicity and minority nationalism—seems to be felt and related to demands for justice predominantly among the middle classes in the West. However, ethnic, national, and some religious movements straddle class and social strata more. Only nationalist chauvinism and perhaps fundamentalist religiosity (but not religious cultism and spiritualism) seeme to mobilize working-class and some minority people more massively than their often nonetheless middle-class leadership. Although most of these people's grievances may be largely economically based through increased deprivation or reduced or even inverted social mobility, they are mostly expressed through allegiance to social movements that pursue feminist, ecological, peace, community, ethnic, nationalist, and ideological demands.

In the third world, social movements are predominantly popular or working class. Not only does this class or stratum have more weight in the third world, but its members are much more absolutely and relatively subject to deprivation and felt injustice that mobilizes them in and through social movements. Moreover, the international and national or domestic burden of the present world economic crisis falls so heavily on these already low-income people as to pose serious threats to their physical and economic survival and cultural identity. Therefore, they must mobilize to defend themselves—through social movements—in the absence of the availability or the possibility of existing social and political institutions to defend them. These third world social movements are at once cooperative and competitive or conflictive. Among the most numerous, active, and popular of these social movements are a myriad of often spontaneous local rural and urban organizations or movements that seek to defend their members' survival through cooperative consumption, distribution, and production. Examples are soup kitchens; distributors, and often producers, of basic necessities like bread; organizers, petitioners, or negotiators; and sometimes fighters for community infrastructure like agricultural and urban land, water, electricity, or transport. Recently there were over 1,500 such local community movements in Rio de Janeiro alone, and they are increasingly widespread and active in India's 600,000 villages. However, not unlike working-class and peasant movements before, these popular movements often have some middle-class leadership and now ironically offer some opportunities for employment and job satisfaction to otherwise unemployable middle-class and intelligentsia professionals, teachers, or priests, who offer their services as leaders, organizers, or advisers to these community and other popular third world social movements.

More often than not, these local community movements overlap with religious and ethnic movements that lend them strength and promote the defense and assertion of people's identity. However, ethnic, national, and religious movements also straddle class membership more in the third world. Ethnic, religious, and other "communal" movements in South Asia (Hindu, Moslem, Sikh, Tamil, Assamese, and many others) and elsewhere in the third world—and perhaps most dramatically and tragically so in Lebanon—also mobilize peoples against each other, however. The more serious the economic crisis—and the political crisis of state and party to manage it—and the greater the deception of previous aspirations and expectations, the more serious and conflictive are these communal, sometimes racial, and community movements likely to grow in the popular demand for identity in many parts of the third world.

The so-called Socialist East is by no means exempt from this worldwide movement to social movements. The 10 million mobilized by Solidarity in Poland and various movements in China are well-known examples, but other parts of Eastern Europe and even the Soviet Union are increasingly visited by similar movements. However, corresponding to the Socialist East's intermediary or overlapping position between the industrial capitalist West and the third world South—if these categories still have any utility or meaning, which is increasingly doubtful—the social movements in the Socialist East also seem to straddle or combine class or strata membership more than in the West or the South. Ethnic, nationalist, religious, ecological, peace, women's, regional, community, and other protest movements with varied social membership are on the rise both within and outside of the institutional and political structure throughout the socialist countries for reasons of, and in response to, changing circumstances similar to those in the rest of the world.

Social Movements and State Power

Most social movements do not seek state power. For many participants and observers, this statement is a truism; since not seeking, let alone wielding, state power is a sine qua non of a social movement, state power would negate the very essence and purpose of most social movements. This incompatibility between social movement and state power is perhaps most intuitively obvious for the women's movement. On the other hand, for both participants in and observers of social movements, it is hardly satisfactory to define or even describe them in terms of what they are not instead of what they are. The most numerous are individual, small-scale, community-based social movements that, of course, cannot seek state power. However, similarly to the women's movement, the very notion of state or even political party power for them would negate much of their grass-roots aims and essence. These community movements mobilize and organize their members in pursuit of material and nonmaterial ends that they often regard as unjustly denied to them by the state and its institutions, including political parties. Among the nonmaterial aims and methods of many local community movements is more participatory democracy and self-determination. These are sensed as being denied to them by the state and its political system. Therefore, the community movements seek either to carve out greater self-determination for themselves within the state or to bypass the state altogether. These community movements have recently mushroomed all over the South and

West, although perhaps less so in the East. Of necessity, in the South the community movements are more concerned with material needs, and often survival itself, while in the West many can afford to devote greater attention to local grass-roots participatory democracy. Of course, most forces of the national and world economy are beyond their control and severely limit the community movements' room to maneuver. Not even national states have sufficient power and do not protect the communities in the face of world economic forces beyond their control. That is why—perhaps ironically, since they are even more powerless—the local communities attempt protection on a do-it-yourself basis.

The other side of this same coin is, especially during the economic crisis, the increasing disappointment and frustration of many people with the economy itself. So many economic slogans and "solutions," such as "economic growth," "economic development," "economic ends," "economic means," "economic necessities," and "economic austerity," do not satisfy people's needs for community, identity, spirituality, or often even material welfare. Moreover, political or state institutions are perceived as handmaidens rather than alternatives or even satisfactory directors of these supposed economic imperatives. No wonder that particularly women, who suffer the most at the hands of the economy, are in the forefront of non- and antieconomic extrainstitutional social movements that offer or seek other solutions and rewards.

Many social movements also respond to people's frustration with, and sense of injustice toward, political economic forces beyond their control. Many of these economic forces—sometimes perceived, sometimes not—emanate from the world economy in crisis. Significantly, people increasingly regard the state and its institutions, particularly political parties, as ineffective in the face of these power forces. The state and its political process either cannot or will not face up to, let alone control, these economic forces. In either case, the state and its institutions, as well as the political process and political parties where they exist, leave people at the mercy of forces to which they have to respond by other means—through their own social movements. Accordingly, people form or join largely protective and defensive social movements on the basis of religious, ethnic, national, race, gender, ecological, and peace issues as well as community and various "single" issues. Most of these movements mobilize and organize themselves independently from the state, its institutions, and political parties. They do not regard the state or its institutions—and particularly membership or militancy in political parties—as adequate or appropriate institutions for the pursuit of their aims. Indeed, much of the

membership and force of contemporary social movements is the reflection of peoples' disappointment and frustration with—and their
search for alternatives to—the political process, political parties, the
state, and the capture of state power in the West, South, and East. The
perceived failure of revolutionary as well as reformist left-wing parties
and regimes in all parts of the world adequately to express people's
protests and to offer viable and satisfying alternatives has been responsible for much of the popular movement to social movements. In
many cases, however, people's grievances are against the state and its
institutions, and in some cases social movements seek to influence
state action mostly through outside—much more rarely inside—pressure. Only some ethnic and nationalist (and in the Islamic world, some
religious) movements seek a state of their own.

One of the major problems of and with social movements, nonetheless, is their coexistence with national states, their political institutions, processes, and parties. An illustration of this problem is the
Green Movement and party in Germany. The originally grass-roots
ecological movement became a political party in Parliament. The real-
ist realpolitik ("Realo") wing argues that the state, parliament, and
political parties are a fact of life that the movement must take into
account and use to its advantage. Influence is best exerted by entering
these institutioins and cooperating with others from the inside. The
fundamentalist ("Fundi") wing argues that participation in state institutions and coalitions with other political parties (e.g., Social Demo-
crats) compromises the Green's aims and prostitutes their fundamentals, including that of being a movement. Ethnic, national, religious,
and some peace and community movements face similar problems.
Whatever they can do outside the state, the pressure sometimes becomes irresistible to try to act within the state, as or as part of or
through a political party or other state institution. But then the movement runs the danger of compromising its mission, demobilizing or
repelling its membership, and negating itself as a movement. The
question arises whether the end justifies the means and is more
achievable through other more institutionalized, nonmovement means.
Moreover, the question arises whether old social movements—which
were often created as mass front organizations of political parties—are
now being replaced by new social movements that themselves form
or join political parties. But in that case, what difference remains between the old and the new social movements, and what happens to
the nonextra antistate and party sentiments and mobilization of many
movement members? Perhaps the answer must be sought by shifting
the question to the examination of the life cycle of social movements
and the replacement of old "new" movements by new movements.

Social Movements and Social Transformation

Social movements are important agents of social transformation and new vision, despite their above-mentioned defensiveness, limitations, and relations to the state. One reason for the importance of social movements, of course, is the void they fill where the state and other social and cultural institutions are unable or unwilling to act in the interests of their members. Indeed, as we have observed above, social movements step in where institutions do not exist, or where they fail to serve, or violate and contradict, people's interests. Often, social movements step in where angels fear to tread. Although many social movements—and particularly religious ones—invoke the sanctity of traditional ways and values, other social moveeents are socially, culturally, and otherwise innovative. Nonetheless, if the circumstances that give rise to and support a social movement disappear, so does the movement. If the movement achieves its aims or they become irrelevant, it looses its appeal. It loses steam and fades away, or it becomes petrified.

Much social transformation, cultural change, and economic development, however, occurs as the result of institutions, forces, or relations, that are not social movements or the political process in national states. World economic development, industrialization, technological change, social and cultural "modernization" were and are processes that are hardly driven or directed by social movements or political or state institutions. Their intervention has been more reactive than promotive. Although state intervention should not be underestimated (as it is by the free marketeers), its limitations are ever greater in a world economy whose cycles and trends are largely beyond control. Even "socialist" state ownership and planning is now unable to direct or even to cope with the forces of the world economy.

This circumstances should make for more realism and modesty about the prospects of social movements—or, for that matter, of political institutions—and their policies to counteract or even modify, let alone to escape from, these world economic forces, but they do not. On the contrary, the more powerful and uncontrollable the forces of the world economy are, especially in the present period of world economic crisis, the more they generate social movements (and some political ideological policies) that claim both autonomy and immunity from these world economic forces and promise to overcome them or to isolate their members from them. Much of the attraction of many social movements, of course, comes precisely from their promise to free their members from the deeply felt unjust threat of deprivation of material necessities, social status, and cultural identity. Therefore, objectively irrational hopes of salvation appear as subjectively rational appeals to confront reality and to serve oneself and one's soul through active participation in social movement. The message becomes the medium, to invert Marshall McLuhan.

Delinking and Transition to Socialism in Social Movements

Social movements today and tomorrow may be regarded as offering new interpretations and solutions to the problems of "delinking" from capitalism and "transition to socialism." For the dependent South, national or state delinking from the world capitalist economy and its cycles proved to be impossible during the postwar period of expansion. Eastern socialist states and their planned economies have been relinked to the world economy and both its cycles and its technological development during the present crisis in the world economy. No national economy or its state and hardly any political parties anywhere in the world today seriously regard delinking a national economy to be a serious practical proposition. Therefore, the thesis about delinking—stop the world, I want to get off—is in for an agonizing reappraisal from those (like the present writers) who have sustained this as an option and a necessity. However, if the nation or state and the economy are not and cannot be independent today or in the foreseeable future, perhaps the idea of "delinking" can and should be reinterpreted rather than abandoned altogether.

The problems of "delinking" may be reinterpreted through the different and new links that many social movements are trying to forge, both between their members and society and within society itself. The women's movement and some green ones are examples. Many social movements seek to protect their members physically or spiritually from the vagaries of the cyclical world economy. They propose different kinds of links for their members to the economy and for society, which they also propose to help change. Perhaps "delinking" should be amended to read different linking or changed links. In that case, it is the social movements that are changing some links into different ones for their members today. This would include those religious and spiritualist movements that claim to offer isolation and protection from the traumas of the secular world to their true believers.

Similarly, the problems and prospects of transition to socialism may be reinterpreted in view of the experience with the current form of socialism and contemporary social movements. The current form of socialism has proven unable to delink from the world capitalist economy. Moreover, despite its achievement in promoting extensive growth by mobilizing human and physical resources, it has failed to provide adequately for intensive growth through technological development. Indeed, the same state planning that was an asset for absolute industrial autocratic national growth has proven to be a liability for competitive technological development in a rapidly changing world economy. The related political organization of the current form of socialism has lost its efficacy at home and its attraction abroad. Most important, perhaps, it is becoming increasingly clear that the road to a better "socialist" future replacement of the present capitalist world economy does not lead via the current form of socialism. As the Polish planner Josef Pajestka observed at a recent meeting at the Central School of Planning and Statistics in Warsaw, the current form of socialism is stuck on a side track. The world—as one of the present authors remarked—is rushing by in the express train on the main track, even though, as Pajestka retorted, it may be heading for an abyss.

The real transition to a "socialist" alternative to the present world economy, society, and polity, therefore, may be much more in the hands of the social movements. They must intervene for the sake of survival to save as many people as possible from any threatening abyss. We must also look to the social movements as the most active agents to forge new links that can transform the world in new directions. Moreover, although some social movements are subnational, few are national or international—in the sense of being between nations or states— and many like the women's, peace, and ecological movements could be transnational—that is nonnational—or people-to-people within the world system. This real socialist transformation, if any, under the agency of the social movements will, however, be more supple and multifarious than any illusionary "socialism in one country" repeated again and again. Thus, even if most movements do not achieve their objectives, their very *movement* itself helps transform social relations and therefore society.

Coalitions and Conflict
among Social Movements

It may be useful—without seeking to give any advice—to inquire into likely possibilities of conflict and overlap or coalitions among different kinds of social movements. Aristophanes already remarked on the relation between women and peace in *Lysistrata*. Riane Eisler has traced this same relation even farther back in human society in her *The Chalice and the Blade* (1987). Today, the women's and peace movements share membership and leadership and certainly offer opportunities for coalition. Substantial membership and leadership overlap can also be observed between women's movements and local community movements. At least women are especially—and in Latin America preponderantly—active in community movements, where they acquire some feminist perspectives and press their own demands, which serve to modify these movements, their communities, and, one hopes, society. In the West, there is a similar if lesser overlap between community and peace movements that expresses itself in "nuclear-free" communities, for instance. Again, environmental, ecological, or green movements in the West share compatible goals and membership with women's, peace, environmental, and community movements—all of which shy away from pursuit of state power and most entanglements with political institutions—and they offer widespread opportunities for coalitions among social movements.

Other areas of overlap, shared membership, and compatibility or coalition may be observed among some religious and ethnic, national, and sometimes racial movements. The movement led by the Ayatollah Khomenei in Iran and some of his followers elsewhere in the Islamic world is the most spectacular example and has the most massive and successful mobilization of recent times to its credit. The Sikhs in Punjab, the Tamils in Sri Lanka, Solidarity in Poland, Albanians in Jugoslav Kosovo, and Irish Catholics in Northern Ireland are other recent examples. Notably, however, these religious-ethnic-nationalist movements also seek state power or institutional autonomy and sometimes incorporation with a neighboring ethnic or national state. If communities are religiously and ethnically homogeneous, there may be overlap or coalition with these larger movements.

There are also significant areas of conflict and competition among social movements. Of course, movements of different religions and ethnicities or races conflict and compete with each other. However, all of them also seem to conflict and compete with the women's movement and often with the peace movement. In particular, virtually all religious, ethnic, and nationalist movements—like working-class and Marxist-oriented movements and political parties as well—negate and sacrifice women's interests. Moreover, they successfully compete with women's movements, if any, which lose ground they may already have gained to the onslaught of religious, ethnic, and nationalist movements. Religion and nationalism, and even more so the two combined, seem to be the worse enemies of the women's interests and movements.

The Impropriety of Outside "Good" Advice
to Social Movements

As long as the social movements have to write their own scripts as they go along, they cannot use—and can only reject as counterproductive—any prescriptions from on high or outside as to where they should go or how they should get there. In particular, the social movements cannot use the kind of imaginary blueprints for the future which Smith and Marx avoided but which have been so popular among many of those who claim to speak in their name. For this reason, also, good advice from intellectuals and other well-meaning people is both hard to find and hard to assimilate for the social movements. Most inappropriate, perhaps, is supposed counsel from nonparticipant observers. On the other hand, many social movements can and do benefit from the vision and organizational skill inputs by participants and more rarely from transient outsiders who transfer some vision and/or experience from other movements, parties, and institutions. Many community movements also benefit from, or even depend on, the support of outside institutions, such as the Church, nongovernmental organizations (NGOs), and occasionally even the state. Such aid and dependence also involves dangers of cooptation by these institutions of individual leaders or intermediaries, the leadership and its goals, or even the social movement itself. Nonetheless, what most characterizes social movements is that they must do their own thing in their own way. In fact, perhaps the most important thing that social movements have to offer both to their participants and to others in the world is their own participatory, self-transforming trial-and-error approach and adaptability. Herein is the hope they promise for the future.

ACKNOWLEDGMENTS

The authors are very grateful for the most useful written comments on our first draft given by Orlando Fals Borda, John Friedmann, Gerrit Huizer, Marianne Marchand, Andree Michel, Betita Martinez, Yildiz Sertel, and Marshall Wolfe, and to other friends for oral comments.

References

Eisler, R. (1987). *The Chalice and the Blade*. San Francisco: Harper & Row.
Moore, B. (1978). *Injustice: The Social Bases of Obedience and Revolt*. Armork, NY: M.E. Sharpe, Inc.

CHAPTER 7

Fraudulent Identification and Biography

Gary T. Marx

Looks are one thing and facts are another.
Herman Melville

Things are rarely what they seem.
Skim milk masquerades as cream.
Gilbert and Sullivan

If this were played upon a stage now, I could condemn it as an improbable fiction.

Shakespeare

Deception regarding identity and biography are common but little commented upon features of contemporary life. Consider the following examples:

• In 1981 Robert Granberg went on a fishing boat with two other men. His companions reported that he fell into the ocean and disappeared. His wife then filed insurance claims for $6 million. In fact, he jumped overboard, swam ashore, and went to England. The four were eventually indicted.

• An engineer in New Jersey working alone set up a number of fictitious companies, obtained bank loans, and fed false information into a credit card service that one of his "companies" subscribed to. He created records for more than 300 nonexistent people and gave them impeccable credit records. He obtained more than 1,000 credit

GARY T. MARX • Department of Urban Studies and Planning, Massachusetts Institute of Technology, Cambridge, Massachusetts 02139.

cards. He was able to operate for 4 years and spent $600,000 before he was stopped.

• Ferdinand Waldo Demara (whom Tony Curtis, aka Bernard Schwartz, pretended to be in the 1960 film *The Great Imposter*) passed himself off as a Royal Canadian Navy surgeon, a monk, a teacher, and an assistant warden of a Texas prison.

• Dorothy Woods, a woman who lived in an 18-room mansion and drove a Rolls-Royce, pleaded guilty to bilking the government out of $377,500 in welfare, food stamp, and medical payments. She opened 12 welfare claims under phony names and contended she had 49 children.

• A study of medical records in hospitals serving the poor found instances where (according to the record) the same person had undergone both a hysterectomy and a prostate operation for the removal of two appendices.

• In Massachusetts an inspector for the Registry of Motor Vehicles pleaded guilty to selling truck operator licenses.

• A San Francisco man posed as a state fish and game warden for 3 months in 1986 before being discovered. He issued citations and confiscated fish. He said he had always loved fish and wanted to be a game warden.

• In the Boston Brink's holdup, the thieves dressed in police uniforms.

• William Cohn, a novelty shop operator from Miami, took Pan American's advice to go to faraway places. Over a 2-year period he flew to London, Johannesburg, Honolulu, and Hong Kong. Pan Am called it theft of $40,000 worth of travel since Cohn pretended to be a flight attendant (complete with a uniform), helped the crew, and rode free.[1]

• Le Beacon Presse appeared to be a classic business success story. Between 1980 and 1984 its sales increased from $15 million to $666 million. That was good enough for 35th place on *Inc.* magazine's list of the 500 fastest-growing companies in the United States. However, the company existed only in the fertile imagination of its creator, Keith Gormezano, a Seattle apartment manager. He obtained listings in Standard and Poor's and Dunn and Bradstreet. He made up phony documents and in a classic move parlayed one listing into another. He also managed to get himself listed in "Who's Who in Black America," although he is white.

• Patty Hearst, Abbie Hoffman, Jonathan Bingham, and Christo-

---

[1] At other times he bought tickets at employee discounts. The case was discovered because he was too good. Passengers wrote letters commending his courteous service. The airline became suspicious when it couldn't find his personnel file.

pher Boyce are among hundreds of thousands of fugitives who have avoided detection by creating new identities.

• Angelos Evert, as police chief of Athens during the German occupation in World War II, saved many Jews from arrest and deportation. He issued them identity cards indicating they were Christians.

• The Chicago Better Government Association had two investigators assume the life of winos and move into a skid row flophouse. They registered under such names as James Joyce and Ernest Hemingway. When the voter lists turned up a short time later, Joyce and Hemingway were on them and actually voted.

• Stella Franklin wrote the book *My Brilliant Career* under the name of Miles Franklin. During the blacklisting era in Hollywood many film writers used noms de plume.

• Recently exposed Arizona newspaper publisher Clarence Tully parlayed brief study at Purdue University into a resumé that listed a Purdue degree and a nonexistent Big 10 football career. He presented himself as a lover of the military. He attended military functions with Barry Goldwater, saluted troops, wore medals and a uniform, and claimed to be a retired air force lieutenant colonel and a hero of the Korean war who flew more than 100 missions when recalled to duty during the Vietnam War. In fact, he had never served any time in the military.

• Boston Celtics basketball star Bob Cousy, "the little guy," was always listed in the program as 5' 10" although he actually was 6' 1½".

• The films *Tootsie* and *Victor Victoria* illustrate gender passing for the purpose of obtaining employment.[2]

• In Los Angeles a tenant received an eviction notice. Unaware of her rights, or that the notice could be challenged, she moved out. She had refused to pay the rent on her apartment after the ceiling in her bedroom fell down and the landlord refused to fix it. The eviction notice led to her being listed in a data base sold to landlords. The woman had a good credit and tenant history and was employed. She went to 15 other apartments but could not find a place to live. One landlord eventually told her she was in the "data base." She eventually found an apartment, but only by changing her name.

A great many other examples could be given: spies and undercover operatives; con artists; racial, ethnic, and religious passers; illegal immigrants with fake documents; transvestites; bigamists; and the more than 4,000 persons given new identities through the Federal

---

[2] This may, of course, be institutionalized. Thus, in Albania there was a tradition that if there were no male children, one daughter would be raised as a male.

Witness Protection Program. There may be more than 500,000 Americans who have fraudulent credentials and diplomas—including a possible 10,000 with questionable medical degrees. One in three currently employed Americans may have been hired with credentials that have been altered in some way (Report, 1986).

If it is correct that charity begins at home, so might sociological analysis: What experiences have you had with identity manipulation as either an actor or a victim? Is your vita a perfect reflection of your biography? Are there any salient omissions or embellishments? Have you ever used a ticket or enjoyed a benefit that belonged to someone else and was not to be transferred? Have you ever used an alias (even if for nothing more serious than making a reservation you were not sure you would be able to keep)? Do you know of any cases where a student took an exam for someone else? Did you (or your children) have fake IDs permitting you to buy liquor, although underage? Do you have any married friends who deny they are married when on business trips? Have you ever been in a situation where someone made disparaging remarks about your ethnic group or religion, not realizing you were a member? What would happen if the IRS were to do an in-depth audit of your taxes, looking especially at deductions and unreported income? Do you ever deny who you are when a telephone caller such as a salesperson or a solicitor asks to speak to you? Have you ever been wrongly charged for consumer purchases or telephone calls made by someone else?

The above examples differ markedly from each other in social contexts and dynamics, legality, and ethics. Yet they all involve fraud in the presentation of self and/or biography.

I think the use of fraudulent identity and biography is increasing in the United States, but apart from whether or not that is the case, the topic is well worthy of study. Plato wrote that "all that deceives may be said to enchant." But beyond its intrinsic interest, this issue has implications for justice studies, social theory, democracy, and the quality of life in American society.

The study of fraudulent identity and biography is certainly relevant to the traditional concerns of criminology and victimology, but what does it have to do with justice studies? Justice involves the distribution of privileges or burdens on the basis of rights, needs, or behavior. Fraudulent identification and biography offer a means for thwarting any system of just distributions. When individuals fraudulently establish an entitlement for rights, the documentation of needs, or the accomplishment of deeds, the system of justice is undermined. We feel that "it's not fair."

An important component of this is respectability and disrespect-ability (Ball, 1970). We anticipate that these will be allocated as warranted and not as a result of the withholding or manipulation of information. Deceptive information deflates the subjective value of both reward and penalty and threatens the legitimacy of the entire system by raising suspicions about its accuracy and thus fairness. The sense of violation felt as a result of being deceived in these matters is usually far worse than is felt as a result of suffering property damage. This negative social response may involve personal betrayal, as well as a sense that a fundamental principle of social order has been trampled.

Our conception of due process involves the idea that the actions of the state will be based on accurate information. In the case of criminal justice, for example, whether the balance is tilted toward punishment and retribution or reform and reintegration, our society values precise information about the individual. The response must fit the criminal as well the crime. The quality of the data on which decisions are made about individuals is a major factor in whether justice is served. Our notion of justice is ill-served when those punished are not guilty, or when the guilty go free, as well as when the deserving are denied, or the undeserving receive, welfare state benefits.

Our ideas about democracy and accountability involve an unprecedented expectation of openness in government. This also extends to personal relations. Our system expects (and even legislates) truth in advertising—whether in products or in selves. This has moral as well as practical underpinnings.

The topic of authenticity in identity goes to the very core of group life, which depends on reciprocity and a degree of trust as central principles. We wish to have confidence that the many people we deal with in secondary relationships are who they say they are and can perform effectively (whether in medicine or in construction). We also believe that people should be true to themselves. Honesty is an important social resource. Yet if honesty is a prime value, it is ironic that much in contemporary industrial society conspires against it.

The topic is theoretically important for understanding modern society. It touches a number of traditional concerns involving deviance and social control, mass society, social psychology, communications, credentials, and technology and society. It can also illuminate the underdeveloped areas of the sociology of deception and surveillance. It offers a good arena to study value conflicts and basic social and psychological processes. By studying the behavior of those who are self-conscious masters at the creation of fraudulent individual and organizational realities, we can gain insight into the more mundane varieties and processes.

Among some of the questions that I find most interesting are these:

• What can be learned from the history of the recording of births, marriages, and deaths and of record keeping by the state more generally (e.g., for taxation and later military draft)? With the rise of the modern state, do rationales become more benign (e.g., an increasing proportion of the data the state collects is to better serve the citizen rather than for the citizen to serve the state)? As wealth increases (along with the possibility of inheriting it) does fraudulent identity increase?[3]

• As the bureaucratic state's appetite for information increased and as social control became more powerful and efficient in the 19th century (the rise of public and private detectives, improved means of communication such as the telegraph, the appearance of nationally circulated wanted posters, the appearance of supposedly more precise means of physiologically identifying people), did the falsification of ID increase? How do practices vary among those states with and without the Napoleonic code?[4]

• When and why did laws regarding impersonation appear? What is the history of offenses such as forgery, theft by deception, impersonating an officer, tampering with public records, and the misdemeanor of false swearing?

• Given the dramatic elements—the theme is prominent in drama, film, and literature—how do the images and descriptions in art compare to real-life case studies?

• How prevalent is fraudulent identification? What are the characteristics of those social situations which require revelation, documentation, certification, and licensing, or, conversely, which protect the individual's right to conceal information? When must individuals identity themselves and what aspects of biography must be revealed? How does this vary across institutions, functions, countries, and time periods? What mechanisms exist to protect anonymity or to create revelation?

• What are the main types?

• How are fraudulent identities created and discovered?

• Is it correct that the use of fraudulent identification is increasing, and if so, why?

Unfortunately, there are few solid answers to such questions. Why an area that is so important to modern society should be so undevel-

---

[3] It is interesting that in the story of Martin Guere, challenges appear only when the imposter tries to gain property.

[4] I still recall my apprehension in staying in a hotel in Europe for the first time and discovering that I had to surrender my passport in order for it to be collected and checked by the police each night.

oped is an important sociology of knowledge question.[5] But we have enough data and ideas to define it more systematically. In this exploratory discussion I cannot do justice to the above questions, but I do examine factors encouraging fraudulent presentations and some reasons why they may be increasing, offer some concepts useful in organizing this material, and conclude with some policy choices. The chapter is neither a review of the literature (there is little social science research to review) nor a report of a finished research project. Instead it is an orienting, issue-raising essay that seeks to inspire more systematic research and to help develop middle-range theory.

I have been collecting file material on fake IDs since I wrote a paper for Professor Erving Goffman in 1961 on ethnic passing.[6] I cast a broad net regarding data sources. The richness of the world (especially when one is interested in studying secret phenomena) requires reliance (with appropriate skepticism) on whatever one can find. The ideas presented here draw from journalistic accounts, novels, interviews, commissions of inquiry, court records, and the how-to-do-it or avoid-it literatures.[7]

The approach differs from that of novelists because of its empirical grounding and concern for cause and explanation. It shares something, particularly in its initial stages, with journalism,[8] but it goes beyond this because of its depth, its development out of an interest in questions raised by theorists of social order and mass society (e.g., Hobbes, Tocqueville, Weber, Simmel, Wirth, Shils, Foucault, Goffman, and Rule), and an interest in generalizing across cases, societies, and time periods.

[5] Part of the answer lies in secrecy. If it is well executed, it may never be discovered and, hence, its full significance not appreciated. It is also a threatening topic since we want to believe that the world is predictable and what it appears to be.

[6] Goffman's work in *The Presentation of Self in Everyday Life* (1956), *Stigma* (1962), and *Frame Analysis* (1974) is directly relevant to the topic at hand.

[7] What this represents is another question. However, I don't think the gap between what is public and what occurs is as great here as in many other areas. This is because of the intrinsic "human interest" that deception entails, the interest victims often have in complaining, and the frequent compulsion to reveal after the fact on the part of perpetrators, or those close to them. Similar methodological issues with respect to data on undercover police are treated in Marx (1988).

[8] I read/skim many general and specialized publications (e.g., *Law Enforcement News, Personal Identity Newsletter, Privacy Journal, Law Enforcement Technology Bulletin,* and *Security World*). I also have participated in an experimental program that brought the AP and NYT wire services over radio waves to my home computer. This was crafted to a number of key words such as *deception, undercover, fake ID,* and *fraud*. In addition, because I have written on aspects of this topic since 1974 (e.g., Marx, 1974, 1979, 1984), colleagues and others occasionally send me cases.

Some Causal Factors

There are examples of the phenomenon that are bizarre and morally reprehensible. Yet the exotic quality of some cases should not lead us into making too sharp a distinction between fraudulent and honest accounts. Rather than seeing the topic in qualitative black/white terms with clear breaks, we would do best to view it on a continuum, moving slowly and unevenly across contexts and identities (although at some point it is useful to talk of hard- and soft-core varieties). Varying degrees of fraudulent identification and biography are an ordinary (in both a statistical and even a normative sense) feature of life in the United States and perhaps in any industrial society.[9] Why should this be the case?

As social observers from Simmel to Goffman have noted, in a mass, dynamic, urban society with extensive interaction with strangers and secondary relations, we are forced to rely on formal factors (uniforms, licenses) to establish the identity of many of those with whom we come into contact. Relative to the small village where individuals are well known to each other, the possibilities for fraud are great.

Our culture and socialization encourage it. Growing up involves learning how to conceal and reveal information. To be human means to be able to take the role of the other. The ability to play roles well is seen as an aspect of mental health. The mass media play an important role. The imaginative taking of roles that occurs when we are caught up in a drama is conducive to thinking about one's self as something other than it "really" is. Advertising attempts to make us imagine we are someone else, and often somewhere else doing something else (e.g., the Marlboro Man or the Fortunoff women, or a "new you" suddenly made over by cosmetics, hair dyes, or personal hygiene products, or on a tropical island, or driving a sports car). Our imaginations are permitted (and indeed manipulated into) flights of fantasy with respect to identity that were unthinkable in earlier time periods. Institutionalized mechanisms such as Halloween, costume parties, makeup, and a wardrobe with clothes for many occasions also support it.

Our culture's emphasis on social and geographical mobility accustoms us to the idea of being someone else and generates pressure to be successful and upwardly mobile. The marketplace mentality en-

---

[9]What Erving Goffman (1962) has observed about stigma (that it is not a unique property of a few individuals but, as both actuality and potential, applies to everyone) also applies to deception in the presentation of information about the self. We all deceive and are deceived. The same also holds for organizational presentations (Altheide & Johnson, 1980).

courages selling selves, as well as products, by placing them in the best possible light. The personal liberty and autonomy that support legitimate exchange and change also support those that are illegitimate. Our expectations of privacy and mechanisms for protecting it provide ample room to omit and alter past biography.

There are many resources available that intentionally or unintentionally aid false presentations. For example, stores that sell or rent uniforms and costumes, mail drops, call-forwarding/phone-answering services, and printing and graphic reproduction services can be used for legitimate or illegitimate ends. Cosmetics and plastic surgery are similar examples. The techniques that change hair color, cover scars, and rearrange facial features are readily available to persons whose motives for altering their appearance goes beyond vanity.[10]

There are organizations that sell fake or questionable diplomas. They exploit the ambiguity in credentialing (e.g., who is a religious leader?) and cater to mobility aspirations. Some states do not even have accreditation laws, and "diploma mills" tend to be found there. In an FBI undercover investigation called Dipscam (diploma scam), an agent was able to obtain 17 advanced mail-order degrees in a short period of time for little or no work. As part of an investigation, Florida Congressman Claude Pepper obtained a Ph.D. from "Union University" in Los Angeles by paying $1,780 and sending in four book reports.

Our tradition of a free press permits an aboveboard how-to-do-it literature. One widely read book called the *Paper Trip*, which has gone through several editions, is a step-by-step guide to creating a new identity. Another called *Ninja 1990* offers clear instructions for how "to change IDs at will/find, hide and transfer fingerprints/get new passports/understand postal covers."

But in addition to these supportive factors, recent changes appear to have resulted in an increase in fraudulent identity. Given the variety of forms and contexts, there are no simple causal relationships. But three broad factors are of particular interest.

If fraudulent identity is increasing, I think to an important extent it can be understood as a function of expansions and contractions in opportunity structures associated with technology and the welfare state.

One aspect of this involves the vast expansion of state benefits

[10]For example, concealing creams ("Cover Creme," "Totally Perfect Cover-Up") are waterproof and long-wearing, and cling to scar tissue. They were developed for those with special needs (e.g., persons with disfiguring birthmarks, pigmentation problems, burns, scars). But they also make it possible for persons who might be initially identified by an obvious scar or tattoo to cover it. In Japan, plastic surgery has reportedly been used even to reconstruct hymens in order to conform to expectations regarding brides.

(e.g., pensions, social security, welfare, health, educational loans, unemployment insurance) that have appeared in recent decades. Persons who cannot legally obtain desired benefits have many more opportunities to defraud the state than ever before.

But there has also been a contraction in opportunities for gain, at least in the sense of restrictions on various kinds of employment. There has been pronounced inflation in educational requirements. College credentials are increasingly required for employment that in the past required only a high school diploma.

There has been an increase in the state regulation, licensing, and control of many kinds of work. This is part of the process of credentialization and professionalization. Not only doctors and lawyers, but hairdressers and morticians must be licensed (there is even a move under way to certify sociologists and criminologists). Given the interdependence between social control and rule violation, enhanced efforts at control may lead to new forms (or an escalation) in violations. Restrictions on employment and increased competition may lead to the use of fraudulent documentation on the part of those who wish to pursue a given line of work but who cannot (or choose not to) formally qualify.

Along with the increased importance of credentials have come new ways of obtaining them. Adult education and outreach programs have significantly expanded the chance to obtain certification, even apart from being on a campus and attending classes. In an effort to serve new constituencies we now see aggressive advertising, televised courses, credit for life experience, independent long-distance study under tutors, and "external degrees." In a phenomenon well known to students of deviance, the extension of legitimate programs creates an opportunity for deceptive operations to purvey their goods as well.

Another restrictive factor that can cause deception is an increase in requirements to divulge information about one's self. As the power and reach of the state and private organizations have grown, more and more information about individuals is in data bases beyond their control. The mandatory provision of personal information is central to the operation of all industrial states. In Sweden, which is often pointed to as the wave of the future, the average adult is in over 100 government data bases. The Swedish citizen is identified in these data bases by a personal ID number given to all persons at birth and which can never be changed. There are benign justifications for this (whether protecting the state or the individual). Yet individuals may find that dossiers thwart their personal goals.

Along with requirements to provide information has come a contraction in the ability to hide one's past that was present before widespread computerization. With the instant availability of computerized information—regardless of whether it is inaccurate or accurate and discrediting[11]—persons may now feel a need to lie about things that in the past were unseen, overlooked, or forgotten. The tightening of the informational net or noose generates structural pressures to fabricate.

The role of technology is complicated and contradictory and overflows the boundaries of any simple theory. On the one hand, biometric forms of identification are adopted precisely because it is believed they are almost impossible to fake (e.g., fingerprints, retinal patterns, palm prints, DNA sequencing—nucleic acid extracted from hair, blood, or semen; computer typing rhythms, signature verification, implanted or manually carried chips or electronic beepers).[12] The elaborate cross-checking of computer data bases makes it possible to verify claimants' stories and hence may identify or deter fraud.

Such devices make it possible to inexpensively and rapidly verify identification and claims. To the extent that near-perfect means of identification are implemented (a very different factor from developing them in the laboratory) we would then expect at least some types of fraud to decline (although systems still might be compromised by bribing or coercing those in positions of authority).

Of course, in a free market economy, means of neutralization may also be available and technologies may be used in ways unintended by their developers. We also can identify some ways in which technology is making document fraud easier.

Computer technology offers rich possibilities for fraud. A document scanner can "read" a picture and "draw" a copy into the memory of the computer. Laser techniques are used to convert the image to digital data. A copying machine developed by Xerox for the Department of Defense as a tool in high-speed map making can also make good copies of dollar bills and driver's licenses.

It is also possible to rearrange images. Document scanners and fast color printers make it easy to fake images and documents. Through digital retouching, computer-generated images can be combined in new ways, unwanted images can be deleted, and colors can be added and changed.

---

[11] Persons who in the past could deceive without altering their identity or biography now find that this is no longer possible. In this sense the basic fraud may not increase, but the use of false IDs to carry it out may.

[12] Cows are now being implanted with identification chips as protection against rustlers. Brands can be altered more easily, but chips are harder to locate and change. A patent has been issued for a locational implant in children that sends out an electronic signal (e. g. implanted in a tooth cavity).

Against the already supportive conditions of a mass society with extensive interaction with strangers, changes in the way we communicate on balance are also making it easier to pull off deception. With the joining of computer and communications technologies, face-to-face interaction is significantly supplemented by interaction that is mediated by distance and time. It is not only that those with whom we interact are strangers, they are not even in our physical presence. As physical location lessens in its importance to interaction, opportunities for fraud increase. Consider, for example, changing records via remote entry. Where remote computer access is possible, the change can occur without even breaking and entering.[13]

In considering the range of factors that are supportive of or encourage fraudulent identification and biography, the question might be rephrased to "Why is it that the manipulation of identification does not occur even more often?"

Types and Dimensions

What are the major forms, types, and cross-cutting dimensions found in fraudulent ID and biography? Given the diversity of the phenomenon, classification is an essential first step.

One means of classification is simply to follow popular descriptive categories. These usually involve a motive, a category of person, or the aspect of identity that is involved. For example, in the beginning of the chapter a number of basic garden-variety types were mentioned (e.g., spies, con artists, occupational and professional imposters, racial passers). Such categories are descriptively but not analytically very helpful. They help define the universe of cases, yet they mix dimensions that should be separated and do not lead to hypotheses. In what follows, I suggest 22 dimensions that can be used for classification. These can aid us in asking comparative questions with respect to different forms, time periods, groups, and societies, and they offer building blocks for hypotheses

1. *Scope:* comprehensive or singular
2. *Temporal:* permanent or temporary
3. *Nature of the deception:* performance (behavior) versus non-performance (claims regarding identity and biography)
      If the latter, this may involve claims about

---

[13]Entry may also be direct, as in the case of a scandal at USC where employees at the computer center sold everything from grade changes to diplomas.

a. *location* (birthplace, residency to avoid out-of-state tuition or obtain some other benefit, or naturalized citizenship given recent immigration law)

b. *temporal*—date or time (birthdate, back-dated documents)

c. entry/exclusion markers (tickets, passes, passports, stamps on the hand)

d. *competency* (experience, health)

This list could be greatly extended. The issue is what element(s) is or are fraudulently presented, how this is distributed, and what the varying dynamics, scenarios, and sanctions are. Are achieved criteria more likely to be used than ascribed? A number of commonsensical hypotheses can be identified: It is easy to obtain a fake college degree or social security number or other counterfeit documents, and relatively difficult to fake a change in gender or race; it is easier to fake accounts regarding *past* biography than to *perform* in a current role.

4. *Documents used:* yes   no

If yes, does the fraud involve a fake document, or a "real" record that is used inappropriately? Is the document a full counterfeit (no such person exists) or is it a genuine document that is fraudulently used or changed (e.g., using an older sibling's ID, a stolen credit card, or a birth certificate of someone who died as a child and is about the same age as the person using it)? This is on the same level as when a "genuine" document is altered; e.g., eye color or race is changed, or a picture of the user is added. Situations where the individual uses his or her own ID fraudulently can be separated from those where someone else's ID is used.

It is easiest to create a paper trail using a real person's birth record or social security number. Yet that also can increase the likelihood of eventual discovery. The systemic and reciprocal aspects are particularly interesting when the fake ID is taken from a real person.

When a person uses the identity of someone else who is living, this often has consequences for the latter. The two are joined in a bizarre connection wherein the person whose ID is fraudulently used is held responsible for the behavior of the usurper. At the simplest level this may involve nothing more than unwarranted charges on a credit card bill. Yet the consequences can be more dire, as with arrests—for example, the case of an Eastern Airlines stewardess who was arrested and held for 5 days as a result of someone's using her identification, which had been stolen a decade before. A Detroit man has been arrested six times as a result of crimes committed by a person who stole his wallet. He was eventually advised by police to change his name to avoid the problem.

    5. *Initiator:* the actor or others

My interest is primarily in cases voluntarily initiated by the actor or subject. However, there are other forms of fraudulent IDs and records that are involuntary from the actor's perspective and that are initiated by others. The actor may be unaware of the fraud. Some gullible people (recent immigrants seem to be disproportionately victimized) are apparently duped into believing that job training and certification programs (often of short duration and inexpensive) qualify them to do things they cannot. Or children kidnapped when they are very young may be given a new identity. Medical personnel may not report the seriousness of a patient's illness. Governments in disinformation, propaganda, and counterintelligence campaigns may create fake records regarding an individual or events. Dirty-tricks political campaigns are another example.

We usually think about fraudulent identities and biographies as things that are strategically put forth by the actor. Yet from Kafka and Orwell to contemporary practices, we have instances where the state and others have the ability to alter the paper record of our biographies and to rewrite history. We assume that the state usually won't alter records, particularly about living individuals, but recent history suggests the opposite, although there is enormous variation among countries.

Implicit here is attention to the issue of blame and responsibility. Is the actor duped, culpable, or heroic?

Errors in record keeping might also be considered here. These also share a profound gap between reality as it is known to be correct by those involved and the image presented to the public, even if intentionality and secrecy are absent.

    6. *Expressed motives when perpetrator is the actor:*
          a. obtain a bureaucratic benefit or avoid a penalty
          b. hide from your past
          c. protect privacy/anonymity
          d. fun, a prank, or a challenge
          e. test a system (Goffman terms this "the vital test")

f. aggression, sabotage

g. obtain information, pretense interviews, infiltration

Attention must be paid to accounts, grammars, and rhetorics. Motivation is, of course, a tricky variable. It is rarely singular and may change
over the course of an event. Actors cannot always be trusted to give
correct accounts, and they may not be fully aware of their motives. It
can also divert attention away from structural and process variables.
Yet one aspect of any comprehensive analysis must attend to the
meaning people give to their behavior. One can sometimes usefully
distinguish between public explanations that legitimize the behavior
and more private reasons.

7. *Implemented via:* commission or omission

Is there a conscious and planned effort to deceive, or is the individual
simply taking advantage of the inherent ambiguity in language and
many social situations to create erroneous impressions? Much short-
run ethnic passing tends to be via omission. The individual simply
doesn't look or act the way members of his or her group are stereotypically believe to act. Commission requires greater effort and is generally seen as morally more suspect.

8. *Nature of the rules violated:* legal (criminal or civil) or norms

There are important historical issues here and this changes over
time. This is part of the folkways/stateways issue. Does law respond
to, or help create morality? There can be a cyclical pattern. For example, ethnic passing in ascriptive societies was probably first an ethical violation that eventually became codified into law that was later
repealed or weakened. India, Germany, Japan, the United States, and
South Africa can be usefully contrasted here. There appears to be
enormous cultural variation in how this is viewed and in the "room"
social orders offer for both legitimate and illegitimate changes in
identity.

9. *Societal response:* sanctioned to tolerated to supported

10. *Audience behavior:* accept to suspect to reject

Such presentations do not occur in a vacuum. They are interactive and dynamic and must be seen as a form of communication with
an intended audience. Audience response is an important variable and
may interact in a dynamic way with the perceptions of the actor.
Awareness contexts suggested by Glaser and Strauss (1964) can be
usefully applied here.

11. *Direction of the change:* a. to higher or lower status
                                            b. entry or exit
                                            c. restorative or new condition

a. We usually think of movement from a lower to a higher status (from black or Hispanic to white and Anglo), yet there are instances of the reverse. In India, some higher-caste persons claim to be untouchables to gain benefits set aside for them. Sometimes the boss's son or daughter will go to work in a manual position under an assumed name.

b. Is the goal of the actor and surveillance agents to keep people in or out? Levi-Strauss writes of control via vomiting out or taking in.

c. This probably affects the morality. For example, a doctor whose license is removed and continues to practice may not be viewed as harshly as someone who plays the doctor role and did not graduate from medical school or never had a license. For the actor, neutralization of the prohibitions against doing this are probably easier for the latter. Formerly licensed doctors may define themselves as still doctors. The case of the New York model whose face was cut and who has undergone plastic surgery and wears cover-up makeup is also an example. It is not clear that she is projecting a fraudulent identity. She can be viewed as trying to create what was once hers. But the same logic does not apply to a dark-skinned person who uses skin lighteners, or a person who undergoes plastic surgery to obtain a more Nordic look. There can be a tension in the cultural emphasis to be all you can be, make yourself over versus being yourself, accepting your identity.

12. *Degree of skill and*
    resources required: high or low
13. *Availability of role models:*   many or few
14. *Directionality:*   reversible or irreversible

Contrast an undercover operation where, with appropriate selection, training, and supervision, the person can come out of the role and resume a traditional enforcement role with a sex change (though what those who have such operations "are" and whether there is any deception is open to interpretation).

15. *Social network/organizations required:* yes   no

Does the perpetrator act alone or with others? Much more complex forms of deception are possible with the support of a social network, but the likelihood of discovery increases proportionally.[14]

---

[14]The Federal Witness Protection program is a very worthwhile topic for study here. The underground railroad that helped slaves gain freedom is another nice example.

16. *Discovery:* inherent or indefinately concealable

Some cases have a self-destruct/disclosure quality with a necessary progression to discovery. In con games, the mark is likely to eventually find out he or she has been taken—the ocean-view land is under water, the Brooklyn Bridge is owned by someone else, the request to withdraw money to test a suspected teller was *not* part of a bank plan. Most undercover operations with prosecution as a goal also are discovered. In contrast, "intelligence moles" may remain in place for a lifetime. Many religious and ethnic passers are never discovered. (How many people knew Cary Grant was of Jewish parents?)

17. *Pace:* sudden or gradual

There may be a gradual process of testing the waters and slowly moving into a fake ID, or there can be a radical break. There are parallels to the process of assuming a deviant identity and changing self-conception. Goffman's work on the moral career is useful here.

18. *Interaction:* face-to-face or mediated

Does the self-presentation involve a face-to-face encounter or does it involve paper records presented at a distance (via mail, computer modems, telephone conversations)? The possibilities for deception are much greater when the fraud is at a distance and involves abstracted, disembodied data images. The sociology of the nom de plume applies here.

19. *Does the event actually occur:* no   yes

This is a fascinating aspect and we lack a vocabulary to adequately capture it. It is relatively easy to define nonoccurrence and to capture the essence of the deception. But when an event occurs, but is still fraudulent, there may be definitional problems. Although it occurs, it does so in such a fashion as to render it inauthentic if the outside observer were to know what the perpetrator does. Contrast a "fake" marriage certificate used as a means of gaining citizenship. In some cases the marriage never occurs and counterfeit documents and/ or entries are made. In other cases the marriage does "occur," a man and wife fill out forms, present a blood test, pay the fee, and are married. Yet in some cases, for the partner who is a citizen, this is done as a business for a fee; in other cases, the citizen may be duped. Insurance fraud offers similar definitional questions. Thus, the car that a person arranges to have "stolen" in order to collect insurance is really missing and likely broken up into its basic parts. The perpetrator of insurance fraud who had a friend cut off his foot with an ax is

For consideration of a contemporary "underground railroad" that helps battered women create new lives, see Ferraro and Johnson (1985).

really missing a foot, even if he claimed it happened in a motorcycle accident. The ambiguity of language offers rich possibility for exploiting "real occurrences" that, nevertheless, are not what they appear to be with respect to identity and biography.

20. *Is a fraudulent role actually performed:* yes   no

For example, college professor Paul Arthur Crafton had 34 aliases. He had 70 credit cards (including 4 American Express gold cards) and five driver's licences. When arrested, he was teaching at three different colleges under different names. He was commuting hundreds of miles a week between Washington, D.C., and Pennsylvania. This obviously requires greater skill and perhaps energy than the mediated identity deception that relies only on paper claims, or where a fake ID is presented for entry or exit.[15]

21. *Origin:* strategic or mental illness

My interest is primarily in strategic, voluntary uses by the actor for a motive that can be conventionally understood in terms of the categories in number 6 above. But with respect to social processes, much could also be learned from looking at neurological cases such as those described in *The Man Who Mistook His Wife for a Hat* (Sax, 1986), or the studies of multiple personalities.

22. *Object:* a. human or nonhuman
           b. individual or organization

a. My interest is primarily in human identity, but some attention could usefully be devoted to nonhuman examples, such as fake pedigrees for animals (dogs, cats, horses). I saw one dog that had its owner's social security number tattooed under his leg. This was registered with the National Dog Registry. Another example involves fake certifications for artifacts such as antiquities, pottery, and paintings. There is a market and incentives for clones to appear once an artist's work becomes well known. It may also be more common for deceased than for living artists. A related area is the fake labeling of mass-produced products, such as Vuitton luggage, blue jeans, and automobile parts. Copyright and trademark violations could be compared to violations involving identity. To what extent do fraud laws differentiate claims

---

[15]Crafton illustrates the ever-precarious nature of social control. Earlier in his career he patented a number of devices, including one used to verify credit card users. Authorities also had trouble "bringing up" his fingerprints because they were so light. That rare condition is usually found only in persons who spend years with their hands immersed in water, such as cement finishers.

Table 1. Four Types of Fraudulent Identity Based on Scope and Time

	Scope	
Time	Comprehensive	Singular
Permanent	1. Fugitives Ethnic passers	2. Denial of arrest record, some religious passers
Temporary	3. Deep undercover operations	4. Teenagers and fake IDs

for the human versus the nonhuman? Many of the same factors that produce increases in the former may operate for the latter.

b. The little existing research has focused primarily on individuals. Yet the topic of fake organizational presentations offers a rich mine. A focus on complex con games or police stings requires attention to organizational as well as individual presentations. The CIA offers a classic case where proprietary fronts (e.g., Southern Air) have been used extensively. Considerable information on this can be found in scattered places. What are the major parallels and differences between fake personal and organizational presentations?

One could go on and list more dimensions, and I apologize for the dizzying impact of throwing a list at the reader. A next step is to decide which are most important and how various values of these may occur in a patterned way. Some basic ideal types can be created by combining dimensions. I offer four tables that I think capture some of the most essential features (or at least the features I find of most interest).

Thus, if we think about the scope and temporal aspects, we have Table 1. New issues and contingencies appear as we move from cell 1, the hard-core behavior that tends to involve complete sociological death and rebirth, to the soft core behavior of cell 4.

Another relevant table involves responses to genuine and fraudulent ID. If we combine audience response with whether the ID is fraudulently or correctly used, we have the typology shown in Table 2.

There are many interesting cases, such as pretenders to thrones and inheritances (Anastasia, Howard Hughes's long-lost relatives). Some of the same dynamics apply even though, in such cases, it is often

Table 2. Audience Response and the Authenticity of Identification

Is ID	Do others	
	Accept	Reject
Correct	1. Most common (gender)	2. Less common (Arthur Miller's play *Focus*, people of age who look young and find their IDs are not believed, people who don't believe undercover or plainclothes police are police
Fake	3. Common (successful deception)	4. Common (effective control mechanisms) fake IDs don't always work

impossible to know where to classify them on the vertical axis since the dispute is about whether they are fake or correct.

Table 3 involves relating what the audience really believes, or knows to be true, to its behavior. This will not always be consistent with overt behavior. In primary relations, and where there is economic advantage for the intended audience, we might expect greater inconsistency.

Cell 4 applies to incentives to project fraudulent IDs and for potential control agents to collude. Liquor stores and bars, for example, have an economic incentive to not look too closely at the IDs they are

Table 3. Audience Beliefs and Behavior

Does audience act consistently regarding the belief?	Does audience believe ID to be valid?	
	Yes	No
Yes	1. Ordinary behavior	2. Failure (from view of holder of the ID)
No	3. Criminal justice framing and cover-ups	4. Collusion, intimidation (M. Guere's wife, some liquor vendors)

Table 4. Document Authenticity and Quality of Role Performance

Effective role performance	Fraudulent documents	
	Yes	No
Yes	1. Thought-provoking	2. Expected pattern
No	3. Incompetent impostors	4. Incompetent professionals

shown. If a credit card is valid, merchants get paid, even if the person using the card has no right to use it. For many situations of false ID, there is a parallel to the relative indifference of the insurance industry to fraud, since costs are diffused and passed on to the consumer. Such externalities reduce the incentive for vigilance.

If we combine whether or not fraudulent documents are used to gain access to playing a role with the quality of the role performance, we gain insight into the important issue of formal versus substantive legitimacy. Such a typology calls attention to what can be the self-serving nature of credentialing and encourages thinking about the relationship between performance and documentation (see Table 4). Placing cases in cells 3 and 4 is less complicated for some groups, such as brain surgeons, than for others, such as barbers or teachers.

Drawing the Line Somewhere

The topic raises issues that go beyond social science in a strict sense to questions of justice, democracy, mobility, and the rights of the individual as against the needs of the state. There are tough public policy questions and trade-offs here.

As automated biometric and object (e.g., autos) identification devices become more efficient and inexpensive, their use will expand. As the cost of computing declines, the demand for ever-increasing amounts of personal data will increase. Credentialing, too, marches onward. The topic is likely to become more salient as a public issue; for example, note the 1986 immigration law with its documentation requirements and the concern over identifying carriers of AIDS. Attention to how the issue has evolved in the last decade can give us a glimpse of the future and the choices we have to shape it.

Chesterton wrote that art is like life and you have to draw the line somewhere. This holds as well for public policy. What degree of risk and disorder do we want to accept in return for maximizing liberty and privacy? We want an efficient and secure society and quality treatment from doctors and electricians. We don't want to see needed benefit programs bankrupt the society because they are shamelessly exploited, and we don't want to put Dracula in charge of the blood bank. We also want a society where, if you have paid a debt, your present behavior is what should count. We want to emphasize achieved not ascribed criteria, and we want to encourage innovation and change. Yet we can't maximize all of these.

As citizens of a democratic society who value equity and liberty, privacy, and a degree of order, how should we view the insatiable demand for more information and documentation and intrusive technologies? Can we have a decent, reasonably efficient, yet loose society? Can we have an open and tolerant society that encourages changes and choices about identity without, at the same time, creating license for rampant and destructive fraudulent identity? Must we choose between the extremes of anarchy and repression?

How leaky or tight do we want our social order to be? To what extent and when and where do we want to extend visibility, accountability, and mandatory disclosure? When do we want to enhance privacy and insulate social actions and personal pasts from visibility? We clearly need better ways to think about these issues and criteria for sorting out what is at stake.

ACKNOWLEDGMENTS

I am grateful to David Altheide, John Hepburn, and Pat Lauderdale for critical comments.

References

Altheide, D., & Johnson, J. (1980). Bureaucratic propaganda. Boston: Allyn and Bacon.
Ball, D. (1970). The problematics of respectability. In J. Douglas (Ed.), Deviance and respectability (pp. 326–271). New York: Basic Books.
Ferraro, K., & Johnson, J. (1985). The new underground railroad. Studies in Symbolic Interaction, 6, 377–386.
Glaser, B., & Straus, A. (1964). Awareness contexts and social interaction. American Sociological Review, 669–679.
Goffman, E. (1956). The presentation of self in everyday life. New York: Anchor Doubleday.
Goffman, E. (1962). Stigma. Englewood Cliffs, NJ: Prentice-Hall.
Goffman, E. (1974). Frame analysis. Cambridge, MA: Harvard University Press.
Marx, G,. (1974). Thoughts on a neglected category of social movement participant: Agents provacateurs and informants. American Journal of Sociology, September.

Marx, G. (1979). External efforts to damage or facilitate social movements: Some patterns, explanations, outcomes and complications. In M. Zald & J. McCarthy (Eds.), *The dynamics of social movements*. Cambridge, MA: Winthrop.

Marx, G. (1984). Notes on the discovery, collection and assessment of hidden and dirty data. In J. Schneider & J. Kitsuse (Eds.), *Studies in the sociology of social problems*. Norwood, NJ: Ablex.

Marx, G. (1988). *Undercover police surveillance in America*. Berkeley: University of California Press.

Report by the Chairman of the Subcommittee on Health and Long-Term Care of the Select Committee on Aging. (1986). Ninety-ninth Congress, Second Session. Washington, DC: U.S. Government Printing Office.

Sax, O. (1986). *The man who mistook his wife for a hat*. New York: Summit Books.

CHAPTER 8

Law as Fair, Law as Help: The Texture of Legitimacy in American Society

Sally Engle Merry

Although many have argued that law somehow contributes to popular acceptance of existing relations of domination by enhancing the legitimacy of those who rule, it has proved difficult in practice to identify exactly how this legitimation takes place (Beirne, 1982; Lachmann, 1986; Scheingold, 1974; Sumner, 1979; Thompson, 1982; Trubek, 1984; Tyler, 1986; Weber, 1978). Some have claimed that legitimacy is simply too hard to distinguish and measure and that the concept should be abandoned (Hyde, 1983), while others assert that it should be retained and defined more carefully (Friedrichs, 1986). Some claim that it can be measured (McEwen & Maiman, 1986; Tyler, 1986). This chapter is an effort to explore the texture of legitimacy for ordinary Americans living in three small urban areas, one of which is rich, one poor, and one in the middle. I argue that legitimacy for these people depends less on a vision of the law as just and fair than it does on an understanding of the law as pervasive, powerful, and, from time to time, effective.

For Weber, legitimacy refers to beliefs about authority that induce actors to comply with the orders of the authority for reasons other than self-interest, habit, or custom; they comply because they see this action as in some way obligatory or exemplary (1978, p. 31). An authority relationship is one in which the exercise of power is justified in the eyes of the person being dominated because he accepts the normative validity of the principle on the basis of which the authority

SALLY ENGLE MERRY • Department of Anthropology, Wellesley College, Wellesley, Massachusetts 02181.

claims power (Kronman, 1983, p. 39). This may occur through the routinization of charismatic authority (Gerth & Mills 1946, pp. 253–264.) There may, of course, be other reasons for obedience operating at the same time, such as self-interest or fear of violence. Actors themselves are often not aware of how far their compliance is a matter of custom, of convention, or of law (Weber, 1978, p. 38).

Critical legal scholars, working within a Marxist tradition, also argue that the world views embedded in legal consciousness legitimate the social order by portraying unjust social relations as either necessary or desirable (Trubek, 1984, p. 597). Critical legal studies scholars seek to discover the false but legitimating world views concealed within legal doctrine and legal consciousness (see also Cain & Hunt, 1979; Kairys, 1982).

These theories consider the implications of general values, beliefs, and orientations toward the legal system for acquiescence to, and support for, the social order. Scholars in the Weberian tradition are particularly concerned with the impact of beliefs that the law is fair and just, and that it provides equal treatment in the sense of equivalent procedures, on compliance with the orders of an authority that appears legitimate.

However, another way of thinking about the legitimacy of law is to ask how people think about it who seek it out to solve their problems. Such people have expressed a willingness to submit to the law's determination of the justice of their claims and to abide by its decisions. They have, in this sense, expressed their belief that the law is legitimate. But in what sense do they conceive of this legitimacy? Is it in terms of fairness and procedural equivalence? Or do they manage to make use of the law without simultaneously accepting the visions of the law that we generally think serve to legitimate its authority?

Legitimacy, defined as that which fosters compliance with authority, is a complex phenomenon derived from beliefs about what the law is like and from ideas about what it can be used for. This chapter investigates to what extent people who use the law do so because of their belief in the fairness and justice of the legal system and to what extent they do so because it is an effective strategy for getting things done. I will examine the cultural meaning of law for experienced users of the legal system, people who turn to the courts for help with their personal problems. When these ordinary citizens take their personal problems to the police, to lawyers, or to court, they demonstrate a willingness to accept the law's supervision over their relations with family, neighbors, and friends. Yet they enter the fray of the courtroom reluctantly, searching for help more than for justice. Such people voluntarily invite the scrutiny of the law over their private lives, but they usually do so out of desperation rather than enthusiasm for legal intervention. In order to grasp something of the range of variation in cultural meanings of law, I will then compare these views with those of low-income urbanites involved in crime and those of affluent suburbanites.

Cultural Meanings of Law among White Working-Class Plaintiffs

This chapter primarily describes research on interpersonal disputes and disputants who have taken their problems to the lower criminal court, the small claims court, and the juvenile court, and to the mediation programs associated with each court. The research was carried out between 1980 and 1984, some in conjunction with Susan Silbey, in two Massachusetts towns. This research involved watching mediation sessions and talking to the participants afterwards about their thoughts, feelings, and understandings of mediation, the court, and the law. In cases that failed to settle in mediation and returned to court, we followed the case back to court and observed the case and talked to the parties there. We attempted in these interchanges to probe beneath the explicit rules and justifications that they provided to their more practical but unarticulated bases for doing and understanding, recognizing the difficulty of making these interpretations in a cultural world that we also take for granted. That they had come to the courthouse for help with a personal problem seemed a significant indication that the law seemed relevant to their personal lives and that it was, in some sense, legitimate to them. They had invited its supervision over their lives.

During the sessions, which often turned into heated arguments, people talked to their opponents in the conflict. For at least this segment of the mediation session, their comments were directed to each other. In the rest of the session, they talked to the mediators, not to the researcher, who simply observed quietly. We also interviewed many of the parties, but interviews yield a different kind of understanding, more "public" statements in a cool and detached interview setting. I observed about 75 mediation sessions myself. Overall, these research projects yielded detailed notes on about 170 sessions (see further Merry & Rocheleau, 1985; Silbey & Merry, 1986). I was not allowed to tape-record the sessions because of the confidentiality of the proceedings, so my descriptions of the sessions are based on detailed but hand-written notes. Many sessions were followed by further informal discussions with the parties and by interviews in their homes. I also did general ethnography on the neighborhoods in which these disputes occurred. The plaintiffs were predominantly working class and mostly white. In an earlier study of urban crime, I discovered that blacks who were part of a social world of criminals also used the courts for inter-personal problems (Merry, 1981). A survey of an affluent white suburb with predominantly upper-middle-class residents offered a rather different vision of the role of law in family and neighborhood life (Merry, 1987).

A Case of Unrequited Love

The following case is typical of the general orientation toward law and use of law shared by many of the plaintiffs who brought their problems to the lower court in one of these towns, a separate community on the fringes of a major metropolitan area. As an old New England mill town, this small city combined old ethnics, Yankee elites, and new immigrants in a changing economy moving from the industrial production of leather and textiles to the provision of retail, financial, and medical services for a larger region.

Bridget Jones (a pseudonym) lived on Green Street, the worst street in town, a dim row of four-story brick tenements built in the 19th century by mill owners to house their recently immigrated mill workers. Her use of the courts to deal with a troubling relationship with her young neighbor, a romantic liaison that misfired, provides one account of working-class legal ideology. Her ideas and reasons for going to court were fairly similar to those of others whose problems ended up in mediation. I have changed names and some personal details in order to conceal the identities of the individuals involved.

Bridget, at 28, was a heavy woman with curly brown hair who looked older than her age. When she brought her problem to the mediation program office in the courthouse, she looked straggly and unkempt, but at the mediation session she had her hair attractively curled and was nicely dressed. My impression was of a strong, caring woman with warmth and vivacity. Bridget came to the court about a problem with a young man, Billy, who was in love with her and called her and harassed her all the time. Billy was 17, a slight, short boy with a meek expression who sat through the mediation session slumped over and silent. He seemed very sad. He refused to be interviewed afterwards, but I talked to her for about 2 hours in her apartment and again when her case returned to court. She seemed very self-confident, he apologetic but angry.

Bridget and Billy lived next door to each other on Green Street for about 2 years; then, a year ago, Bridget moved out. While they were neighbors, Billy baby-sat for Bridget's three children, ages 5, 7, and 10, and spent a lot of time at her house, talking to her and playing with her as well as the children. She was separated from her husband at the time and confided her problems to Billy. However, when Billy wrote her a love note, she told him that the relationship was off. He began to harass her, attack her and pull her hair, lie in front of her car to prevent her driving away, and call her at work all the time. He threatened to kill himself by jumping off the roof if she did not change her mind. He sometimes sat in her car and waited for her, and once she had to call the police to get him out of her car. This situation lasted about a year. Bridget said that she had threatened many times to go to court if he did not stop harassing her and had finally filed a complaint with the clerk charging him with harassment. Billy was very surprised and hurt that she had.

Billy lived with six or seven brothers and sisters and a mother who was often absent for weeks at a time. In the follow-up interview, Bridget told me that Billy was often left to take care of the younger children, including one 7 and one 10 years of age. She said:

> It was really kind of sad. He would spend all day cleaning up the apartment when his mother was coming home, and she would just come in and not notice it at all or say anything. He would do the same thing for me, clean my apartment from top to bottom. Once the little boy, the 7-year-old, and another boy, set a mattress on fire and fortunately Billy came home in time to call the fire department. But they are too young to be left alone without anyone to watch them. I guess that Billy or his older brother provides food for them.[1]

When she kept calling the police about her troubles with Billy, the police urged her to take out a restraining order against him (for which she was not eligible, since they did not live in the same apartment). She thought that they were eager for her to take him to court since they thought he was a troublemaker. In light of my observations of similar cases, however, I suspect that the police also grew tired of coming.

At the time of the mediation session, Bridget was working as kitchen help in a local school and Billy was working in a temporary job in the post office. He had dropped out of high school. Bridget also worked off and on in a local bar. Both lived in rented apartments.

The mediation session lasted 70 minutes. The mediation coordinator told the two mediators that this was a problem of a young boy with an attachment to a married woman, and that their role was to

---

[1] I did not tape-record interviews, so that this quote, based on notes I took, is my best recollection of the conversation.

tell the boy that he had to end the relationship and stop harassing her. Bridget began the session with her statement of the problem, which shows a strong undercurrent of caring about Billy and a sense that she has turned to the court for protection in a situation that has strained her beyond endurance. She does not, however, talk in terms of legal rights.[2]

> The problem is that he won't leave me alone. He is calling at work, bothering me all the time. This is really aggravating me and it has just got to stop. He calls me out of work down the hall to the phone several times a day. It is making me sick and getting me so aggravated. It has been going on for two years now. And furthermore, I was at a friend's house cooking dinner one day and he sent me a letter saying that he would kill himself if I didn't leave the house. It was a male friend. He is very jealous of my male friends and gets very upset if I ever talk to them. I live in the next town now, but when my husband and I were separated, I lived near Billy. He would bother me then. His sister used to baby sit for my children, and I got to know him then. He would come over and play with my children. He needs someone to care about him and listen to him, and I always did that, I was always there for him. I helped him in his relationship with his girlfriend. I did this when I lived near him, but now I have moved to the next town, and this continues. He calls me when I am at the club [a local bar], he calls my male friends there, and he called one a black bastard. He gets very upset about all my male friends.

When the mediators asked Billy for his side, he responded only, "I have nothing to say." In the private discussion with the mediators, Billy said only that he had his reasons for harassing her, that she hurt him very much, but that he would not talk about it. When they asked Billy if he knew why she did not want to see him anymore, he replied: "I don't know. I guess I am harassing her. She says so, so it must be true. And besides, she took me to court, didn't she?" He seemed hurt and later very angry that she had taken this drastic step, and he had called her several times that morning so complain to her about it. Both seemed to assume that invoking the court for this problem was very serious.

When the mediators asked him if he could treat her like a total stranger, he replied: "It would be hard, but I could do it. And I have to, because if I don't, she will take me to court. But I could take her to court too. I could charge her with statutory rape."

Not only does this comment suggest that there were sexual relations between them, but it also implies that Billy could also have used legal weapons against Bridget, and powerful ones, but refrained from doing so. His comment suggests a more equal bargaining position in the legal arena than the rest of the mediation session implied.

---

[2] Since I was not allowed to tape-record mediation sessions, these statements are reconstructions based on the detailed notes I took as I observed the sessions.

When they asked what he would like in the agreement, Billy said that he would like her not to come into his neighborhood at all. When the mediators replied that this was not fair, that she still had friends there she wanted to visit, he replied that there was nothing that he wanted. When the mediators urged him to make another demand, claiming that this was not a one-way street, but an agreement for both of them, he replied, "But she always has a one-way street, and the complaint is against me." It was obviously very important to him that the case was in court.

In the private discussion with the mediators, Bridget said that she doubted that he would stay away from her, although he had agreed to, because when she threatened to take him to court before, he threatened to take her to court on charges of rape. She thinks he needs counseling, but he has refused, saying that he is not crazy. She acknowledges that they used to be really good friends until he wrote the love note about a year and a half earlier. She describes him as a "super person." When the mediators ask about Billy's mother, Bridget replies:

> Billy complains that his mother is never home. She leaves for weeks at a time and leaves him to take care of the children, and there are a lot of children he is responsible for. His older brothers beat him up. He breaks out all of the windows in his bedroom, which are now covered with boards. When I go to my girlfriend's house near his house, he sees me and then the police always get involved. He knows I go out with my friends on Friday and Saturday nights, and he always waits for me. I want him to stay away from me. He seems to be in shock, ever since I went to court. I don't think he thought I would really do it.

The mediators work out an agreement in which Bridget agrees to drop charges of harassment against Billy providing he stops trying to see her or talk to her. Both agree to treat one another as total strangers should they accidentally see one another. The third clause reads, "Billy realizes that Mrs. Jones will immediately reactivate her charge of harassment and pursue it in court if there is the slightest breakdown in the agreement." The mediators inform them, as they sign the official-looking document, that a copy will be given to the clerk and one will stay with the program, but that there will be no record of criminal charges.

Six months later Billy came into the mediation office to say that Bridget was still bothering him. The mediation program wrote to Bridget, who had moved back to Billy's neighborhood, and she came into the office to say that he was still harassing her, calling her five times a night in the bar where she now worked, and that she had filed a complaint against him in court. The charge is harassment and assault and battery with a knife and rocks. On the complaint application form she described the facts of the case as follows: "This kid refuses to leave me alone on a constant basis. He constantly harasses me and my children with his threats. If I don't talk to him he gets very violent and starts to cause trouble. All I want is this kid to leave me alone. Mediation did not work. Everybody on Green Street knows everything he does to me." In the blank for date, she wrote, "Everyday."

During a 40-minute hearing in front of a court clerk to determine whether or not a complaint should be issued, the clerk tells Bridget that he cannot do anything about this case since she needs to provide specific dates, times, and incidents, not a general pattern of harassment. Billy did not appear, although he was summoned by the court. The clerk assures Bridget that if anything else happens, she should come right into court with the specifics, but as it is, he can do nothing. Harassment is not a crime. Threats are, however, and when he asks if Billy threatened her, she brightens up and says, "Yes, all the time." But he threatens to call the Children's Protective Services about her mistreatment of her children, not to hurt her. The clerk says that is not a threat. As she tells him more of her problems and the physical violence, he seems more sympathetic but still says that he must have a better legal case in order to do anything, that there is not much to go on. She describes assaults with rocks and a knife, but he asks her if she has medical records. "Dates are very important. Do you know when these incidents happened? If this goes upstairs [i.e., to the judge], and the district attorney asks you for specific dates and you can't provide them, you will lose it."

The clerk advises her to call the police, but Bridget points out that the police have stopped coming. She keeps saying, "This has been going on for three years. Something has got to be done." She points out that she already tried mediation. When the clerk refuses to issue the complaint, she keeps repeating, "Does that mean nothing can be done? That he can just get away with this?" The clerk counters, "But this is also your fault, in a way. You have let this go on and on. You should have done something sooner. Now it doesn't look so convincing. And the incident you mention [which precipitated her complaint application and the mediation session] was too long ago, it is now seven months ago. The judge will say, why didn't you do something sooner? If he touches you again, come right down." (There is an element of Catch 22 to this reply: you have waited too long, so I won't do anything now.) Bridget sighs and looks disgusted. Her friend, who came with her to the hearing, says, "Bridget, they have to do this legally, you know." The clerk concludes: "I advise you to stay away from that bar. Get some beer and go home and drink it. It is better for your kids, anyway. If there is any more trouble, just come in and I will issue a complaint. You let too much time go by."

After she leaves the hearing, the clerk confides to me that she is the type who goes to bars and drinks, and that although he has not seen her before, he knew the friend who came with her, who is "no prize either," and he knows the bars they drink in. He also knows the neighborhood they come from, which is a bad one, and knows that the police will not do anything there. He has seen the boy in and out of juvenile court many times and is sure that he will go to jail sooner or later. His older brother is in trouble with the law as well. The clerk says, "This is a serious case; it is assault and battery with a dangerous weapon, but without any dates or evidence, they will throw it out upstairs." Six months later, he told me that he never heard from her again and presumed that he had settled the case (see further, on role of clerks, Yngvesson, 1985).

Ironically, the court insisted that the problem be fixed in time and place in order to act, yet it was precisely the repeated and ongoing quality of the problem that motivated Bridget to take the step—which both she and Billy regarded as drastic—of filing a complaint in court. She refers repeatedly to how long the problem has been going on in asking for more assistance from the court, while the clerk replies that without specifics the court can do nothing, and, in fact, he implies that the judge will think him a fool for issuing the complaint. Bridget was not interested in punishing Billy for past acts; her concerns were directed toward the future, toward stopping the situation of harassment. She wanted to go to court rather than mediation because, she said, "I needed somebody higher to say something." If the mediation agreement failed to stop the harassment, she intended to use the court again, not mediation.

Neither Billy nor Bridget was a stranger to the court. The court clerk knew Billy's family and said that Billy had been in and out of juvenile court for years. Bridget said that he was accused of stealing a car. According to the records of the mediation program, Billy's mother appeared in mediation 1 or 2 years earlier as a plaintiff in a dispute with another neighbor, Judy, whose 10-year-old boy she accused of inspiring her 5- and 8-year-olds to fight and to set fire to a mattress. Billy's mother went to court and was referred to mediation.

Bridget has also had considerable experience with court. In an interview, she described two times when her husband was a defendant in criminal court as a result of fights with his acquaintances. The charges were all dismissed or dropped. She once spat on a police officer who put her into a cruiser and charged her with assault and battery. This case was continued without a finding. Four years earlier she got a restraining order from the probate court against her husband for attempting to throw her out of a window. She thought that it worked very well; the police came up often to see how things were going and searched the house for him. When Judy, the neighbor Billy's mother took to court over the mattress fire, hit her over the head with a stick, she charged her with assault and battery and the case went to the judge, who put the woman on probation for 6 months, according to Bridget. Bridget thinks that Judy was angry because the state was taking away her children for neglect. While Bridget lived in the Green Street tenement, her little girl, then 3 years old, fell off her third-floor porch and got a bad concussion. The railing was very weak and Bridget had complained about it to the landlord many times. She stopped paying rent and filed a suit for $30,000 against the landlord, a notorious slumlord. When I interviewed her, she had not yet settled the case, but she said that her lawyer told her she had an excellent case. When the accident happened, Billy was very upset and came over and started hammering up a new railing, pounding and pounding on it in anger.

Nor are Billy and Bridget unusual. Records of 239 cases that were referred to the mediation program from the town over a period of about 1½ years indicate that the neighborhood in which they lived had almost the highest rate of cases per capita in the town. There were almost 16 cases per thousand residents in the Green Street neighborhood (21 cases from a population of 1,400), in comparison with a town average of 6 per thousand (239 from a population of 40,000) and a rate in the most suburban neighborhood of 2 per thousand (3 cases from 1,900 people). Only one neighborhood had more, 16.5 per thousand (11 cases from 670 people). These numbers refer to mediation program referrals, of course, not to court filings. But the mediation program inspected the cases filed in the clerk's office every day for interpersonal disputes, so that these numbers represent a rough approximation of the number of interpersonal cases that arrived at the court under citizen initiative.

What does the law mean to Bridget? What was her view of its legitimacy that led her to turn to it repeatedly with her problems? Was she inspired by a belief that the legal system was fair and just? Her discussions in mediation and court suggest that she saw it as a place for getting help. She explained why she needed help from the law in terms of very broad claims to the need for freedom from being bothered and attacked when she had done nothing to deserve it rather than in terms of particular rights, injuries, or legal claims. In fact, the language of therapy is far more pervasive in her talk than the language of law. Nor does she talk of evidence. In fact, her complaint application to the clerk and the discussion in the clerk's office both suggested that she was unfamiliar with a discourse of evidence and claims. Instead, she talked of her needs and Billy's needs.

The court was, it seems, a familiar way of dealing with problems that involved fairness and protection in a very general way. She saw the court as a service to which she was entitled, useful for problems such as her husband's violence and the landlord's failure to repair the railing.[3] Getting help from the court in violent personal relationships is part of her cultural repertoire. When the court fails to help, she is disgusted but not disillusioned. She did not go to court with illusions about its equality, fairness, or justice.

One of the most intriguing features of the case is that a person like Bridget, who in many ways is powerless in the American social order, went to court at all, that she feels that she has the right to use the court for help and to be disgusted when it refuses. She and others like her believe in the power of the law but not in its justice. When they do not find it particularly fair or just, they are not surprised or disillusioned. But when they find it has no power—when it is not effective—then they are disgusted. They use the court because it is the nearest institution which exerts some moral authority, to which they can bring claims based on a general sense of morality in human relationships, and which offers a more civilized alternative to violence. As we can see in the case of Bridget and Billy, the court is not a preferred strategy, but one used in desperation, as a last resort, when the problem seems destined to stretch into an intolerable future. They view the courts as personalistic and influenced by personal contacts and political pressures, but they believe that, in general, the world runs on favors and that those with more education and money have more power.

Bridget and Billy are typical of the kinds of people who appeared in mediation with their personal problems. Many were marginal workers, unemployed, retired, or employed intermittently. They had factory jobs, food service jobs, jobs in small stores as clerks, or custodial jobs. Many had ethnic heritages, but very few were recent immigrants. Instead, the bulk were descendants of the major European migrations of the 19th and early 20th centuries—people whose ancestors had come from Ireland, Italy, Poland, and French Canada. These were people who had grown up as Americans, of American parents, feeling that they belonged in American society and that its institutions—political, legal, educational,—were for them. They felt entitled to go to court.

At the same time, this group, in the Boston region as well as in other cities of the Northeast in the 1980s, was under increasing pressure of job loss with the disappearance of many stable blue-collar jobs as industry moved to other regions and overseas, and under pressure

---

[3] I am indebted to Austin Sarat for this perspective.

of housing loss, as gentrification and urban redevelopment chipped away at existing supplies of low-cost rental housing (see Bluestone & Harrison, 1982, Sheehan, 1984; Susser, 1982). Newcomers moving into these poorer districts, such as Hispanics into the Green Street area, exacerbated the pressure and generated conflicts over housing and space that took on ethnic overtones. For this group, use of the court to handle problems is part of an aspiration to middle-class status, to membership in American society, to dealing with problems in the way defined as respectable by a law-oriented culture. These plaintiffs are not strangers to welfare, government regulations, or the courts. Their past experiences with the legal system, both as defendants and as plaintiffs, have simply increased their skill at maneuvering through the legal arena in order to get something done.

Survey Evidence

In order to get a more quantitative assessment of how these plaintiffs felt about the legal system, we interviewed 81 people who had brought a problem to court or to one of the mediation programs. Two-thirds of the plaintiffs interviewed were women, and almost two-thirds (63%) had had some previous experience in court. After 21 less-structured interviews, we asked 60 plaintiffs a series of closed-ended questions about the fairness and effectiveness of the courts. These court users were almost all white and working class in occupation and income, were in their 30s, on the average, and generally earned between $16,000 and $20,000 a year. About half had some education beyond high school.

Each person was presented with a series of statements about the legal system and asked to indicate the extent to which he or she agreed or disagreed with these statements. Although each person was asked to make a distinction between five degrees of assent or dissent, I have collapsed these five categories into three for the purposes of analysis: agree, disagree, and don't know. Obviously, questionnaire data of this type are extremely limited in their ability to capture the complex nuances of meaning and context that individuals bring to a problems such as their view of the courts. However, they are of some utility in making possible a comparison among perspectives on different aspects of the legal system. I regard them as only a pale supplement to detailed ethnographic accounts, however (see Table 1).

These responses indicate that people who take their problems to the court tend to see it as fairly powerful and effective, although they do not generally believe that everyone is treated the same or that po-

Table 1. Plaintiffs' Attitudes toward the Courts[a]

	Agree	Don't know	Disagree
Courts can get things done, they can force people to obey the law and punish them if they don't.	82%	10%	8%
You have no choice but to follow the orders of the court, even if you don't agree.	73%	7%	20%
There is a legal obligation to follow the orders of the court, even if you don't agree.	88%	7%	5%
The courts treat rich and poor, men and women, racial and ethnic groups the same.	18%	8%	74%
Police, judges, and people who work in the courts can be influenced by personal contacts.	84%	12%	4%
If you, yourself, were accused of a crime, you could expect to get a fair trial.	65%	12%	23%
Judges are generally honest and fair in deciding each case.	60%	17%	22%
Courts generally provide justice.	65%	10%	25%

[a]In the tabulation of these responses from all mediation users, defendants (N = 92) as well as plaintiffs (N = 60), revealed substantially the same pattern of answers.

lice, judges, and people who work in the courts are immune to personal influence. Eighty-two percent agreed, "Courts can get things done, they can force people to obey the law and punish them if they don't." Almost as many (73%) agreed, "You have no choice but to follow the orders of the court, even if you don't agree." Fully 88% agreed, "There is a legal obligation to follow the orders of the court." On the other hand, only 18% agreed, "The courts treat rich and poor, men and women, racial and ethnic groups the same," and only 4% did not think, "Police, judges, and people who work in courts can be influenced by personal contacts." About two-thirds felt that they themselves would get a fair trial, that judges are generally honest and fair in deciding cases, and that the courts generally provide justice. They do generally expect fair treatment, but less often than they expect that the court is a powerful institution that must be obeyed.

These court users were not persuaded that the courts are blind to differences of race, gender, and class among individuals or that they functioned without reference to personal contacts and influence. Yet they went to court anyway because, it appears, they think the law is sufficiently powerful, controlling, and effective in imposing its decisions to be worth a try (see further, on lower courts, Silbey, 1981).

The Criminal Underclass

In an earlier study in Boston in the mid-1970s, based on 18 months of participant observation in an inner-city housing project, I talked to a number of young men and women—about 15—who were or had been involved in crime along with their relatives and neighbors (1981). They lived in a multiracial inner-city housing project with black, white, Hispanic, and Chinese neighbors. Most were black, a few were white. Some were actively involved in crime. The young men were experimenting with burglaries, robberies, and car thefts; the young women with prostitution and shoplifting. Others in the group were simply girlfriends or sisters of the young men trying out crime. I say trying out because for many of these young people, crime is a phase in their lives that they will probably drop in the future. Only a few are likely to become career criminals; for the rest, this seems a temporary job.

These people know the criminal law. If often regulates what they do, and they often use it. These young people are sophisticated as defendants and persistent as plaintiffs. They use the criminal courts because they know how they operate, yet they do not believe they are fair or just. They see the system as alien, run by whites, and out to get them. They have often felt its grip as they are taken to court and sometimes to prison for burglaries, robberies, and auto thefts. They feel that the law is used by whites against blacks, often against them, and that blacks are often accused of crimes they did not commit because they are black. They feel that white police officers are generally hostile to blacks. The young men in particular contrast this system of law to "people's law," by which they mean their own rules of social life. The notion of "people's law" presumes that society is ordered by law, but that the legitimate law is not that of the state but of the local community. As the following account of an interpersonal dispute demonstrates, however, people's law is much like state law in its form.[4]

---

[4]I was present to observe this discussion of the incident, and I talked to several of the participants over the next few days. However, I did not go to court, so my description of what happened in court is their description of the event, not mine.

A Case of Love and Jealousy

A young black man, George, hit his girlfriend, Renee, in the eye and she ran home crying. Several friends gathered to discuss the event in the playground in the middle of the housing project. Wilson, a 27-year-old man who was a friend of both, witnessed the incident and thought that George was jealous because Renee had been riding in a car with George's rival, another young man. Renee's brother arrived, looking for George, with a pipe thinly concealed in his pants, and her mother came brandishing a chair leg. Both threatened to beat up George if they found him. George was nowhere to be seen. This group waited 2 hours for him, but he did not return. Although George lived only 2 minutes' walk away, no one went to find him. When I asked why not, Wilson said that if anyone went there and George killed him, he could claim he was justified, "maybe not legally" but according to "people's law." Later that day, Wilson's sister arrived saying that "Renee's mother had sworn out a warrant for George's arrest and that Renee had signed it. Renee said that she had done the same thing (pressed charges for assault and battery) against George 2 years earlier and he had gotten a suspended sentence.

The night before the case came to court, George had a bitter fight with the rival for Renee who had taken her in the car. The next day, in court (I was told), Renee's brother told George he was going to die, and George told the brother that he was "going to get it." George took out a case against the brother for these threats. On the day of the next hearing, the docket listed cross-complaints: Each had lodged charges against the other. According to George, the judge threw it all out but said that he would put both cases on file. George was not sure what that meant, but he was mad at Renee for "messing up his record." He said that the judge decided it was a family fight. George moved out of the project within hours of this incident. About 5 years earlier, he had had another violent fight with the same rival over Renee. George sadly told me that one of his former girlfriends first thought of taking a case to court against him, and he gave the idea to Renee when he told her about it.

Other black residents of this neighborhood, mostly women, also filed criminal charges against their boyfriends, neighbors, and husbands. It is men who are usually taken to court and women who take them there. In 18 months of participant observation in this small project of about 1,200 residents, I heard reports of seven interpersonal disputes in which one party charged the other in court and three more in which court was threatened. (This rate of about 6 per thousand is the average of the town discussed above and far less than in Green Street, but, given the very different ways I gathered information in the two studies, it is not certain that these people actually used the court less than Green Streeters, although it seems possible.) Of the seven filings, four of the plaintiffs were black women, one was a black transvestite boy, one was an elderly white man, and one was George, when he filed a cross-complaint against Renee's brother. When a white woman went to complain to the older black grandmother of a boy who was bothering her daughter, she took her German shepherd with her for protection. As the dog approached, the boy came out with a butcher knife, but his grandmother said, "No, we will handle this legally." She did not file charges, however, but only threatened to.

When these plaintiffs go to court, they find out that little happens. Complaints are likely to be thrown out if they are "family fights." As with the white working class, these people discover that the courts do not treat their interpersonal problems seriously but regard them as trivial or "garbage" cases. After repeated encounters in court, some people in each group come to see the courts as less awesome, powerful, and effective, but that is another story (Merry, 1986). As long as there is the possibility of powerful intervention, people will continue to try. Sometimes plaintiffs among the criminal group get results because the courts and police are trying to catch the people they have accused anyway. If the defendant is a "known troublemaker" the charges are much more likely to produce some results. The police often encourage these plaintiffs to take the step of going to court when the accused is someone they consider a "troublemaker." Catching and identifying a burglar or a robber and building a case that will stick in court is very difficult, but if the police can seize on an existing complaint based on an interpersonal dispute, the problems of firmly identifying the accused evaporate. The police encourage and support this kind of case in order to "get" the men. Of the three cases in which the defendant was either sent to jail or put on probation, each one already had other pending criminal charges against him. The rest of the cases were simply dismissed. Thus, when people have a bad reputation with the police, they are vulnerable to attack through the courts by relatives and neighbors.

Litigation is a weapon in a struggle for these people, no more. There is no talk about justice, fairness, or getting heard by the system. Instead, they talk about particular judges, police officers, probation officers, and their prejudices and peculiarities. As they come to know it better, they regard the system as lenient, riddled with holes, and personalistic. Going to court is a way for women to challenge the power that men exercise over them, and for older people to challenge the power of youths. It is seen as a potentially powerful political strategy, but one that substantially escalates disputes and angers defendants.[5]

These young men and their girlfriends, wives, and female neighbors use the courts in ways that are very similar to those of the white working class. They also see going to court as a symbolically serious step invoking potentially powerful weapons, a strategy to be used in a struggle against a powerful adversary. Neither group sees the law as providing fair and just treatment for all, although the young blacks involved in crime are far more cynical than the working-class whites. Both use the law and, in a sense, demonstrate their acceptance of its legitimate supervision over their lives, more because of its perceived power to help than because of any image of fairness and equal treatment.

The White Upper-Middle Class

In order to develop a broader comparison by social class, I interviewed 35 residents of an affluent suburb outside of Boston about their views of the meaning of going to court with personal problems. They strongly opposed the use of the courts and police for personal problems, emphasizing the value of personal and family privacy, yet they willingly and extensively used lawyers, police, and courts for regulating neighborhood life and property relationships. Indeed, even when they overheard neighbors fighting and screaming at each other, they hesitated to call the police for fear of invading their privacy. Yet they were quite willing to call the police for problems involving noise, dogs, teenage parties, and suspicious outsiders. Ninety-one percent said that they had called the police at some time, and 86% said that someone they knew had called the police. Most thought it was a good idea in certain situations, such as crimes, accidents, or noise in the neighborhood. Most thought that the police were effective. None of the 35 interviewed had been a plaintiff or defendant in court over an interpersonal dispute, but 74% said that they had a lawyer, 86% said they had

[5]Middle-class blacks, both those who lived in this housing project and those I talked to during the mediation research who lived in other neighborhoods, held very different ideas about using the criminal courts for personal problems. Going to court was "like washing your dirty linen in public," something a respectable person would wish to avoid. A medical technician in one mediation program said that she thought people should be handling their own problems, not taking them to court. For these people, court means criminal court, not civil court. Although class is a slippery concept, I suspect that these attitudes reflect more middle-class orientations toward the use of criminal law for personal problems and parallel white middle-class attitudes.

consulted a lawyer at some time, and all said that they knew how to find one. Half (17) said they had been to court in some capacity: 1 in criminal court, 7 in civil court, 4 in divorce court, 1 in small claims court, and 4 in some other setting. Of the 17, 3 had appeared as plaintiffs, 3 as defendants, and the rest as witnesses, jurors, or observers.

The people interviewed were willing to use legal or legalistic strategies to deal with property problems, such as boundaries, trees, building rights, and land use, and with neighborhood annoyances, such as barking dogs or cars left unregistered in driveways. On one street, for example, the neighbors signed a petition complaining about the loud parties of one family's teenage children and presented it to the offenders. One woman said, about taking a case to court: "Everyone has certain rights. If something is radically wrong or against the law, you have to make it known." Several people interviewed said that if they had a problem, they would talk to a lawyer first, and several had friends who were lawyers. For most people, going to court was a possibility only if their rights had been seriously infringed, not for cases of barking dogs, for example. They preferred to call the police or to talk to a lawyer first. In this town, the police are perceived as friendly and effective and the lawyers are likely to be friends or relatives. Thus, these people share with the other two groups the sense that recourse to court is possible, but only for severe problems. They differ, however, in their greater access to private lawyers. They often conceptualize their differences and problems with neighbors in terms of legal categories.

Law, for this neighborhood, meant primarily civil law, and insofar as interpersonal squabbles developed, they were converted into civil cases, much as property disputes in the working-class neighborhood were converted into criminal cases. They were taken to lawyers, who negotiated them privately. The number of restraining orders in domestic violence situations enforced by the police force is about 15% of the number in the first town, although its population is not much larger (35,000 in comparison with 27,000). The homogeneity of the neighborhood, in terms of social class and family structure, and the security of the town's social status reduced the frequency of problems such as dogs, noise, and vandalism, which were a constant source of difficulty in more urban neighborhoods, particularly transitional neighborhoods changing in ethnic, racial, or class identity (Merry, 1987). Homogeneity here was not ethnic but was based on life-style, education, income, and a "professional" identity.

The professional people who live in the town—lawyers, doctors, teachers, business executives—are part of the groups in power that have directly or indirectly shaped legal institutions to conform with their ideas of fairness and justice. The residents of this town are, in a sense, the architects of the law's supervision. They do not support the use of law as a model for ordering intimate social relationships within the family or friendship circle, yet they welcome its supervision of more distant and commercial relationships, even, within limits, relationships between neighbors as these too become distant and instrumental (see also Baumgartner, 1988). They willingly subject themselves to innumerable town regulations about dogs, noise, and unregistered cars, and to elaborate zoning and building codes. They too, along with the two other groups, see themselves entitled to use the police and courts in their social lives, particularly in battles with neighbors and strangers. Although they are more reluctant to seek legal intervention in conflicts with family and friends, this is primarily because they do not want to use a public agency, such as the court, not because they do not see law as useful. They will consult private lawyers. They lack the cynicism and alienation of the other two groups, yet they also view the law as a basic and effective tool for shaping an orderly neighborhood life, and they certainly turn to agents of the law, such as police, for help on innumerable occasions.

Conclusion

People in different social positions, defined by class, race, gender, and experience in court, seem to have somewhat different perspectives on the legitimacy of the law, both in their willingness to use it and in their perceptions of it. Like the blind men examining an elephant in the fable, some of whom saw the elephant as a long, thin object and others as a flat or columnar one, the legal system takes on different appearances depending on where the viewer is standing and what he or she is looking at. Those who are the architects of the legal order regard it with more enthusiasm and are more likely to see it as embodying principles of fairness and justice than those at the bottom who are the objects of its control. Even among groups that use the law, they use different parts: the white working class uses the criminal law, as do the blacks at the fringes of the law, while the affluent suburbanites use civil law and private lawyers.

Underlying these variations is a common implicit understanding of the law as help. For each, the law represents a resource, a service to which they are entitled when rights and interests are seriously threatened. They use it instrumentally, to get things they want. Over time, it becomes for some a familiar strategy. Although the middle- and upper-middle-class people I spoke to spurned the criminal courts for this purpose, they too used legalistic strategies to guarantee individual protection and security, such as zoning ordinances and civil suits. The pronounced element of strategy and pragmatism in the criminal underclass and the white working class is in some ways similar to the way elite lawyers and their clients look at law as a tool to be shaped to particular purposes. While we are accustomed to this stance toward the civil law, here we see users of the criminal law adopting the same approach. We are familiar with this instrumental approach to the law among elite lawyers, who manipulate it to promote their client's interests; here we see the same orientation among other social groups as well.

But the less powerful groups I talked to do not generally think that legal ordering has produced a fair and just society. More often, the law serves as a resource in struggles over control, so that disappointment with its intervention leads to disgust but not to disillusion. Legitimacy has many facets; it is a matter not only of beliefs and values but also of social practices and strategies. Perhaps the power and resilience of the legitimacy of legal authority in American society, despite its failure to live up to its claims of equity and fairness, is the result of its utility as a secular moral authority to which people can turn for help with personal relationships in a society that eschews violence as well as religious authority for dealing with these problems.

ACKNOWLEDGMENTS

The author is grateful to Gray Cavender, Nancy Jurik, Pat Lauderdale, Austin Sarat, and Susan Silbey for insightful comments and suggestions on earlier drafts. The research described in the chapter was supported by a grant from the Law and Social Sciences Program of the National Science Foundation, No. SES 86-06023. Additional funding was provided by the Wellesley College Braitmeyer Foundation Fund, the W. T. Grant Foundation, and the National Institute of Justice and National Science Foundation in earlier grants.

References

Baumgartner, M. P. (1988). The Moral order of a Suburb. New York: Oxford University Press.
Beirne, P. (1979). Ideology and rationality in Max Weber's sociology of law. Research in Law and Sociology, 2, 103–131 (special edition, S. Spitzer (Ed.), JAI Press, Greenwich, CT). Article reprinted (1982) in P. Beirne & R. Quinney (Eds.), Marxism and law (pp. 44–62). New York: Wiley.
Bluestone, B., & Harrison, B. (1982). The deindustrialization of America: Plant closings,

community abandonment, and the dismantling of basic industry. New York: Basic Books.

Cain, M., & Hunt, A. (1979). Marx and Engels on law. New York: Academic Press.

Friedrichs, D. O. (1986). The concept of legitimation and the legal order: A response to Hyde's critique. Justice Quarterly, 3, 33–50.

Gerth, H. H., & Mills, C. W. (1946). From Max Weber: Essays in sociology. New York: Oxford University Press.

Hyde, A. (1983). The concept of legitimation in the sociology of law. Wisconsin Law Review, 379–476.

Kairys, D. (Ed.). (1982). The politics of law: A progressive critique. New York: Pantheon.

Kronman, A. T. (1983). Max Weber. Stanford, CA: Stanford University Press.

Lachmann, R. (1986). The cultural bases of legal legitimacy: Edgerton's Pictures and punishment. American Bar Foundation Research Journal, 301–313.

McEwen, C., & Maiman, R. (1986). In search of legitimacy: Toward an empirical analysis. Law and Policy, 8, 257–273.

Merry, S. E. (1981). Urban danger: Life in a neighborhood of strangers. Philadelphia: Temple University Press.

Merry, S. E. (1986). Everyday understandings of the law in working-class America. American Ethnologist, 13, 253–270.

Merry, S. E. (1987). Crowding, conflict and neighborhood regulation. In I. Altman & A. Wandersman (Eds.), Neighborhood and community environments (pp. 35–69). New York: Plenum.

Merry, S. E., & Rocheleau, A. M. (1985). Mediation in families: A study of the children's hearings project. Cambridge, MA: Cambridge Family and Children's Services.

Scheingold, S. A. (1974). The politics of rights: Lawyers, public policy, and political change. New Haven: Yale University Press.

Sheehan, B. (1984). The Boston school integration dispute. New York: Columbia University Press.

Silbey, S. S. (1981). Making sense of the lower courts. Justice System Journal, 6, 13–27.

Sumner, C. (1979). Reading ideologies: An investigation into the Marxist theory of ideology and law. London: Academic Press.

Susser, I. (1982). Norman Street: Poverty and politics in an urban neighborhood. New York: Oxford University Press.

Silbey, S. S., and Merry, S. E. (1986). Mediator settlement strategies. Law and Policy, 8, 7–32.

Thompson, E. P. (1982). The rule of law, reprinted from Whigs and hunters: The origin of the black acts. In P. Beirne & R. Quinney (Eds.), Marxism and law (pp. 130–138). New York: Wiley.

Trubek, D. M. (1984). Where the action is: Critical legal studies and empiricism. Stanford Law Review, 36, 575–622.

Tyler, T. R. (1986). Justice, legitimacy, and compliance. Paper presented at the Law and Society Association Meetings, Chicago.

Tyler, T. R. (1987). What is procedural justice? Criteria used by citizens is assess the fairness of legal procedures. Law and Society Review, 22, 103–137.

Weber, M. (1978). Economy and society (G. Roth & C. Wittich, Trans.). Berkeley: University of California Press.

Yngvesson, B. (1985). Legal ideology and community justice in the clerk's office. Legal Studies Forum, 9, 71–89.

CHAPTER 9

The Origin of Order and the Dynamics of Justice

Laura Nader

Introduction

In the United States, discourse on law and order are often juxtaposed to discourse on social justice. Indeed, throughout American history, corrective justice (as with punishment) has often been found in opposition to distributive justice (as when all individuals get their fair share in life). Proponents of corrective justice call for law and order to prevent disruption of the social order, while opponents look to social justice as the means for creating a more orderly social system. Some have explained the disagreements over order and justice as rooted in the pluralistic nature of American society (Pound, 1906). Others have argued that what you see depends upon where you sit (Black, 1976; Chambliss, 1982; Nader, 1986). Whatever the origin of the dissensus, debates about order are really debates about justice. However, it may be that discourse centered on law and order or social justice does little more than sustain the status quo, while discussion of injustice would force an examination of concrete events rather than abstract ideals and interrupt the oscillation between government programs to cure law and order problems and government programs to address questions of social injustice. The central question of this chapter is a conceptual one—what type of discourse would work to produce needed social transformations. As I will show, discussions centering on order will not do because it is possible to have order without justice. It may also be true that discussions focusing on justice would not work to produce social transformations because a discussion of justice

LAURA NADER • Department of Anthropology, University of California, Berkeley, Berkeley, California 94720.

centers on abstract ideals. Instances of injustice, on the other hand, reveal the impediments to both order and justice.

My purpose here is to critically examine the relationships between concepts such as law and order, and law and justice—concepts that have been coupled so frequently in the rhetoric of law that they have seemed to be inseparable. Those who see the social system as *just* argue that the law must maintain order so that the existing social structure can be preserved. Those who believe that social inequities sustain an *unjust* social system argue for government programs to remedy injustice. Each has a way of speaking about law as principally related to order or to justice. Advocates of law and order believe that order can be maintained by controlling deviants through enforcement machinery. Advocates of justice, however, pursue the same goal by ridding the system of inequities they deem unjust through the use of the courts or Congress. Supporters of both these positions utilize government social engineering to achieve their goals without having to alter the basic design of an industrial structure that hides the inequalities of income, race, gender, and age.

Discourse on law and order also obfuscates issues of injustice by associating disorder solely with street crime, despite increased public awareness of the high incidence of white-collar and business crime in the United States. American citizens have had to deal with the contradictions of a model emphasizing vindictiveness in handling selected classes of defendants, and leniency in dealing with the powerful (Nader, 1986). The resulting social tensions are components of the dynamics that move public policy from social reforms (like the New Deal) to harsher penalties for "criminals" and extrajudicial alternatives (like the Alternative Dispute Resolution movement) for civil cases. The voices of the victims or potential litigants are not fashioning change policies; instead, one has the feeling that it is the dialogue between the order people and the social justice people that stimulates the oscillation between poles, that for the most part do not address the origin of order problems.

What has been missing in the debate is an adequate testing of the assumptions about order theories or about social justice theories. Is it true, for example, that more law or more law enforcement automatically leads to more order? It is true that government programs for the victims permanently alter their position in society?

It is now well recognized in the social science literature that order is not solely, or even most commonly, achieved by law enforcement policies, or those akin to the New Deal. Order and disorder are largely the products of the social and cultural systems within which they occur, and of the ways in which these systems address patterns of injustice. In many of the societies studied by anthropologists, order is found in the absence of courts, police, and the like. We have discovered a wide range of checks upon human conduct that contribute to societal ordering without being coupled to social scale, complexity, or national wealth. As I will explicate in the following section, a small Mexican Zapotec community may regulate violence and disruption effectively, but small New Guinea villages (or Eskimo villages) seem unable to control their violence. Communist China was able to achieve a state of social order in which vandalism, juvenile delinquency, rape, murder, and theft are rare. In the United States, however, we have increasing (albeit fluctuating) rates of street and corporate crime, despite public policies aimed at resolving problems of crime. The relationship between social structure and social order is one that merits increasing attention at least to understand the varieties of social orders.

Implicit in the relationship between social order and justice is a second assumption, one that relates order to justice. Data indicate that the two are not coupled; the presence of order does not correlate with the presence of justice, nor does the absence of social order necessarily indicate an absence of justice. As we know, fascism may provide order without achieving individual or social justice, while democratic states may maintain order while ignoring social inequities based on class, race, or sex. Yet the rhetoric of law becomes important in those societies where the people's demand for justice is not being met because of their position in the social structure, or, more specifically, because of the existing legal system. Lawrence Friedman (1975) comments on the rhetoric of the 1960s and 1970s by focusing on legal rights:

> At present, the United States seems to be passing through a time of accelerated demand, of volcanic eruption in claims of right. . . . The "rights explosion" is revolutionary but in a peculiar way. Many of the "rebels" do not feel themselves rebellious at all. They ask only what is coming to them legally and ethically. The minorities demand mainly that society take down barriers which kept them from enjoying their rights. The claim is revolutionary only because a whole social system grew on the assumption that they would not claim or demand certain rights. (p. 232)

It is at this point that the discourse reflects the "groups and classes and interests, understanding each other none too well" that Dean Roscoe Pound spoke about in 1906 (pp. 399). The conflicting ideas of justice are related to *order* on the one hand and *injustice* on the other.

Order and Social Structure: Four Examples

In 1926 the eminent anthropologist Bronislaw Malinowski argued that the rights and obligations that bind people together serve to maintain social order. Malinowski (1926) had studied the Trobrianders, a

Pacific Islands people who had no law as we understand it, but nevertheless had law. As he states:

> The rules of law . . . are sanctioned not by a mere psychological motive,
> but by a definite social machinery of binding force, based, as we know,
> upon mutual dependence, and realized in the equivalent arrangement of
> reciprocal services, as well as in the combination of such claims into strands
> of multiple relationships. The ceremonial manner in which most transac-
> tions are carried out, which entails public control and criticism, adds still
> more to their binding force. (p. 55)

The idea that social organization and its underlying ideology (the
principle of reciprocity among the Trobrianders) is the same as a system of social control is not new today. Most ethnographic studies
demonstrate how social life is conducted by means of regulated arrangements of social relations, like corporate kin groups, which coor-
dinate social activities and maintain order, or which sabotage collective cooperation through factionalism or feud.

The influence of social organization on the maintenance of order
can be identified by comparing two villages—one orderly, one violent.
In the mountain Zapotec village of Talea, Mexico, I have identified
the forces of social organization that contribute to order (Nader, 1990).
Klaus Koch, on the other hand, examined the social organization of a
village in the mountains of West Irian New Guinea—a social organization with few institutions for the peaceful settlement of disputes,
where conflicts were likely to escalate into serious societal disrup-
tions (Koch, 1974).

In the social organization of Talea, the ties linking citizens are ties
of kinship, locale, common work interests, friendships, and shared
obligations and values. These ties are organized by principles of social
control operating outside of any governmental organizations. The
principles are related to hierarchy (vertical integration), leveling (horizontal integration), and cross-linkage (composite integration).

First, all groups in Talea, whether kin, governmental, or religious,
are ranked hierarchically on the basis of sex, age, wealth, and/or experience. Family members are ranked by sex, generation, and age. In
the civil and religious organizations, a ladder system prevails. In moving up the ladder, individuals assume more responsibility, authority,
and respect. How far they climb, and the number of positions in which
they serve before retirement, varies with the size of the town and the
qualifications of the candidate. Since this hierarchy involves rank relationships, where each person's role is defined as subordinate to the
one above, leveling, influenced by the value placed on symmetry (or
equality), may be seen as complementary.

The concept of leveling operates in many of the hierarchical relationships described above. Leveling mechanisms mediate the harsher aspects of hierarchy, without undermining the virtues of superordinate/subordinate relationships. In the family, for example, older brothers have authority over younger brothers, yet all children are supposed to inherit equally. While women owe obedience to their husbands, when they separate, the man is expected to pay the woman retroactively for her service as housekeeper if she asks for it. The richer people in the village must bear the cost of fiestas—again a leveling device. Among these mountain Zapotec, it is both unappealing and dangerous to be too rich, too poor, too pretty, or too ugly. Asymmetry (or inequality) is often the underlying cause of envy, witchcraft accusations, or disputes in court. So leveling lessens the likelihood of disputes arising as a result of social inequality.

The dimension of cross-linkage is to be found in the village social structure, unlike the dimensions of hierarchy and leveling that permeate daily activities. Cross-linkage brings a number of people together, integrates them as groups or individuals while also dividing them by linking some of them with different groups. Members of the same savings and loan associations are not also members of the same musical organization. People living in the same section of town share membership in the savings and loan association with people from other parts of Talea.

The exact manner in which hierarchy, symmetry, and cross-linkage operate as social control mechanisms is affected by internal and external changes and by individual-to-individual relations. Stresses, strains, and divisive activity usually result in conflicts that end up in court or functionally equivalent settings. This occurs because (1) the above-described dimensions of Talean social organization are insufficient to control certain behavior, (2) this behavior falls outside the controlling influence of these dimensions, or (3) specific standards of conduct are neither homogeneous nor universally shared. In all of these contexts, including the legal one, the dimensions of hierarchy and symmetry serve to buttress traditional and contemporary values (which may often conflict), while cross-linkages ensure the presence of third parties to handle disputes both inside and outside the courtroom. Third-party dispute-settlement mechanisms cannot develop without a social organization characterized by links and cross-links between individuals and groups. The social structure is built on patterns of groups and relations that act as a shield against the escalation of conflict.

The intrinsic nature of certain types of social structures in different societies may promote or discourage conflict by determining the ways in which people handle disputes. For example, Talea is a village populated by individuals who, over time, came from outside of the region and from other villages in the region. It is likely that people moved as individuals or, at most, as nuclear families. This, in turn, probably encouraged the proliferation of secondary nonkin groups to act as backup supports in the absence of extended families. Taleans evolved what, in another context, anthropologist Alfred Kroeber (1917) referred to as a "marvelous complexity guaranteed to guard against segmentation, rift, or fission" (pp. 86–87). In Talea, the musicians' groups, the savings and loan associations, and the patrons are all potential dividing agencies if their members were not linked in other ways as well.

In contrast with Talea, any conflict can escalate into a war among the Jale of Western New Guinea. Klaus Koch (1978) informs us that "the political realities of interpersonal and intergroup relations often make it difficult to settle conflict by peaceful means" (p. 41). The Jale are a farming people who live in villages divided into two or more wards. Each village consists of residential compounds containing clusters of domiciles, the largest being the men's house, with smaller housing built for married women and their uninitiated sons and unmarried daughters. The wards form the principal war-making units in intravillage and intervillage conflicts. There are no political and judicial offices, and so self-help—often in the form of violent retaliation—is an institutionalized method of conflict resolution when negotiation fails. As Koch describes the situation: "If a confrontation develops into a fight between parties' supporters and someone suffers an injury, the skirmish may mark the beginning of a round of battles and retaliatory raids lasting for weeks, months, and even years" (p. 41).

Escalation is a common experience for the Jale. In Jale law, liability is not only absolute but also corporate—i.e., shared by the agnatic kin group of the party whose action caused the injury. They also do not distinguish between intent, negligence, inadvertence, and accident as aggravating or extenuating circumstances. Under these conditions, orderly social life is precarious, and Koch details how devastating a single conflict can be for continuing peaceful relations within and between communities. In addition, Koch (1978) found that Jale conflict management is inadequate for several reasons. Inadequate procedures to deal with grievances create what he terms a "snowball effect." If there are no authorities capable of settling conflicts, then even minor disagreements may escalate into war between whole villages. A second problem is that every retaliation has the potential of generating new disputes. The only checks against this volatile situation are provided by kinship and residence, which are not strong enough to prevent escalation of any particular conflict.

Koch's study supports my contention that the style of conflict resolution and the incidence of conflict both derive from a society's principles of human association. Koch (1974) concludes that the lack of a third party institution and the correlated prevalence of violent self-help to obtain redress result from a combination of interrelated sociological and psychological factors; namely, the absence of cross-cutting group affiliations, the formation of corporate agnatic power groups, the existence of multiple, independent, political units within a local community, and patterns of socialization that develop an aggressive and vindictive personality" (p. 166).

The observation of disorder and, particularly, violent confrontation has led Koch to seek and identify the social and cultural preconditions for such phenomena. His question as to what has stunted the institutionalization of peaceful means of dispute settlement among the Jale was addressed by analyzing order and disorder in the broadest social context rather than viewing violence as a psychopathology or genetic abnormality.

The Zapotec and the Jale suggest how order may be maintained and how disorder may be generated by the social structure in small-scale societies. Examples of large-scale societies could be used to illustrate the same point. Communist China and the United States are examples of large-scale societies. In comparing the two states, I will rely partly on Victor Li's (1977) monograph *Law without Lawyers*. According to Li, in Communist China there is an underlying principle that the law should be broadly based rather than the province of elite professionals. The Chinese system reflects the belief common to the Confucian tradition that a ruler should govern through virtue rather than law, and operates under the assumption that more laws do not create a better or more harmonious society. Courts in the People's Republic of China are feared and avoided. Instead, the massive program of public education about law through the media is a major source of legal norms. The nonlegal areas of childhood and adult socialization processes, religious influences, and education are also very important aspects of Chinese "criminal law." According to Li, it is difficult to distinguish between the manner in which a "criminal" matter is handled and the treatment of a social, moral, or political matter. Thus, a person who punches his neighbor might be treated very much like someone who is lazy at work or neglectful of children. As Li states:

> Lacking both a large number of lawyers and an active judiciary, the Chinese legal system obviously does not perform the same functions as the American legal system. This does not mean that problems dealt with by legal mechanisms in the United States do not arise in China, or that they arise

but are neglected. On the contrary . . . these problems are handled by a
different group of actors and institutions employing a different set of methods. (p. 31)

Chinese law focuses on prevention instead of waiting for criminal
acts to occur before dealing with them. Li describes the handling of
deviancy in the United States as analogous to falling off a cliff, whereas
in China, the handling of deviancy is referred to as sliding to the bottom. His point relates to prevention. In China, potential deviants receive help at the early stage of deviance rather than after they have
committed a serious antisocial act. Laymen play a very important role
in this process. One county with a population of over half a million
had 300 police and several thousand neighborhood volunteers. The
many eyes in the community serve to control the incidence of crime.

An important observation that Li makes is related to the existence
of community in Chinese rural and urban areas. There is little mobility in Chinese cities; each neighborhood has a formal social organization that regulates local relationships and responsibilities. Chinese society appreciates the importance of individuals while placing greater
emphasis on their relationship to the larger group.

The point of the comparisons presented thus far is not to roman-
ticize or idealize or denigrate. My intent is first to question widely
held assumptions about law and order in the United States. More police do not automatically reduce the crime rate, more lawyers do not
necessarily provide more order and justice, and small communities
are not always peaceful. Furthermore, a high crime rate may be a
symptom of injustice.

The second objective is to underline the close association between the presence of order and peaceableness through law and forms
of social organization. Certain forms of human association, ties that
bind and cross-link, act as brakes on the escalation of conflicts and,
indeed, may prevent them from occurring. In contrast, we have seen
that a social organization of two opposing factions may induce confrontation and preclude the presence of third-party action. We have
also learned that in complex societies, crime is not a necessary fact of
life but something that results from the structuring of human groups,
and their approach to the problem of order may be changed by human
groups. The Chinese example is an experiment in the use of human
groups to prevent deviant behavior or reduce its socially harmful potential in the absence of either great numbers of police or lawyers but
with the strong backing of a state structure. In our own society we
may have developed a social organization that encourages the kind of
criminal behavior that cannot be remedied by more police or more
lawyers, judges, prisons, and regulatory agencies. The evolution of this

social organization may be traced by presenting an outline of changing New England towns.

The history of New England towns demonstrates that changes in the social organization, culture, and economy of these communities have contributed toward an increase in the incidence of crime and/or disorder. Historian Michael Zuckerman (1970) describes the principles and ideology connected with the peacefulness to be found in these communities. He identifies the patterns of shifting authority between the villages, the government at Boston, and the mother country, and describes how village governance finally rested in the villages themselves prior to the Revolution. He describes the closely packed settlements as having a premium on peace, and on the strict control of aggression. These are consensual communities; the Puritan had an obligation to think for himself, but also to think as his neighbors thought. This stress on harmony and homogeneity probably goes as far back as the founding of the Massachusetts Bay Company, whose advice to new colony leaders was to be careful to maintain peace and unity and to suppress disputes.

While historians may argue that Zuckerman's findings are more applicable to the 17th century (see Kenneth Lockridge, 1970), the picture of New England society is the direct antithesis of Victor Li's (1977) description of United States law in the 20th century. Public welfare was given priority over private interest, and unity was seen as the source of public happiness. The townspeople avoided appearing before the judiciary because their practice of seeking peaceful solutions to disputes was not within the law. These towns had no real capacity for coercion or opposition. Public opinion had to be unanimous, and mutual consent meant something more than majority rule. The social organization of these towns implied what historians have argued was a disdain for direct democracy, not a model for the United States in the 20th century, which is based neither on homogeneity nor on the concept of class exclusivity.

Residents of these towns—those born there and disciplined from childhood, and those who had passed the elaborate entrance requirements—defined their identity in terms of social solidarity. They proclaimed peaceful communion as the predominant public value, and they used the town meeting as a place where consensus was reached on issues and where individual disagreements were subordinated to group opinion. When there were disputes, the remedy was accommodation and conciliation. Highways were built or improved on the request of the townsmen they would serve, and with the assistance of the whole town. Accommodation was made in potentially disruptive areas—taxes were remitted for villagers furthest from facilities, and

towns that had only one schoolhouse refunded a portion of the rebates
to the parents of those children who could not easily attend. Separation from the community was the ultimate solution to disputes that
could not be handled by accommodation and conciliation. Splinter-
ings of settlements occurred from the very early years. As Zuckerman
(1970) notes:

> The culture simply could not contain conflict . . . discord dictated divi-
> sion because division could restore peace. So for differences in religion,
> occupation, ethnic origin or anything else, hiving off was seen as the only
> solution. Harmony required homogeneity; there was no possibility of
> structural diversity. Order then is structured in these towns by values of
> harmony and homogeneity in both the political and religious spheres by
> consensus rather than majoritanism. Peace here was not just a character-
> istic or a byproduct; it was a peace consciously structured, a peace which
> tolerated no differences. (p. 139)

These towns had no place for cultural pluralism and demographic
diversity, no compassion for the downtrodden or tolerance for
dissenters.

Changes in the social organization of New England towns and the
ensuing changes in law and order are also revealed through the history of the small mill town in Connecticut in which I was born and
brought up. In the early 19th century, this was an agricultural town,
essentially homogeneous, and in many ways not too different from
what Zuckerman describes for an earlier period. During the 1930s,
this town was bustling with activity; the solid red-brick factories were
the scenes of action. With immigration, and then industrialization, there
was an increase in occupational, ethnic, and religious diversity. Yet it
was a time of plenty. Economically the town was booming, and order
was not a serious problem, although ethnic and religious differences
were reflected in the issues discussed at town meetings. By the time I
went to college, however, companies had already started moving out
of New England and into the South, where labor was cheaper.

Today, New England is still trying to recover from the mass exo-
dus of the factories built at the end of the last century. My town has
become essentially a bedroom community to the state capital and other
industrial zones in Connecticut. The town itself is characterized by
loss of pride in local culture, high and chronic unemployment, depen-
dency, and families who no longer share space in the same town by
day, while visually the place has fallen into decay. The increase in
drug consumption, sometimes associated with the increased incidence of delinquency, is a common pattern, along with burglary and
people worrying about break-ins. The police are now highly equipped,
impersonal, and trained in urban areas for urban problems that they

themselves, sometimes unwittingly, help create in this small town. There is little community—the population is dependent on other towns for employment, court services, and hospital services, on the state for unemployment, and on the federal government for subsidies.

Here Li's observations do apply. Private interest has come to supersede public interest—a trend justified by the belief that society ultimately benefits from the pursuit of individual gain (Dumont, 1977). Despite the large number of legal actors, unless one is fairly wealthy or very poor, legal and extralegal services are inadequate. The most visible sign of law in my hometown are the police—not lawyers, judges, courts, or anything else. All of the problems existing here are exaggerated several hundredfold in our cities. Our process of industrialization has meant that the social system has been restructured increasingly around the individual, rather than around such groups as the family, neighborhood, or entire community. The traditional communal values of American culture that used to dominate social life, have now become subordinated to individualism (Bellah, Madsen, Sullivan, Swidler, & Tipton, 1984). We now have laws that are not being applied and courts that cannot be used. We have increasing numbers of legal personnel who confront a persistently high crime rate in the corporate suites as well as in the streets. And, as we will see, the recommendations for alternative dispute-resolution mechanisms to deal with these problems continue to approach them as cases of individual justices rather than developing aggregate solutions that join remedies for particular complaints with prevention of their causes. New directions in law would entail expanding the debate over law and order to include concerns not normally the fare of legal scholars.

Justice and Social Structure: The American Case

In my discussion of order in the first section, I have focused on order as the absence of conflict. When we move to a discussion of the relationship between order and social structure, we are focusing on order in a different sense. The concept of social structure implies a focus on the regular, repetitious patterns of behavior—those things that make social life appear "ordered" to the observer. The discussion of justice focuses on people's subjective evaluation of the fairness of this system of order.

The evolution of social structure and its relation to justice as perceived by participants in the system can be illustrated from a decade of research on economic grievances that focused on the process of consumer complaints (Nader, 1979, 1980). In this work, I examined the ways in which Americans voiced their complaints about products and services, the little injustices that plagued their lives because they were not so little. In their quest for justice, these people reacted with outrage, shock, and anger, and in the final analysis with hopelessness and disappointment. As one consumer said in the film Little Injustices, "There's gotta be some justice somewhere."

A striking case that we investigated concerned a stove that turned itself on and off unexpectedly. By the time the owner sent Ralph Nader her 3 inch thick packet of correspondence, she still could not claim to have attracted the helpful attention of those to whom she had written: the seller, the producer, the utilities, and a dozen government offices. Finally, her house burned down in a fire caused by the defective stove.

In our analyses of thousands of cases, we found that the very advertising techniques and packaging devices that companies use to sell their products are the source of people's expectations of justice—and also of their widespread disillusionment and lack of faith. The very fact that people of all socioeconomic classes write complaint letters is an indication that they are motivated to write by a sense of injustice rather than by simple economic need. One does begin to believe in the existence of a universal justice motive, particularly on observing that when people do receive an honorable response from a company or a service, they are willing to give credence and are glad to discover that decency still exists.

In a study done as part of our overall research on how Americans complain about products and services, Best and Andreasen (1977) found that when consumers do take their problems to third parties (in about 1.2% of the cases) they come away satisfied only about one-third of the time. One reason is the extreme inequality of power between complainer and complainee, which permits producers to wage psychological warfare against those who complain. For instance, a strong anticomplaint ethic is part of the ideology sold to consumers along with goods and services ("You're the first person to complain"). Complaintants are labeled deviants. Another factor in the failure of complaint mechanisms is that some of our most cherished values—the primacy of the individual, the principle of confidentiality—can get in the way.

The enormous toll of unresolved complaints is now well documented. Unresolved complaints have a pernicious effect on the machinery of government, on the mental health of citizens, and on the crime rate. Grievance feeds frustration, anxiety, and friction. Living with an intermittently unreliable product produces repeated psychological strain, because one does not know what might go wrong next. Grievances waste money, time, and resources for individuals and for the economy in general. Moreover, the lack of prosecution serves to encourage criminal behavior among those who, consciously or unconsciously, capitalize on the fact that the American criminal-justice system is not organized to handle what, in some cases, amounts to widespread petty thievery accomplished by small economic crimes against individuals and, in other cases, results in the loss of life.

The historical events that have led to the present economic grievance process are a necessary part of any descriptive theory of the relationship between injustice and social structure. As I have indicated in earlier work (Nader, 1984a), the American justice system did not adjust to the changing relationship between producers and consumers over the past 300 years. As the primary economic activity in the United States switched from subsistence agriculture to industry and the roles of consumer and producer became separated, the balance of power shifted. The absolute powder that consumers had previously enjoyed by also being the producers of what they consumed diminished with the separation of roles. By the latter part of the 19th century, the greater power of producers over consumers could be measured by their organization of personnel and resources, by the quantity of complaints received and left unsettled, and by the number of social movements created to remedy this power shift (Nader, 1980). The state became a participant in mediating issues raised by consumers and took an interest in basic needs: food and drugs, dairy products, prices, truth in advertising. The issues voiced by consumers were viewed by the government as concerns common to this class of people. These problems were addressed not as individual ones but as class problems to be remedied by legislative and regulatory action. Consumer issues were the law-and-order problem of the day. By the late 20th century, however, the absolute power positions of consumers, producers, and government have changed. Now, both organized producers and organized government have considerably more power than dispersed consumers, and the strength of each of these parties varies with their respective access to legal services. Regulatory procedures set up by the political government were not structured to handle minor economic complaints that involve major economic crime. Procedures set up by the corporate economic government were based on an ideology and organization designed to minimize long-term gains for complaints.

The one-by-one approach to complaints gained favor with the growth of government bureaucratization in the 20th century that accompanied the increasing erosion of the consumers, status, and influence. The issue was no longer class justice but individual justice, for as producers became distanced from consumers, consumers themselves became distanced from one another.

In 1906 Dean Roscoe Pound made the observation: "Our administration of justice is not decadent. It is simply behind the times" (p. 416). He might not be so generous were he alive today. If law is to respond to justice—that is, to human needs and the equitable distribution of rights, opportunities, and remedies—then the manner of practicing law would be different.

Over the past decade from 1976 to 1986, there has been a quiet revolution in American law. Prompted by the Office of the Chief Justice of the U.S. Supreme Court, Justice Warren Burger, the Alternative Dispute Resolution movement has swept into American law schools and across the nation. Extrajudicial procedures were to replace courts as forums for justice. While our assessment of this revolution is still in process, some results are clear: The law is being increasingly privatized, the lives of individual Americans are subject to more state control, while citizen participation has not grown (Abel, 1982; Nader, 1984b). These extrajudicial alternatives provide no increased provisions for remedy, display little interest in prevention, and exert more control over potential litigants (Abel, 1982; Nader, 1980). This movement was a response to the "explosion" in the demand for rights described by Lawrence Friedman (see page 191 above). In the recent words of Chief Justice Burger (1984):

> Our distant forebears moved slowly from trial by battle and other barbaric means of resolving conflicts and disputes, and we must move away from total reliance on the adversary context for resolving all disputes. For some disputes, trial will be the only means, but for many, trials by the adversary context must in time go the way of ancient trial by battle and blood. Our system is too costly, too painful, too destructive, too inefficient for a truly civilized people. To rely on the adversary contest as the principal means of resolving disputes is a mistake that must be corrected. (p. 66)

In the same address, the chief justice refers to representatives of private justice institutions that strive to formulate compromise solutions as "healers of conflict" (p. 66). Notice the words the chief justice uses. He is interested in efficiency, in compromise, in healing. There is no mention of injustice.

During 1985–1986, I directed the research of a young anthropologist interested in pursuing the meaning of the phrase "healers of conflict." Bjorn Claeson (1986) explored the privatization of justice by studying a private justice corporation, located in the San Francisco Bay area, whose purpose is to manage the worker compensation claims for a large corporation. Claeson examined the relationship between the worker and the private justice "healers" and explored the conceptions of illness among the injured workers within the worker compensation procedure. Early in his study he maintains:

As these healers are in fact hired by the Esco Corporation to defend its interests, they are in reality antagonists to injured workers. Injured workers are then visible to their actual antagonists. It is their visibility that makes them controllable; it permits a nonviolent, but efficient control. Furthermore, as the patient-healer relationship conceals the antagonism between employer-employee (private justice) representatives are in effect invisible—unknown—to injured workers. Control is then covert and exercised anonymously, and cannot be effectively resisted. Consequently, Esco can realize its goal, namely, to reduce its costs in worker's compensation payments.

Claeson points out in his conclusion that the ethic of treatment has replaced the ethic of right and wrong, only in the situation at hand *it is not the legally insane defendant in criminal law cases that is being treated, but the legally sane plaintiff in civil law cases*. Treatment by means of the harmony model facilitates a control of injured workers by fictionalizing the conflict between the worker and the corporation. According to the "healers," conflict is nothing but confusion and misunderstanding that can be dissolved by proper communication. Claeson goes on to explain how he believes the transformation in ethics from right and wrong to treatment has occurred since the turn of the century, and he concludes, "When the ethic of treatment is dominant, the existence of conflict is no longer relevant for determining a course of action" (p. 78). And I would add that when we do not recognize the conflict, we are once again masking injustice. As Zuckerman (1970) said of the 18th century: "The culture . . . could not contain conflict. . . . Harmony required homogeneity; there was no possibility of structural diversity" (p. 139). The continuity is striking.

Injustice and the Transformation of Order

Discussion of both order and justice have a static quality about them. Both order and justice are abstractions. Both bring to mind an ideal set of standards, an ideal society, an ideal solution, more procedural and immediate than far-reaching. But as Edmond Cahn (1964) has observed, "the response to a real or imagined instance of injustice is something quite different; it is alive with movement and warmth . . ." (p. 13). "Justice," Cahn tells us, "means the active process of remedying or preventing what would arouse the sense of injustice" (pp. 13–14).

The dynamics of justice then require us to look at specific instances of injustice, to remedy or prevent. Neither the vocabulary of law and order nor the vocabulary of justice accomplishes this task; rather they serve to maintain the status quo. In discussions of the origin of order, attention is paid to principles of association. Discussions of justice lead to treatment rather than the prevention of wrongs. But a concern with social injustice leads inevitably to a concrete instance. It is his attention to injustice that led Cahn to define justice as an active process. Yet his discussion reflects a contradiction—perhaps it is only by means of social injustice that people can be mobilized to change. Justice is contemplative; a concern with wrongs in dynamic, linked with change rather than status quo.

Discussions of order elicit passivity rather than action. It is creative disorder that will promote needed social transformation. For example, a complaint about the production of Ford Pintos could spark a "disordering" in the American automobile industry. The adovcates of corrective versus distributive justice in the debate on law and order described in the introduction are one and the same. Both parties are interested in maintaining order and the existing social structure, albeit by different methods. Insight by centering attention on injustice would distinguish injustice from the act of assault (whether being mugged in Central Park or being engulfed in flames from a Ford Pinto, known to be defective during production) from the injustice experienced by the absence of remedy for the victim of the assault (as in the inability of a worker to receive adequate compensation for work injuries). It is not law and order that is at issue in the dynamics of justice but law and injustice and order and injustice. In my research on the economic grievances of consumers, it is the consumer's concern with injustice that has changed the relative power of consumers vis-à-vis government and business, necessary as a prelude to change. Things seem to change in history when people no longer accept the usual discourse strategies, in this case involving the concepts of order and justice rather than injustice.

Two directions for fundamental transformation are suggested in this essay. The first has to do with an American conception of order. When Americans realize that we need not be trapped in the binary opposites of more state control versus more crime, our options will increase. We can choose to lessen industrial violence by transforming the structure and organization of the industrial corporation, with its limits on the freedom of internal dissent, and its relentless focus on short-term profits. New directions for public problem-solving in the area of street crime could impel us to discuss once again for our times the Commons and its relation to community and family fragmentation, alienation, inequality, and unrestrained competition in the marketplace, all related to overall societal order. The second direction has to do with the automobile industry; disorder generated by a sense of injustice may be the force that keeps industry creative and innovative. Fundamental transformations in the social order will occur when Americans realize that we need not be trapped in the binary opposites of more state control versus more crime. An important part of change is the vocabulary we use in elaborating change directions. Law and order theorists would become community breakdown theorists, justice philosophers would become injustice specialists, and rights specialists would make room for wrongs specialists. The terms we use shape the policies for change as the questions shape our theories. How is the fact that we speak regularly about order and about justice affecting the analysis and practice of law? How would it be different if we spoke about law and injustice, and wrongs? Sometimes things will change when we break out of accustomed ways of discoursing. Imagine a department of injustice.

References

Abel, R. (Ed.) (1982). *The politics of informal justice, Vol. 1. The American experience.* New York: Academic Press.

Bellah, R., Madsen, R., Sullivan, W. M., Swidler, A., & Tipton, S. M. (1984). *Habits of the heart.* Berkeley: University of California Press.

Best, A., & Andreason, A. R. (1977). Consumer responses to unsatisfactory purchases: A survey of perceiving defects, voicing complaints and obtaining redress. *Law and Society Review, 11,* 701–742.

Black, D. (1976). *The behavior of law.* New York: Academic Press.

Burger, W. E. (1984). The state of justice. *American Bar Association Journal, 70* (April).

Cahn, E. (1964). *The sense of injustice.* Bloomington: Indiana University Press.

Chambliss, W. J. (1982). Toward a radical criminology. In D. Kairys (Ed.), *The politics of law.* New York: Pantheon.

Claeson, B. (1986). *The privatization of justice: An ethnography of control.* Honors thesis, University of California, Berkeley.

Dumont, L. (1977). *From Mandeville to Marx.* Chicago: Chicago University Press.

Friedman, L. M. (1975). *The legal system: A social science perspective.* New York: Russell Sage Foundation.

Koch, K.-F. (1974) *War and peace in Jalemo: The management of conflict in highland New Guinea.* Cambridge, MA: Harvard University Press.

Koch, K.-F. (1978). Pigs and politics in the New Guinea highlands: Conflict escalation among the Jale. In L. Nader & H. L. Todd (Eds.), *The disputing process* (pp. 41–58). New York: Columbia University Press.

Kroeber, A. L. (1917). Zuni Kin and clan. In *Anthropological papers, XVIII.* New York: American Museum of Natural History.

Li, V. (1977). *Law without lawyers: A comparative view of law in China and the United States.* Stanford Alumni Association, pp. 1–103.

Lockridge, K. (1970). A New England town: The first hundred years. New York: Norton.

Malinowski, B. (1926). Crime and custom in savage society. London: Routledge.

Nader, L. (1964). Talea and Juquila: A comparison of Zapotec social organization. University of California Publications in American Archaeology and Ethnology, 48(3), 195–296.

Nader, L. (1974). Perspectives on the law and order problem. In M. Lerner & M. Ross (Eds.), The quest for justice: Myth, reality, ideal (pp. 65–81). Toronto: Holt, Rinehart & Winston of Canada.

Nader, L. (1979). Disputing without the force of law. Yale Law Journal, 88(Special Issue on Dispute Resolution), 998–1021.

Nader, L. (1980). No access to law. New York: Academic Press.

Nader, L. (1984a). From disputing to complaining. In D. Black (Ed.), Toward a general theory of social control (pp. 71–94). New York: Academic Press.

Nader, L. (1984b). A user theory of law. Southwestern Law Review, 38(4), 951–963.

Nader, L. (1986). Enforcement strategies and the catch they yield at the SEC. Harvard Law Review, 99(6), 1362–1373.

Nader, L. (1988). The ADR explosion—the implications of rhetoric in legal reform. Windsor yearbook of access to Justice. Windsor, Ontario, Canada.

Nader, L. (1990). Harmony ideology: justice and control in a Zapotic mountain village. Stanford: Stanford University Press.

Nader, L. & Sursock, A. (1986). Anthropology and justice. In R. L. Cohen (Ed.), Justice: Views from the social sciences (pp. 205–233). New York: Plenum.

Pound, R. (1906). The causes of popular dissatisfaction with the administration of justice. American Bar Association Report, Part 1, 29, 395–417.

Zuckerman, M. (1970). Peaceable kingdoms: New England towns in the eighteenth century. New York: Knopf.

CHAPTER 10

Terror of the Simulacra: Struggles for Justice and the Postmodern

Stephen Pfohl

Translator's Preface: Questions of Access and Excess

To write ethnographies in the model of collage would be to avoid the portrayal of cultures as organic wholes, or as unified realistic worlds subject to a continuous explanatory discourse. . . . The ethnography as collage would leave manifest the constructionist procedures of ethnographic knowledge, it would be an assemblage containing voices other than the ethnographers, as well as examples of "found" evidence, data not fully integrated within the works of governing interpretation. Finally it would not explain away those elements in the foreign culture which render the investigator's own culture newly incomprehensible. (Clifford, 1988, pp. 146–147

This text is an ethnographic text, if somewhat surreally. It invites the reader, not so much to agree with the evidence and the analysis set forth by its author, but to enter actively into the process of researching one's own historical and biographically given position within what might be described provisionally as "the postmodern scene" of contemporary America (Kroker & Cook, 1986). It begins with a terrifying fragment of this scene, the image of Lt. Col. Oliver North, Jr., telling the truth about the "facts" of U.S. foreign policy. This scene is terrifying, precisely because for many of us there was an other side, or several, to North's truth. There was "factual" knowledge of the dead and mutilated bodies of others who opposed this country's right to

STEPHEN PFOHL • Department of Sociology, Boston College, Chestnut Hill, Massachusetts 02167.

imperial domination. And there was the terror that facts of "the other side" make little difference within the consumptive mediascape of postmodern America—that any facts are all too easily converted televisually into their opposite and then recirculated ritualistically into a fascinating amalgam of truths. Truths that feed vampirically upon images of apparent contradiction, amassing more and more information, data-banking everything, giving nothing in return, inoculating themselves against structural contradictions with periodic mass-mediated spectacles of scandal.

> Lt. Col. North: Those are the facts, as I know them, Mr. Nields. I was glad that when you introduced this, you said that you wanted to hear the truth— the good, the bad, and the ugly. I am here to tell it all, pleasant and unpleasant. . . . I was provided with additional input that was radically different from the truth. I assisted in furthering that version . . . I was provided with a different version of the facts. They were, I believe, transmitted to me in a note, a PROF note or an actual memorandum that is basically what's here, that is inconsistent with what I knew to be the truth.
>
> Mr. Nields: Did you say to Mr. McFarland, "That's not the truth"?
>
> Lt. Col. North: I don't have a specific recollection of that conversation. . . . I am saying that I decided that I would continue to participate in preparing a version of the chronology, not necessarily what would be the final historical internal version, but a version of the chronology that was inaccurate. . . .
>
> Mr. Nields: In any event, my question to you, sir, is: There were reasons on the other side, were there not?
>
> Lt. Col. North: Would you—would you give me—I, I don't understand your questions about "reasons on the other side."
>
> Mr. Nields: There were reasons—well, I'll give them to you, and see if you agree. First of all, you put some value, don't you, in the truth?
>
> Lt. Col. North: I've put great value on the truth. I've come here to tell it.
>
> Mr. Nields: So, that was—that would be a reason not to put forward this version of the facts?
>
> Lt. Col. North: The truth would be a reason not to put forward that version of the facts, but as I indicated to you a moment ago, I put great value on the lives of the American hostages. I worked hard to bring back as many as we could. I put great value in the possibility that we could . . . have ended the Iran-Iraq war . . . and that we had established for the first time, a direct contact with people inside Iran who might be able to assist us in the strategic reopening and who were at great risk if they were exposed. And, so, yes, I put great value in the truth, and as I said, I came here to tell it. But, I also put great value on human life, and I put great value on that second, second channel, who was at risk. (North, 1987, pp. 13, 43, 49)

This is a true story of vampirism, of living death, and of the electronic simulation of what's empirically given within an almost fully industrialized economically stratified, racist, imperial, and patriarchal Western society. It begins, "Once upon a time," as all stories or all theories do with an image, or rather with a set of images. Oliver North, Jr., delivers the facts, Vanna White speaks, Bill Cosby becomes both black and white at the same time in space. What's the difference? Sincere or cynical talking heads providing fascinating information about the sex lives of star politicians, the selling of the summit, the accumulation of toxic wastes, and the exact number of inches of precipitation expected day after day after day after . . . Nothing is lost, it seems, to the I/eye of the camera, the I/eye of the screen. More and more information, faster and denser, more and more facts, data, empiricities, batting averages, body counts, stock market reports, numbers of homeless, AIDS victims, tooth decay, car sales, foreign trade deficits, inches of snow, records of temperature. All clearly explained. More white than white. More real than real. More sexy than sex. More news than new. A moving spectacle of even more fashionable body parts: his rippling biceps, her exposed thighs, its smooth metallic shine, digitally impregnated, perfectly copied. Advertising the desire for desire and for designer bodies modeled after models modeled after models. Mechanically toned, pharmaceutically adjusted, or anorexically emptied bodies, always lacking, always wanting to want more or less. Restless bodies, ecstatic yet bored. Bodies invaded, panicked, made anxious by nightly broadcasts of the latest fashion in dress, dining, or murder, economic setbacks, third world rioting, high-speed auto crashes, and scientific breakthroughs or breakdowns. Images of missing children who find themselves participating interactively in shaping their futures and the ends of history as they enter the screen electromagnetically in assisting Captain Power to again and again escape mortality and so ritually enact a particularly violent historical materiality, a new mythic American empire of the senseless.

This is a true story. And yet, once in those (im)possible spaces, before that "once upon a time" where this story, the history of our (hegemonic) present, is mythically constructed, there are Other beginnings, Other narrations of the birth of what's real. They begin perhaps with the weaving of a plethora of different colors, different foods, tastes, smells, geographies, and sound waves. Or with periodic unweaving, dissolvings, reconstructurings, rememberings. They begin excessively maybe in a brown earthy womb or in black thick waters or with breathy rhythms or fiery flows of spiraling chaos. Perhaps under the sign of a crescent moon returning to difference. Or with a different language uncastrating, discontinuous, as attentive to noise as to music. A menstrual, pregnant, or voodoo language. Expensive, giving itself away. Not a nostalgic language inducing desire for a lost garden of wholeness. Nostalgia is the language of the postmodern mediascape, the language of lack, a language that fills its communicants with sacramental longings for a present that never comes, for the gift that never arrives, for apocalypse both now and forever.

We must move socially to the other side of nostalgia, if we are to be touched erotically, politically, or in laughter by a language that dissolves itself festively. A language that opens out to or is embraced by Others. "[Not] because it was ever once like that, but because [within the dominant material imagination of our hierarchical present] it never was and never will be able to be otherwise" (Levi-Strauss, 1986 p. 22). Languages of excess, the excessing of language, (non)places of death not deterred but incestuously coming again and again in sensuous waves of ecstatic multiplicities. Poetic spaces. Spaces that resist proper names, proper economies of grammar. The other sides of any certain climax, the other sides of power and its fetishized chronology of lawful time circulated measure for measure.

These other spaces have become relatively inaccessible to those among us possessed hegemonically by the hierarchical pleasures of that fetishized and accumulative order of things in time in which we find ourselves commodified, freeze-framed, or commonsensically real or realistic. Why?

> Mr. Nields: In any event, my question to you sir, is: There were reasons on the other side, were there not?
>
> Lt. Col. North: Would you—would you give me—I, I don't understand your questions about reasons on the other side. (North, 1987, p. 43)

Why? Why are spaces the other side of the dominant ordering of what's real seemingly so inaccessible or unmemorable? This text invites you, its readers, to entertain the suspicion that, for some time now, the experience of what is accessible to us has been (or is being) altered historically by a radical material simulation of excess. In other words, excess is being reduced to the self-same realm of access. Stated another way, those experiences that had previously exceeded or fractured the socially constructed "common sense" of the modern order are today being manufactured in a simulated form and then fed back for our consumption without their once disturbing potential for creating a critical difference. This has been happening for some time. Perhaps since the electronically mass-mediated invasion of our time and of many (if hopefully not all) of our minds embodied within the dominant televideo, computerized, and increasingly cybernetic confines of the culture of advanced transnational capital.

In using the term *excess* to connote what is being simulatively accessed by the postmodern media, I wish to evoke an image of what can never by perfectly imaged or properly named. I am referring to those pure and heterogeneously embodied experiences of ourselves becoming Other, becoming sacred, soulful, effervescent, or contagious. The historical realization of such excessive spaces is crucial for social movements aimed at radically changing an existing order of things in time. Without ritual access to those other sides of the dominant or mythological stories in which people find themselves inscribed in history, it is virtually impossible to imagine other and hopefully more justice ways of practically organizing our lives together. Unfortunately, this is exactly what is being denied us in the emergence of postmodern society. The more we move within the dense and high-speed world of image simulations that characterizes the postmodern, the more we find excess modeled to fit prepackaged formats of access and then sold back to us so that we might consume what's different and what's the same all in the same bite/byte. Reasons for this terrifyingly new telecommunicative form of vampirism may be found in a careful study of the "reality effects" manufactured by postmodern technologies of image management. These images and their power are today being produced for profit by the most advanced institutions of transnational capital.

In *Everyday Life in the Modern World,* an early attempt to critically theorize the coming of postmodern society, Henri Lefebvre (1984) distinguishes modern societies in which hegemonic power is reproduced by a mix of both force and ideological influence from an emergent postmodern social formation, the society of bureaucratically controlled consumption. In this latter type of society, ideology functions less by the power of signs to provide rationalizations for an existing order than by the fascinations evoked by drawing the consumer of signs into an almost endlessly productive network of informational effects and nearly instantaneous electromagnetic feedbacks. The "fatal attractions" of such a society are found in its seeming parasitic abilities to erase those previously critical spaces between what's on the inside and what's on the out, between the selfsame and its other, between access and excess. What becomes increasingly important are material rituals of "signing," those almost electromagnetic processes by which people are seductively drawn out from within the subjective or modernist confines of one's own skin into a postmodern mechanics of signmaking itself. Drawn into the dense, high-speed, and electronically pulsating structural operations of telecommunicative mass marketing, many of our bodies are quite really invaded and then extended outward hyperreally into the networkings of the media itself. Multiple channels of information converge on and through us, not so much as to persuade as to still an uncanny if somewhat panicky oscillation between what's feared and what's fascinating. Perhaps this is because those of us most subject to the code of the postmodern find ourselves situated physically within such a serial swell of data that even our most intimate senses of what's real become extended outward into ever more enveloping informational networks. At the same time, the sensational effects of these network hookups return within, reconstituting our sensory imaginations of what's (empirically) possible and what's not.

Here human subjectivity is called out into a decentered hyperspace. Do you hear the call? How can you resist it? Within this emerging postmodern space, people's embodied imaginations of themselves and of Others are preprocessed through complex networks of biotechnological feedback, videoloops, prerecorded sound systems, Sony Walkmans, and talking cars. All within a solid liquidity of capital, a dark thick ocean of white noise. A ritual bombardment of sensory stimuli produced for our fearful and fascinating consumption by a profitable historical conjuncture of corporate, military, civil-state, and scientific institutions. And positioned so as to hegemonically dominate the manifest destinies of these institutions—an upward classification of skillful or compliant white men of power, whose visions of the most profitable ways to work this planet constitute the core economic, sexual, and racial images upon which the informational simulations of postmodernity are modeled masters of the universal, *Masters of the Universe.*

This is the show the young white girl is watching, enthralled by. I am sitting having coffee with her mother in the next room. Her mother is single, bored, and anxious. She is unemployed. These are my neighbors. It is Saturday morning. Maybe 11:20 a.m. The young white girl in the next room is exposing herself to a television set. It strikes me that she is daydreaming with the machine. Her eyes are moving rapidly but her body remains still. She sits, knees curled within her dress, biting her nails, clutching a doll. Wide eyes/it's electric. She is watching "Masters of the Universe," taking in the information, the story, its repertoire of images. Something is really happening in this room with the young white girl and the machine. Is this the end of history? Is this the beginning of the (non)history of the postmodern code? Is this the advent of the truly functionalist society? A society of cybernetic programming of productive consumptives? The young girl enters the room where her mother and I are talking. She opens her mouth, recirculating desire. I hear the following words: "Mommy, mommy. They showed a K-TL 191 with screaming rearview blinkers and a flashing rotary rocket launcher with a digital tracking unit. It was only $29.99 but for one time only it's $19.99. But you have to call right away. Can we, Mommy? Can we? Can we get the K-TL 191? Can we? Can we? All you have to do is call."

The young girl informs her mother breathlessly of a 1-800 number. Her mother does not appear to understand. Perhaps she is less acquainted with this code. Suddenly the young girl again hears the voices of the Masters of the Universe. And so, without waiting for her mother's response, she efficiently returns to the televisionary site in which she finds herself called out in mind and body, interpellated with a desire for consumption. Offscreen there are other events. The young white girl does not notice. There are plant closings in the northwest midwest, U.S.-supported death squads in Central America, a growing number of homeless families, teenage suicides, and longer prison sentences for blacks and Hispanics. There is a young black male child in another part of this city. He stabs another young black child, his neighbor, to get control of a "boom box," a sound system, a point of access into the media. The young white girl does not notice. Perhaps she is not hooked into these events, or hooked up.

Are we here witnessing a new form of social memory, a new tele-communicative theatricalization of what's real? How fascinating and how fearful? That possibility that a postmodern society has already come upon and within us is explored throughout the remainder of this text. For the moment, permit me to elaborate upon the suggestion that the emergence of such a society dramatically forecloses many previously accessible spaces for exceeding the limits of what has been historically represented to us as real. The suggestion here is that, unlike earlier modes of Western social organization, postmodern society is no longer staked upon a simple sacrificial exclusion of otherness. As complex as such simple hegemonic exclusions have been in the past, something else is today beginning to take shape. Something more terrifying, more eschatalogically final. Today, exclusion is simulatively undone then mechanically doubled. All in the same operation. Before the blink of an eye/I within the empty curved space of the self-mirrored narcissistic eye/I within. Or both. Postmodern society is that society which is ominously becoming technologically capable of inoculating itself against its Others. First, by producing an exact simulative double of the modality in which its other sides have been previously arrested or frozen outside the time of their own exclusion from modern society. Imagine here a vast array of stereotypical images of the economically oppressed or of women, nonwhites, nonwesterners, or any Others excluded from reciprocal participation in the social structuring of the real life of modernity. In postmodernity, however, these images are not simply excluded. They are simulated or doubled again. Made into almost picture-perfect copies, not of what's real but of what had already been stereotypically reproduced. These iconic images of otherness, seductive simulacra or simulations of what's different, are then fed back or consumptively incorporated into the communicative informational circuitry that constitutes the ever-expanding data base of postmodern empiricities. Thus, what may have previously exceeded or resisted being incorporated into the "true" and violent stories of modernity is today accessed by the vampiric tendencies of a postmodern organization of power.

Within the "signing" practices of the postmodern scene everything becomes possible. Even those previously critical (im)possibilities in excess of the modern order. Throughout modernity those in power were constantly threatened by a "return of the repressed," by the shadowy traces of those others excluded by modern capital, patriarchy, racial and imperial hierarchies. Postmodern culture promises a masterful end to all of this. This is a society of eschatalogical fulfillments, a nuclear-powered society aimed at the end of history, the end of anything other than what's knowable within the self-adjusting code of an already reproduced and ungiving order of things simulated. The perfect clone. The perfect copies. Not a real illusion but illusionary reals. Reel after reel. The hyperreal. The "thing-in-itself," sui generis, finally realized or realizable, fixed or fixable without end, without difference, and beyond a shadow of a doubt.

This is a space without the shadow of the predigested Other. Is it also a time of the living dead? Vampires cast no shadows. Nor do televisionary projections of what might be bought, sold, or stolen. And what of viral implants or genetic mutations of the codes of biological production? Is this a time where the brightest dreams of Western man might at last be realized within the technological machinery of a "male mothering," the actual materialization of the word made flesh? An ultramodern social world without end? And most terrifying, without the possibility of returning to Other impossible beginnings? Terror of the Simulacra.

This is a true story. But is it also a story that remains relatively inaccessible if we, as readers, remain confined, somewhat illiterately within that realm of empirical (or categorically imperial) reality that is today modeled upon "the already made," the previously given, the perceptual set theorization of what's real in terms of what was "once upon a time" collectively represented, then mechanically reproduced and subsequently and quite seductively simulated as the "real thing"? Coke or Pepsi. Max Headroom or Ronald Reagan. What's the difference?

In the early years of television, before such media-scattered events as the mass marketing of computer games, the almost unmemorable

U.S. invasion of Grenada, the May 13, 1985, police helicopter bombing of a community of Afro-American radicals in Philadelphia, or the daily "eclipse of reason" in what may seem like the almost random violence of impoverished, hyperbored and technopharmacologically stimulated male inner-city youth gangs, C. Wright Mills (1956) used the term *cheerful robots* to evoke a sense of the historical materialization of a terrifying new American character type—persons whose primary modes of production had become consumption. Three decades later, French social theorist Jean Baudrillard again employs a science-fiction-like vocabulary to alert us to the possibility of an even more dramatic transformation. According to Baudrillard, the media infestation of a great many of our historical embodiments has advanced to such a state-in-excess that we are no longer so much manipulated, like robots, as that we have become materially accessed by the postmodern media itself. That we have been seduced into taking the media within ourselves; its screens and its terminals now functioning as our most intimate organs of sensation, erasing previously imagined differences between the public and private, the personal and the political, the cognitive and the carnal. Baudrillard's contention is this: that we are becoming possessed by the productive consumption of media icons to such a degree that there appears to be nothing outside the magnetically looping narratives in which we find ourselves close-circuited. We are thus invaded and occupied by a seductively recurrent recycling of sensations of difference into the same old story. We are the media! We are the television! We are or are becoming the living screen for the filmic projections of accumulation of dead or temporally frozen moving images. We are (or are becoming) the Living Dead, claustrophobic vampires in a coffin that only appears always open but that, in fact (or in the historically materialized fictions in which we find ourselves empirically), is open to nothing but the simulations that haunt everyday perceptions of what is really happening. Thus, we alternate between infinitely refracting mirrored opposites, between binary poles of pleasure and terror in the new but old, different but same, digitally programmed narrative structures of love, ambition, fear, power, and inflationary desire. Hence, what's real today hegemonically is largely a matter of simulating what's been materially imaginable in the time before. Everything returns almost magnetically to the available plot structures of the time before. Nothing is lost. Thus, if something appears radically different in one flashing instance and almost exactly the same in the next, it should come as no surprise. For in a world of simulative ready-made experiences, it is the uncanny sense of the familiar, of the *déjà vu*, that renders "all things considered" accessible, meaningful, or commonsensically real.

   This is a true story, an ethnographic text. And yet it attempts to
exceed the ordinary channels of (socially scientific) access into which
so many of us have become empirically (or imperially) attuned. For
certain readers this will mean that the text fails. This is a risk. The
second channel, of whom Oliver North, Jr., speaks truthfully, will remain unprotected. And the third, and the fourth, and the fifth. On my
television set there are 91 channels. The average U.S. household is
exposed for over 7 hours each day. For *other readers* the experience
might evoke a sense of those (im)possible truths that lie beyond the
transnational mediascape that is rapidly becoming the dense and ni-
hilistic base for the reproduction of hegemony with the *USA Today*.
This is a hope. Here lies the material basis for what I consider to be a
more effective strategy for radical first world writers and artists to organically participate in an activist struggle for justice within and against
the historical confines of postmodern America. Within the body of
this text this strategy is referred to as "the allegorical method of the
fifth person plural, or whatever."
   In closing this already too lengthy preface, let me briefly address
a few additional issues concerning access into the excessive project of
re(w)riting that follows. Since the task of what I read as the text's
(dis)autobiographical opening to history is already dealt with substan-
tively in resisting the singular confessions of its author's I's/eyes, I
will consider but two further aspects of its structure—why the concern with Walter Benjamin and how to delineate the historical "origins"
of the postmodern.
   Walter Benjamin (1892–1940) was a major German Jewish social
theorist whose writings on the media, the politics of art, and the epistemological foundations of a historically material practice of social
theorizing anticipate many of the themes of today's debates about
postmodernism. In his essay "The Work of Art in the Age of Mechan-
ical Reproduction," Benjamin (1969) makes an argument concerning
the critically reflexive possibilities of an activist engagement with media that resist the transcendental aura of mystifying genius or artistic
"originality." More ominously, Benjamin also considered the emergence of a Fascist "aestheticization of death" as a simulative incorporation of otherness within the violently hierarchical confines of the
Fascist state itself. In much of this text, I treat the life and work of
Benjamin as an important precursor to the theoretical and political
challenge of postmodern culture. Indeed, in juxtaposing scenes of Nazi
Germany with those of the America of Ronald Reagan and Oliver North,
Jr., it is my intention to recommend Benjamin's writings as important
contributions to present strategies in the struggle for justice. In this
regard, Benjamin's work needs no better reference than that provided

by postmodern theorist Jean Baudrillard, who underscores the terrifying connection between postmodern and Fascist forms of power.

> There is no doubt that fascism . . . is the first . . . violent reactivation of
> a form of power that despairs of its own rational foundations. . . . [A]s
> the violent reactivation of the social in a society that despairs of its own
> rational and contractual foundation, fascism is nevertheless the only fas-
> cinating modern form of power. . . . Fascist power is then the only form
> which was able to reenact the ritual prestige of death, but (and most im-
> portantly here) in an already posthumous and phony mode, a mode of one-
> upmanship and mise-en-scene, and in an aesthetic mode—as Benjamin
> clearly saw—that was no longer truly sacrificial. Fascism's politics is an
> aesthetics of death, one that already has the look of a nostalgic fad; and
> everything that has had this look since then must be inspired by fascism,
> understood as an already nostalgic obscenity and violence, as an already
> reactionary scenario of power and death which is already obsolete the very
> moment it appears in history. (Baudrillard, 1987, pp. 61, 62)

As to the historical "origins" of postmodernism, I suggest several
beginnings. The first three are places of considerable hope; the last
two are strewn with pessimism. The first revolves around a break with
modernist social science research and involves the surrealistic ethnographic practices of a collectivity of French theorists and artists in the
years between the world wars in Europe. "Historically situated between a revolutionary refusal of France's colonized Others to submit
to the homogenizing gaze of Western anthropological imperialism and
a practical political desire to counter the epistemological lure of fascism, certain critical French social theorists, writers, and artists were
drawn into a desire for a deconstructive displacement of the facts of
everyday Western social life, and of the [modern] rules of the sociological method that theoretically secured their reign" (Pfohl & Gordon,
1986, p. 595). Radicalizing the critical epistemological investigations
of Emile Durkheim and Marcel Mauss, theorists such as George Bataille, Michel Leiris, Roger Callois, and other "ethnographic surreal-
ists" advocated an ethnographic de-realization of the imperial construction of the hierarchical Western I/eye (Clifford, 1988; Hollier, 1988;
Richmond, 1984). Rather than interpretively mastering the facts of "the
other," these theoretical predecessors to French poststructuralist analysis
advocated a critical corrosion of taken-for-granted modern realities when
confronted with the historically structured presence of "others" sac-
rificed to the imperial construction of modernity itself. In this regard
it is significant that this early gesture toward a critical postmodernity
was joined by Walter Benjamin, who attended the Parisian cafe sessions of the "College of Sociology" organized by Bataille, Leiris, and
Roger Callois in the late 1930s. Indeed, much of what we know today
as the writings of Benjamin were passed to us by Bataille, who was

entrusted as the caretaker of a number of Benjamin's manuscripts when the latter was forced to flee Paris and the Gestapo agents of his "aestheticized death."

A second place of hopeful beginnings for a critical postmodernism may be found in the uncertain writings of certain radical feminists. Understanding the project of Western modernity as founded, in part, upon the exclusion of heterogeneous feminine languages, embodiments, and desires, a diverse yet convergent ensemble of feminist writers materially imagine sensations of renewed beginnings the other side of patriarchal modernism. "They say, we must disregard all the stories relating to those of them who have been betrayed beaten seized seduced carried off violated and exchanged as vile and precious merchandise. They say, we must disregard the statements we have been compelled to deliver contrary to our opinions and in conformity with the codes and conventions of the cultures that have domesticated us. . . . They say that there is no reality before it has been given shape by words rules regulations. They say that in what concerns them everything has to be remade starting from basic principles. They say that in the first place the vocabulary of every language is to be examined, modified, turned upside down, that every word must be screened" (Wittig, 1971).

Consider the following passage from Mary Daly and Jane Caputi's *Wickedary*. This theoretically poetic text conjures the possibilities of a "positively revolting" feminist language in excess of modern patriarchy's dictionary of defined meanings. In the following passage, readers are cautioned against the polar inversions of meaning that are today a commonplace of ultramodern mediaspeak.

> Many of patriarchy's reversals are the products of director's inversion. . . . Thus Ronald Reagan is called "The Great Communicator." The MX missile has been called "Peacekeeper." Animal Rights activists who oppose violence against any creature are labeled "terrorists."
>
> The same mechanism is observable when groups opposing women's right to choose abortion—groups manifesting callous indifference to women's lives and to the lives of unwanted children—label themselves as "pro-life" and "right-to-lifers." In a society that accepts such inversion, Coca-Cola can pass as "The Real Thing" and makeup can be labeled "The Natural Look," while women who refuse to wear makeup are called "unnatural." (Daly & Caputi, 1987, p. 250)

Other radically feminist writers, such as Kathy Acker, descend into a material collage of unsettling political poetics. Acker's spiraling texts scream of the pornographic violence tattooed across the bodies of women, who like the female protagonist in her re(w)riting of *Don Quixote*, discovers that "BEING BORN INTO AND PART OF A MALE WORLD, SHE HAD NO SPEECH OF HER OWN. ALL SHE COULD DO

WAS READ MALE TEXTS WHICH WEREN'T HER" (1986, p. 39). Or
to radically re(w)rite these texts the other side of what's modern.
Because of a commitment to styles of (w)riting that refuse or
transformatively resist the homogenizing phallocentrism of modernist
prose, many radical feminists also often encounter questions about the
accessibility of their texts to the generalized (predominantly male) audience of scholarly discourse. To demands for access, Luce Irigaray,
whose critical texts exceed the normative boundaries between theory
and fiction, responds as follows: "No clear nor univocal statement can,
in fact, dissolve the mortgage, this obstacle . . . being caught, trapped
in the same reign of credit. It is as yet better to speak only through
equivocations, allusions, innuendos, parables. . . . Even if you are asked
for some *pre'cisions* [precise details]" (Irigaray, 1985, p. 178).

A third space of critical postmodernism is embodied in the diverse
intellectual and artistic labors of people of color within the televisionary borders of the United States and its ultramodern allies. And in the
antiimperialist voices from south of those borders, from those whose
continued real economic underdevelopment constitutes a transnational foundation for the emergence of a culture of hyperreality within
vast sectors of the first world itself. One need only read the opening
pages of Toni Morrison's *The Bluest Eye* (1970) to be confronted allegorically with stark ethnographic truths concerning the "whiter than
white" narrative gardens of the ultramodern story of Dick and Jane,
their ever-smiling happy parents and running dog Spot. These white
pages are staked historically upon the consignment of racially inscribed others to that "unyielding . . . plot of black dirt" that has
been the fate of so many peoples of color under the modern imperi-
alities of Western enlightenment.

Indeed, what is all too homogeneously labeled as modernity has
been a time of enslavement or colonization for many who await the
other side of what's modern as—for realizing social justice. When
George Jackson (1970) writes that an enforced version of whitened
reality from St. Augustine on is *the* problem, or when Zora Neal Hurston (1981) and Ishmael Reed (1988) remind us that beneath the apparently Christian surface of popular Black American culture lies the
complex and challenging material spiritualities of "Neo Hoo Doo," or
when Houston Baker (1984) locates the "crisscrossing impulses" of
African-American signing practices within the living historical tonal-
ities of a "blues matrix," we are confronted with the possibility of
cultural spaces that lie beyond the disembodying hyperrationality of
the modern West. Related challenges are heard in what many first world
readers perceive as "the surrealist" tendencies of Central and South
American fictions or in the political allegories of African and Asian

authors. Such writings presage in diverse ways a more hopeful construction of "life after modernism." In the meantime, and within the densely white media of ultramodernity, we are provided with rhythmic word-soundings of encouragement by Afro-American scholar, poet, and musician Gil Scot-Heron, whose song "B Movie" includes the following postmodern lyrics:

> Just keep repeating that none of this is real.
> And if you're sensing that something's wrong
> Just remember that it won't be too long
> Before the director cuts the scene
> Cause
> This ain't really your life
>   ain't really your life
>   ain't really nothin' but a movie. (Scott-Heron, 1981)

As to more troubling or more pessimistic beginnings of the postmodern, I will but mention their names in passing. Each represents a major portion of the themes examined at length in the following text. Fascism and the televisionary culture of transnationalized capital. As to the hegemonic relations between these two dark forms of postmodern enlightenment, I offer an allegory—*Terror of the Simulacra*.

Author's Preface: Re(w)riting Other Sides

It is July 9, 1987. There is television and I write. I watch the image of a lieutenant colonel pose dramatic. "Indignant," states the Boston *Globe*. A manufacturer of truths that lie. An evocation of fascism in the name of democratic resistance. ABC updates its public with polls that show a 70% favorable response. "Oli-mania!" says the *Inquirer*. This lieutenant colonel calls our (congressional) representatives to task for abandoning the terrorists, the contras, the mercenaries we support with money taken from school lunch programs, from drugs and weapon sales, from a cybernetic obfuscation of what's real. This lieutenant colonel and those he says he loves represent themselves as the *true* heirs to American democracy. They are. He sits poised before the screen, speaking of terrorism, a new American hero. This is the truth. This is an image.

> The simulacrum is never that which conceals the truth—it is the truth that conceals that there is none. The simulacrum [the image] is true. (Baudrillard, 1983, p. 1)

The above words preface Jean Baudrillard's terrifying text, "The Precession of Simulacra." In a preface to the 1843 edition of *The Es-*

sence of Christianity, Ludwig Feuerbach (1983, p. 1) states, "Without doubt our epoch . . . prefers the image to the thing, the copy to the original, the representation to the reality, appearance to being." These are prophetic texts. Feuerbach was a materialist. Materially speaking, our epoch, an epoch of advanced transnational capital, has effectively erased, or is in the process of effectively erasing, all significant differences between a copy and its putative original. The representations by which we locate ourselves materially and imaginarily in history are nothing but copies of copies. There is no real beyond the images with which we fix ourselves spatially in time. Or such is the thesis offered to us by Jean Baudrillard, whose disturbing ethnography of the economic, political, and cultural structures of an almost fully industrialized West suggests this image—*TERROR OF THE SIMULACRA*.

According to Baudrillard, the electronic informational systems that constitute the advanced technological machinery at the core of transnational capital have so transformed the code of everyday Western social life that we are today controlled by a seemingly endless precession of mass-mediated images of who we are, what we desire, and where we are going. Is Baudrillard's frightening picture of this picture-perfected world correct? Has the historical project of modernity come to an end? Has the enlightenment's dream of ever-increasing rational and calculative control of the things of nature been superceded by a dark, irrational, and omnipresent programming of consumptive desire? Have we entered (or are we entering) the postmodern, a world of simulation in which we find ourselves modeled materially in relation to the imaginary confines of an electronically narrated story of our times, the "days of our lives" made real fantastically in the spectacular digital array of shimmering dots that have come to occupy our thoughts and dreams, our feelings and bodies, our fears and fascinations? Have we entered the "hyperreal," the vast, unconscious, and imperial recesses of commodity fetishism as it plays itself through our embodied imaginations, turning us on before the television, just as it erases our senses of history, represses memories of that erasure, and "naturalizes" our fix within a powerful set of social, economic, racial, and sexual hierarchies? Has this new empire of power and knowledge crept upon or within us so subtly and so completely that it has seized control without notice? Of the hidden rule of postmodern culture, Jean Baudrillard remarks, "Disneyland is there to conceal the fact that it is the "real" country, all of the "real" America, which is Disneyland (just as prisons are there to conceal the fact that it is the social in its entirety; in its banal omnipresence, which is carceral)" (1983, p. 25).

Questions posed by the (possible) advent of postmodern culture

are of great significance for struggles for justice in contemporary society. By struggles for justice I mean this—heterogeneous but convergent efforts to deconstruct institutional social apparati that currently
position us in relations of economic, political, heterosexist, racial, and
imperial hierarchies, to deconstruct hierarchical relations so as to reconstruct relations of reciprocity, relations of power-reciprocal social
exchange. As such, in the text that follows I will attempt a preliminary reading—that is, a re(w)riting—of some central features of the
historical context and of the substantive, epistemological, and practi-
cal-political effects of what Baudrillard describes as the world of the
hyperreal, a seemingly endless stream of simulated images that refer
to nothing but other images, copies of copies, ghostly doubles of nothing but the pulsating electronic adverts that occupy our minds and
stir our bodies with even greater and more deadly desires for self-
consumption.

Some Notes about What Appears Next

A preponderance, but not all, of the ethnographic materials interrogated in this text concern the codified simulation of heterosexist
hierarchies. Why this critical concern with heterosexist as opposed to
other advanced capitalist simulations, for instance, in the realms of
economic life and public political practice, or in the reproduction of
racial or imperial domination? There are a series of answers.

First, as suggested previously, this is a preliminary investigation.
I have no intent of privileging postmodern struggles against heterosexism over other forms of hierarchy. Nor should it be thought that heterosexist practices are uniform across boundaries marked by other historically material sites of power. Two further distinctions are needed.
First, the precession of heterosexist simulacra act hierarchically to
dominate both women in a variety of public and private spheres, and
women and men who desire a heterogeneity of intimate sexual or erotic
engagements, a gay heterogeneity of pleasures that a homo(geneous)
sexual economy—that is, generally, a homophobic sexual economy—
typically reduces to the misnomer "homosexuality." A second quali-
fication is this—a recognition of significant differences in construction
of heterosexist hierarchies by relations of race, class, religious orientation, and imperial positioning within an international division of
labor.

In more personal terms, materials relating to heterosexist control
practices are those that most now occupy my own theoretical practice.
They consume my attention in that given "order of things" in time in

which I discover myself called out or interpellated. In an uncertain way, it might be said that I am working through these imaginary materials. In another sense, it might be written that the site through which these materials work imaginarily is me. What site is this? What constitutes this site? My mind, emotions, desires, fears embodied. He almost always hadn't noticed. His eyes upon her ankle turn to gaze upon the calves high-heeled the image before his "I" secured. The terminal images remembered; they recalled him to remember a certain self, its other and the sacred canopy that "naturalized" his relation to the other as a universal and categorical imperative to act normatively within this world in a given manner. This is a sociological critique of pure and practical reason. It re(w)rites Kant in the wake of interventions by Emile Durkheim and Marcel Mauss.

The terminal images remembered at Boston's Logan Airport before boarding the plane that would carry him to Phoenix to deliver these words—three signs. The first: "Boston's best unarmed security jobs," an advert for the unemployed to guard some warehouses. Other words: "The ideal job for those with limited time." Time, he thought to himself, it seems forever limited, cut up, measured, sequentially ordered in a linear progression of exactly equivalent units; a repetitive foreclosure of the future in terms of the present. The ideal job for those with limited time: security. A second sign, a second weapon: a wet dripping image of a string bikined torso of a woman. Arms behind her back and red-nailed fingers teasing a spray of fluid that shoots from the head of a bottle she caresses. These are its words. They read: "Snap of schnapps. Squeeze of fruit. Splash of soda. Fletcher and Oakes." This is the image of something he might purchase. A third sign bears the same words but a simulacrum that appears, at once, different and not different. This is a different image that appears much the same. This time she is coming wet but is turned facing his eyes. Her eyes are covered over with steamy goggles that block her vision. She cannot see him gazing at her red lips parted roundly, open, "O" like a circle or like a zero. What's the difference? An erasure of difference: the circle, once sacred, now a zero profaned before his eyes, his "I's."·A terminal precession of simulacra he sees before boarding the plane to deliver these words. "Boston's best unarmed security. . . . The ideal job for those with limited time" linear.

Why this critical concern with heterosexist as opposed to other advanced capitalist simulations? A second reason is this. These simulative practices are not in opposition. They work together. Simulacra of heterosexist hierarchy converge with other hierarchical image practices in giving shape to the hegemonic structuring of power and knowledge within the advanced capitalist West. Her image sells his products within a terminal secured by so many other terminals. A microchip network of terminals produced in Asian electric sweat- shops—employing high-tech circuitry screened by eye/I-damaged women competing for obscenely low wages within the debt-driven economies of an imperial periphery displacing jobs once promised to nonwhite U.S. workers crowding factory-closed cities in decay and searching restless for release from the oppressive constraints of trans- national corporate control of time measured linear. Release produced with a given price—the commodified ecstasies of sex, drugs, and vio- lence. These prepackaged vacations from the constraints of the normal and normative consume but a present pain, while displacing attention with such alleged liberties as the "privilege" of voting for well-fi- nanced white males who take aim on pornography and the "drug cri- sis," sending arms and military advisors into the southern hemisphere to quell threats to that simulacrum they call democratic freedom.

Why this concern with the relation between heterosexism and the postmodern? One more reason. The historical project of the progres- sive, rationally instrumental and linear conquest of time that has de- fined the modern West is itself staked upon a fundamental suppres- sion of sexual difference. Characterized by what might be referred to as the twin rule of the phallocentric and the logocentric (Spivak, 1974), this project has, from its "origin," revolved around a singularly vio- lent sacrifice—the sacrifice of human relations within the life cycles of nature, erecting in its wake a certain precession of simulacra privi- leging the enlightened presence of "Man," solidly above nature, look- ing down upon what he sees, from his terrifying vantage point in his- tory, as a deadly dark black hole void liquid and unruly. She awaits his penetrating light in order to be made over until the end of a time that never comes, world without end, Amen. This is the violence of a perversely Western form of "primitive classification." He ritually in- scribes her otherness and appears the master. He speaks and she is silent, or so the story goes: the imperial story of the modern capitalist West.

Hence, in concluding this preface—three reasons for weaving these several possible stories together, the weaving of a strategic, if uncer- tain, critical intervention, the weaving of a socially deconstructive practice of theory.

Why Theory?

We all have opinions
Where do they come from?
Each day seems like a natural fact
and how we think changes how we act. (Gil & King, 1981)

The three reasons for interweaving stories relating to the post-modern, struggles for justice, and heterosexist domination: (1) a pre-liminary autobiographical or ethnographic depositioning of a white male American author in history, (2) the hegemonic conjuncture of the heterosexist with other social structuring practices within a given social formation, and (3) the suppression of sexual difference as a con-stitutive feature of Western modernity itself.

Two final quotes to seduce you into the text that follows; then a poem. The quotes are from Gayatri Spivak. The first reads:

> I do not see how . . . criticism can do more than decide to deny its desire as master, nor how it can *not* attend to the conditions of [its own] intelli-gibility. . . . The text of criticism is of course surrendered to the play of intelligibility and unintelligibility, but its decisions can never be more self-subversive than to question the [historical material] status of [its own mode of producing] intelligibility. (Spivak, 1987, p. 12)

This is how I read—that is, re(w)rite—Spivak's deconstructive in-tervention. Criticism can do no more than to decide to deny its desire as master, but perhaps it can do less as well. Perhaps it can begin to undo itself, just as it power-reflexively re(w)rites the provisional au-thor(ity) of its imaginary and material positioning in history in rela-tion to others. This is a strategic project of unlearning. To quote Spi-vak a second time:

> Unless one is aware that one cannot avoid taking a stand, unwitting stands get taken. . . . [W]riting is not simply identical with the production of prose and verse. It is the name of a "structure" which operates and frac-tures knowing (epistemology), being (ontology), doing (practice), history, politics, economics, institutions, as such. It is a "structure" whose "ori-gin" and end are necessarily provisional and absent. (Spivak, 1987, p. 147)

And now the poem: a social science fiction.

Desire for Allegory: Notes on Theoretical Method and the Fifth Person Plural: A Letter

Dear person who addresses me without naming:

There is anarchy in the warm spring air and I recollect myself on paper. It is Saturday and afternoon. Celie she's a cat and haunches nearby. First eyes over me than drawn to prey upon the image of a bee investigating the ivy beyond the screen that shields the tower within which I write she watches: a text that unfolds me before it; thereafter I am drawn.

"A text is made of multiple writings, drawn from many cultures and entering into mutual relations of dialogue, parody, contestation, but there is one place where this multiplicity is focused and that place is the reader, not, as was hitherto said, the author. The reader is the space on which all the quotations that make up a writing are inscribed without any of them being lost; a text's unity lies not in its origin but in its destination" (Barthes, 1977, p. 148).

Dear reader:

I'm about an hour's time from my destination, Boston. I'm up in the air, I reset my watch and remove my pen. Sometime earlier I sat in the Phoenix airport; tired emotions outpoured me and intensity overwhelmed my eyes welling toward release. I was wearing dark glasses and paused before the tears. I'll fall to sleep on this plane, I thought. These last few days have been explosive in talk, gift exchange, critique, play, and unlearning. I awake this morning in her bed debating within myself with her imagined: excessing quotes remembered or rewritten from the night before, turning over everything before coffee. I had been transgressing gossip allegorically and claiming this as related to a deconstructive theoretical practice and radical. I was concerned with the hegemonic narration of our desires at this time in history, in the industrial West, and with the mass-mediated phantasms that consume us materially and in the imaginary confines in which we gossip. The privatized confines of gossip, a place of romantic violence and cleansing. We've been washing our hands with soap operas since the 19th century, but not much before. But this is another story, not new but repetitious. "A story that classifies us," he whispered privately. This is gossip. "A story that classifies a story that classifies us," I said venturing into the public realm, a realm denied us politely and with discretion, that is with discretionary violence. I thought myself exhibited impolitely, an indiscretion, a violence doubled. This is allegory. I was within the text complicit yet speaking out impurely but with hope for somethings other. You read this as a contradiction you refused participation with and said, "This is not a new story. I've heard enough vileness. I refuse to hear anymore." Were you really this pure or had your desires been mediated so much less by television? When I was 5, I marched through my mother's kitchen with a coonskin cap and plastic rifle, searching for Indians to kill and a girl to marry herself to my desires. I bet you hadn't marched in this fashion.

This conversation disturbed me greatly. I found myself sliding from some self centered in a given story into a desire for somethings other. I awoke the next morning, that is this morning, in your bed, debating within myself with you imagined: excessing quotes remembered— turning over everything before coffee. I was allowing your position to question mine. Over breakfast with others you said the same, that is you talked of difference. You spoke of difference within a story and from without. The question of complicity hung in the air, as did I sometime later approaching my destination, Boston. I'm up in the air. I reset my watch and remove my pen. Over breakfast with others talking about the representation of evil in 19th-century Paris you referred me to a book about vampires and said I should read it and, "Goodbye. I'm glad you came. I'll see you later."

Several weeks passed before he received her letter. When he opened it, he found quotations from the book she had referred him to in her handwriting but without either his name or her signature. What he read was not the origin of this text but its destination. It stated simply: "Evil with infinite gradations and without guilt." This made him think that there was much more to write about the relationship between allegory and gossip. He was up in the air when he reset his watch and removed his pen. "I'll rewrite her letter," he decided, "and begin with this quote rather than with a proper name."

The letter, it began this way: "Evil with infinite gradations and without guilt." It had begun again earlier this morning on the rug. He was exercising his body and remembered time entwined with an other. This other, she knew his name or at least wrote his name on the outside of an envelope and licked the stamp. It was delivered and he found pleasure in the fact she called him Stephen; and she in his lack of knowledge of her proper name. Earlier this morning on the rug, he was exorcising a memory of time entwined with an other, time that passed through his body in history like her and he was consumed, then emptied.

> "You don't understand him!"
> I fought it, kissing her, I wanted to shower her with kisses, her cheek, her lips.
> "No, I understand him only too well," she whispered to my lips, even as they kissed her. "It is you who don't understand him!"
> I fought it, kissing her, I wanted to shower her with kisses, her cheek, her lips.
> "Love's blinded you," she said. "[Y]our fascination with his knowledge, his power. If you knew how he drinks death you'd hate him more than you. . . . I tell you I'm in danger!"

Early the next night, I left her, convinced. . . . (Rice, 1976, pp. 251–252)

A Note on Method. This is straightforward, a suspension of allegory. What I did was circle sentences and mark the margins of passages I read myself through the other day and night. Actually, it was several days and two nights that I positioned the text, as always, before me. And now in re(w)riting:

I journey through its traces; the spaces that mark my reading last time now
operate upon me and so I re-collect them and copy. I copy-(w)rite. I never
fail to be taken off guard. I am flipping through the marked up text and
suddenly the words before me read: "Aren't there gradations of evil? Is
evil a great perilous gulf into which one falls with the first sin, plummeting the depths?" (Rice, 1976, p. 237)

I sat in the Phoenix airport wearing black glasses and paused before the tears. I had slept in your bed while you dreamed elsewhere
and you asked, "How do you fly when you're dreaming?" This is not
an exact quote, but neither is it unlike the way you repeatedly quoted
me from within one time into another. And so I heard myself differently when I was with you. In this I found an uncertain pleasure,
remembering that you had said to me I was someone who you could—
No, let me quote you inexactly. You said, "I was just thinking that
maybe you're someone who I could—Who I could—"
THIS IS A WORKING DRAFT.

. . . .

. . . .

. . . .

. . . .

. . . .

THIS IS A PICTURE OF A DRAFT OF ME. I BEGIN TO (W)RITE, again
and again, that is repeatedly ruining myself conceived the moment
before, undermining my position, displacing the "I" who authors. I
am at work and remember Benjamin (1986, p. 81), who wrote, "The
work is the death mask of its conception."

The death mask of Wagner is a central visual image in Syberborg's
film of the opera *Parsifal*. Syberborg makes use of this image in
re(w)riting the 19th-century German quest for the grail. Throughout
his cinematic palimpsest, moving pictures that superimpose one story
in relation to another, ruins of Nietzsche and Marx abound. In France,
the collective representation of origin was destined for difference. Ruins
of Durkheim abound.

Benjamin, melancholic and self-destructive, left Germany for Paris
just as Nordic fascism projected its ruinous real upon the imperial
screen of a state bureaucratized in history. They were shooting images
of purification and blood sacrifice into the blond veins of those for

whom primitive romance had become a CAPITAL idea and Benjamin
fled before the rattling of iron cages and the thirst for death dark and
post-Christian. Tremors were felt in the cathedrals and banal lust cir-
cled all synagogues with savage terror. An eclipse of reason.

The Paris through which Benjamin wandered, losing his self with
each street crossed, was full of gossip. In the "dream wave" of surrealism in which he found himself ruined, "the threshhold between
waking and sleeping was worn away . . . the steps of multitudinous
images flooding back and forth . . ." (Benjamin, 1986, pp. 178–179).

He awoke in your bed, debating within himself with you about
the difference between gossip and allegory. You had taken issue with
what you heard as gossip and said, "This is not a new story. I've heard
enough vileness. I refuse to hear anymore." You stated that gossip was
vile to others, but he thought he had been ruining only himself. He
thought he had exhibited himself impolitely, indiscreetly, or with a
violence doubled back upon his own words, but now he wondered.
He desired to quote to you from Benjamin who had written: "To live
in a glass house is a revolutionary virtue par excellence. It is also an
intoxication, a moral exhibitionism, that we badly need. Discretion
concerning one's own existence, once an aristocratic virtue, has become more and more an affair of petit-bourgeois parvenus" (Benjamin,
1986, p. 180). Is this gossip? Kathy was there, a third person to this
conversation and remarked that what we had been calling gossip, she
heard as allegory.

"Allegories are, in the realm of thoughts what ruins are in the
realm of things." Benjamin wrote this and was later quoted to this
effect by Susan Sontag (1981, p. 120).

But why am I (w)riting this to you and so often in the third person? Shouldn't I fear the ruin of our relationship? This is an allegory.
She had invited him to see the ruins, he thought. This was the origin
of their relationship. No, this was its destination. They had driven
into the desert and she said, "There's nothing new in this story." He
had been talking about gossip and she said, "That's not something
new!"

The Problem of a NOVELTY: Gossip

"The last journey . . . death. Its destination: the new." He was
quoting Baudelaire. That is, Benjamin was quoting Baudelaire and he
was quoting Benjamin another time. That is, Benjamin was now in
another time—his. She too was in another time. Of this he was certain. He was in the men's room, late for the talk he was to give when

Pat appeared. Pat reminded him of the time and laughed affectionately at the "fact" that she probably hadn't even realized how much
time it took to get from her bed to his talk. Here they were, standing
in the men's room, the two of them laughing affectionately at the "fact"
that she was in another time. Now it was later than before. He hurried
to his talk without reminding Pat that he too was nearly always in
another time, perpetually late to class. In high school, he had been
taken aside and told that this represented a latent resentment of authority. He was surprised. He had thought this more manifest. Then,
in another time, she told him how she had studied anarchism and
said, "That's not something new!"

   " 'The last journey . . . death. Its destination: the new . . .' Novelty is a quality independent of the intrinsic value of the commodity.
It is the origin of the illusion inseverable from the images produced
by the collective unconsciousness . . . whose indefatigable agent is
fashion. The illusion of novelty is reflected, like one mirror in another, in the illusion of perpetual sameness . . . the phantasmagoria
of 'cultural history,' in which the bourgeoisie savors its false consciousness to the last" (Benjamin, 1986, pp. 157–158), deferring its
ruin, postponing its relation to death in time.

   This is the melancholy Marxism of Benjamin. He told her that
he too was often melancholy and she asked, "Don't you ever stop
working?"

   "The style of work of the melancholic is immersion, total concentration. Either one is immersed, or attention floats away. As a writer,
Benjamin was capable of extraordinary concentration" (Sontag, 1981,
p. 128).

   He was reading this one day just as she called from the telephone
she did not have in her home. She had no telephone at home, only a
simplicity of things, spatially sparse. Her sense of time was different
also and she wore black converse sneakers and offered him her bed
while she dreamt elsewhere. He had been reading an essay by Sontag
on Benjamin one day just as she called and now he was (w)riting her
a letter. She reminded him of Benjamin in a certain way. This is not
to say that he thought she was really like Benjamin. It was just that in
relation to her, he was reminded of Benjamin. He had been dreaming
in her bed and now he was writing her a letter. "Don't you ever stop
working?" she asked.

   "Even the dreaminess of the melancholic is harnessed to work,
and the melancholic temperament may try to cultivate phantasmagor-
ical states, like dreams, or seek access to concentrated states of attention offered by drugs . . . to furnish all the material needed to work.

Benjamin always working, always trying to work more, speculated a good deal on the writer's daily existence. . . . Part of the impetus for the large correspondence he conducted, was to chronicle, report on, confess the existence of work" (Sontag, 1981, pp. 126–127).

The Fifth Person Plural: Gossip Doubled with a Question

You wrote me again. This time stating directly that you "assume that I still exist." I am quoting you, re(w)riting. In so doing, my voice shifts from the third person I inscribe as "existent-other" to a fourth person I recognize as "a ruined self-sameness." But what if I (w)rite myself within this ruin toward something other? "Is this gossip?" he asked, repeating himself. What if I (w)rite myself over again from within a melancholic acknowledgment of the material and imaginary contingencies of my existence, the carnal and cognitive effects of the relations in which I find myself decentered genealogically within history, with you and with others? I remove my pen only to find myself fractured before the television, desiring a story that escapes me. If I (w)rite myself from within this fourth person what is left? What comes fifth and plurally?

Why these melancholy questions at this time in history: the death of the author? Some attribute this line of inquiry to the fashionable intellectual chic of French poststructuralist thought. That's not something new. The wanderings of Benjamin suggest a more historically material story of this NOVELTY. Benjamin, melancholy and self-destructive, left Germany for Paris just as Nordic fascism projected its ruinous real upon the imperial screen of a state bureaucratized in history. They were shooting images of purification and blood sacrifice into the blond veins of those for whom primitive romance had become a CAPITAL idea. And now in another time and place we are shooting these images into ourselves: the thirst for death dark and postmodern. He turns himself on before the television, before the image of an actor posing presidentially against terror with violence, re(w)riting history like the movies, a loss of the real. This is what this actor is doing, fascinating us with pictures of anonymous Hispanic men, lifting a large bag into or out of a boat somewhere. This is what this President is saying: PICTURE this—Important officials in the Nicaraguan government shipping cocaine to a playground in Indiana, where it will feed upon the minds of our youth. Communists, it seems, will stop at nothing. They must be stopped and the children must be drug tested and the workers. This is what this actor is doing, fascinating us with pictures of F1-11 attack routes and of maps of an evil city, a haven for terrorists and mad dogs and for the dead bodies of dark-skinned children murdered in the night. This is what this President is saying: "I made it clear we would respond as soon as we determined conclusively who was responsible for such attacks. . . . Our evidence is direct, it is precise, it is irrefutable. . . . Today we have done what we had to do. If necessary, we shall do it again."

He turns himself on before the television, close-circuiting the ruins before him. He sees her fingers unzipping his pants, palm flat against his groin aroused. Hot. Heavy. Hard. These adjectives: they circumscribe his mind, stir his body. Where do these images come from? What do they mean? These questions fascinate him like the images. Images of imperial mastery, patriotic purity, and patriarchal obsession with the pornographic: the things we count upon daily, just as we are counted among their number. Market research: it informs us of our desires. Can you buy these ideas? The latest overdetermination of CAPITAL; the full surrealization of consumptive desire; the digital reproduction of quality in quantity; a repetitious deferral of ruin; a postponement of death in time; the fascination with a linearity without end, Amen, and with fascism; the electronic simulation of desire within the third person singular.

But what if reflexively we recognize this ruinous third person? Is it too late to do this? Should we try another time? Picture this: a collective deauthorization of "he" who (w)rites his destination before the television; a ruinous transformation of this existent voice, the third person, singular, already ruined, into a fourth person, unsingular and uncertain. Benjamin offered a related picture: the death of the author. He sought points of transformative resistance within the complex and contradictory theater of mass-mediated desire. To stray with Benjamin is to stray complicitly from within. It is to seek out spaces of mediated fracture from within which we find ourselves vibrating between the practical exigencies of production and the ecstatic excesses of self-consumption. There is nothing easy about this search, this research. Moreover, it demands another sense of time. All revolutions do. Benjamin envisioned time differently. He was a melancholy Marxist and this was his material imagination of history: a collage of collective re(w)ritings in the fifth person plural. A reclamation of the public sphere: gossip doubled ruinously with a question of communism. This was his hope: that we might un(w)rite ourselves, loosen the confines of self simulating NOVELTY.

This is an allegory. It demands another sense of time.

Primitive Romance: The Ruins of Intercourse, the Ruins of Gossip

It had begun earlier this morning on the rug. He had been exercising his body and remembered a time entwined with an other. They had come to desire each other, like in the movies. They longed to intercourse as only the stars knew how. She pressed her body against his alone within his space and made him shudder. Her fingers unzipping his pants, palm flat against his groin aroused. Hot. Heavy. Hard. These adjectives: they circumscribe his mind, stir his body. She is his now he imagines. But how does he know? He guides his hand slowly between her thighs for the evidence: her moan and the typical wetness. It is late at night and evil. They had taken shelter from the moon on his rug. Her nipples were erect but her eyes hesitant and he was trying not to think about his performance, like in the movies. He wanted her to lose herself in him, that he might be credited in the production of her pleasure. He thought that credit was important. He bared her shoulders and thought to himself, "She's flirting with death. This is to my credit." He found it pleasurable to have a good credit rating. She would rate him highly. This was the meaning he made of her image. TERROR OF THE SIMULACRA!

She was trembling pleasurably within the confines of his story. Where did this story come from? Her story was different. She realized that they didn't even know each other's proper names and speculated that maybe he'd kill her and hide the body. This frightened her. Why was she here? What was the meaning of her desires? Where did these meanings come from? What came before? What comes next?

"Images and language take precedence," declared Benjamin (1986, p. 179). "Not only before meaning. Also before the self." But what if we reflexively recognize this ruinous third in which we find ourselves inscribed meaningfully in desire? Is it too late to do this? This frightened her. She lifted her blouse above her head, exposing her neck with a filmic gesture of sex. Why was she here? She's flirting with death, he thought to himself. This is to my credit. Is it too late to ruin this image, that is, to recognize this image as a ruin and ruin that ruin. To double the ruins of gossip, to collectively fracture the singular confines of mass-mediated desire—this demands another sense of time: the fifth person plural or whatever.

Is it too late to do this? Too late in what—capitalism, the machine age, the narrative confines of cybernetically simulated desire? This question is occasioned today by at least two spaces of potential resistance. In time, there may be more. The first space: impure and complicit. This space is made possible, in part, by a contradictory grant

from EXXON, Xerox, IBM, and other multinationals. It is a space of
contradictory effects. For just as these giant conglomerate institutions
of late capital depend on the electronic language of mass-mediated
imagery to interpellate or call out our desires to consume, so simultaneously do they present us with an increasing body of material evidence concerning the ruins we've become. The consumer is made, at
once, more restless and more programmed. The restlessness of the
consumer within capitalist society—that is not something new. The
desire for more, the yearning for the consumptive fix, for another purchase, increased ownership, although certainly exaggerated by mass-
mediated advertising, this has been a desire within the capitalist narrative since its beginnings. But the realizable programming of consumption, this is something new, a twisted NOVELTY that threatens
the dominant illusions that capitalism has traditionally offered its
privileged bourgeois classes. For the bourgeoisie the narrative destiny
of capitalism offered the following: the promise of authorial mastery
of world history, the masculine dream of rational and calculative control of the things of nature, and an endless deferral of death in time.
Over the last several decades, the future of these illusions has been
visibly contradicted by the institutional practices of capital itself, by
the advent of the realizable programming of consumption. I hum the
Burger King tune all the way to work each morning and feel deliciously different. Instead of death's deferral and the rational control
of things, an electronically mediated structure of capital seems capable of effecting a deferral of life and the control of people by things
that hum them deliciously: the death of the illusion of authorial mastery, the death of the author.

This is new, a twisted NOVELTY, realized materially in the historical wedding of advanced electronic communicative technology with
an existent bourgeois culture orchestrating the maximization of profit
by the most efficient means available. The most efficient means: electronic advert upon advert, a terminal procession of desire-producing
images without end: the darkest nightmares of science fiction realizing
themselves before our eyes, the full operationalization of the machine
body, the simulacrum, the death of the author without renewal, rebirth or resurrection, the robotic hell of the living dead. You wrote me
a letter inquiring about my existence. Quite honestly I might have told
you that I hummed the Burger King tune all the way to work and felt
deliciously different. This, I'm afraid, is new, a twisted novelty and
deadly. Benjamin, melancholy and self-destructive, left Germany just
as fascism projected its ruinous real upon the imperial screen. And
now in another time and place, we are shooting these images into
ourselves: the thirst for death, dark and postmodern.

This is a fundamental contradiction of late capital: a confrontation between the restless desires for authorial bourgeois mastery of consumption with the haunted and starkly new, digitally programmed death mask of the consumer itself. This frightened her. What was the meaning of her desires? Where did these meanings come from? What came before? What comes next? These are frightening questions. They emerge from within the contradictory space occupied uneasily by reflexive bourgeois theorists who recognize themselves inscribed within the imaginary and material confines of late Western capitalism society. The restless authorial consumer is not the happy robot, at least not yet, not completely, not everyone. This is a melancholy hope: that it is not too late, that we might yet loosen the confines of our self-simulating NOVELTY, that we might stray repeatedly and together, impurely and with an acknowledged complicity with the narrative against which we struggle to (w)rite ourselves out from within toward some others.

This is the first space of potential resistance: contradictory and fearful fractures within a class of bourgeois theorists, artists, and activists previously privileged by the illusions of authorial mastery. Robbed of the material base for such illusions by the electronic image culture of late multinational capital, some of these deauthorized intellectuals may be drawn (organically?) to ally their decentered selves with the revolutionary narrative practices of others excluded from that historical illusion, that is the historical reality of bourgeois mastery. There is no idealism in this analysis, simply a hope for another site of material resistance. It comes from other worlds. Not from one other world, third or whatever, that is a primitive romance for the privileged. It comes from a heterogeneity of others excluded in the reductive simulation of the same. It comes from other worlds less complicit with the narrational practices of primitive romance because the imagined pleasures of that masterful story were never realized as their own. In other words, (w)riting without the confines of the third person singular is nothing new for those condemned to the historical margins as human junk, ruinous fourth persons, unsingular and uncertain.

What names are these others given in the inscription of proper grammar, in the material and imaginary rituals of power and knowledge? These peoples of color, women, the colonized, the classified, those who desire sex differently, the mad, the bad, the Other. Proper grammar silences or ruins the voice of these others. We hear them only when they double the violence of grammar in revolt, when they re(w)rite themselves the ruins in time. This is the heterogeneous voice of the fifth person plural, a violence doubled, a return of the repressed. It operates upon history with another sense of time. Refugees

from the ruinous simulations of the bourgeois world may ally themselves with this voice but first they must unlearn the grammar that
confines them in a certain time. That is, they must learn another sense
of time, a time of the ruined self, the death of the author in and as
history. Is this the time of allegory?

I was sitting drunk with my parents before the world's largest
stage. Huge video screens and Stars Wars fighters were being lowered
from above. A dazzling filmic projection of flight formed a backdrop
for the simulated landing of a full-size airplane, a 707, really the world's
largest stage, and everyone applauded. A life-size shell of a huge metallic bird delighting the mass of enchanted vacationers here to drop
their dollars. From its womb a stream of nearly naked dancers: showgirls
twirling star-spangled tits and young men posing with tight asses to
the hoots of the American work force on holiday. It was Reno, Ne-
vada. My brother was the manager and my drinks were free.

The world's largest everythings are on display in Reno. Just read
the signs: the world's largest gas station, the world's largest slot machine, the world's largest casino-food-give-away. Nobody's hungry in
America, said Reagan. Reagan's been to Reno. Free food, free enterprise you consume largely while you gamble. Just read the signs: the
world's largest cock, the world's largest asshole. Is this true? Just read
the signs. I was sitting drunk with my parents before the world's largest stage and each of us was nodding before four of the world's largest
cocktails, four each before the show: spectacular. My brother was the
manager and I hallucinated an image of our ruin. Our multinational
corporate destiny? The parade of nearly naked dancers was suddenly
cut up by a terrible spray of machine-gunned bullets. Members of the
African National Congress had arrived and found no pleasure in our
filmic projection of white flight, star-spangled tits, and young men
posing with tight asses in the wake of another world's history we
plunder violently to under(w)rite our story, the world's largest mass
of fatty flesh drunk with spectacle. Blood splattering everywhere, the
veneer of innocent pleasures, the death mask of Western decadence
exposed doubly and in time ruined. A double exposure this violent
hallucination. I was sitting drunk with my parents before the world's
largest stage and suddenly I had become melancholy. Is this the time
of allegory? Just read the signs.

Melancholia, Marxism, and the Spatialization
of Time in Allegory

We had been talking of Benjamin's Marxism as a reconceptualization of melancholia. You pointed out that Benjamin's melancholia

was also a reconceptualization of Marxism. It was my intent to offer Benjamin's work as one of several historically specific means for modifying the methods of a critical theoretical practice, to circumscribe theoretical practice within the narrative confines of late multinational capitalism, the dominant story of our time. You were concerned about the practical political implications of this methodological shift in theory and raised questions about the ill-fated character of Benjamin's own practical struggles with the capitalist spectacle of Nordic fascism in another time and space, in history. That morning, I had been talking about the methodological implications of Artaud's work in a related fashion. This led you to question the practical adequacy of the position I was opening. Artaud hadn't exactly fared that well in the practice of everyday social life. Nietzsche, Poulantzas, and Althusser hadn't fared all that much better. In *Madness and Civilization* Foucault (1973) adds the names of Goya and Van Gogh, and just that morning I'd been reading texts by Kathy Acker (1978): screams that tremble in the night without an author. Each refused identity before the mirror of perpetual sameness cracked. That is there was no NOVELTY in what they (w)rote they screamed.

The scream. He saw it loudly. He awoke in a sweat, cold, and saw it staring at him, silent. And what of Benjamin? What was the narrative destiny of his melancholic story. Let's be honest. "Benjamin was probably not exaggerating when he told Adorno that each idea in his book on Baudelaire and nineteenth century Paris 'had to be wrestled away from a realm in which madness lies' " (Sontag, 1981, p. 129). But if madness lies no less than truth, what is the difference? He asked this not to construct some primitive romance about madness, but to ruin the deadly truth of things in time.

" 'Allegories are, in the realm of thoughts what ruins are in the realm of things.' . . . The culminating allegory of this mournful vision lay in the multiform emblematic renderings of death: 'Melancholy betrays the world for the sake of knowledge. But in its tenacious self-absorption it embraces dead objects in its contemplation in order to redeem them.' Thus the historical ruin has its bodily equivalent in the depiction of the human physis as a corpse, the *memento mori* . . . (S)uch chosen objects self-reflexively reveal the nature of the allegorical literary process itself, in which 'life flows out of' the things of this world and they 'signify' in inorganic ways such as montage" (Lunn, 1982, pp. 186–187).

When Benjamin wrote melancholically of such matters he evoked another sense of time. This was Benjamin's most recurrent theme: the spatialization of time, "his notion of ideas and experiences as ruins. [For Benjamin] To understand something is to understand its topography . . . to know how to get lost [within time's space] . . . [T]ime is the medium of constraint, inadequacy, repetition, mere fulfillment. In time, one is only what one is: what one has always been. In space one can be another person. . . . Time does not give much leeway: it thrusts us forward from behind, blows us through the narrow funnel of the present to the future. But space is broad, teeming with possibilities, positions, intersections, passages, detours, U-turns, dead-ends, one-way streets. Too many possibilities indeed [S]ometimes one has to cut one's way through with a knife. Sometimes one ends by turning the knife against oneself" (Sontag, 1981, pp. 116–117).

Is this the time of allegory, the death of the author? I quote Gayatri Spivak (1977) and am ruined. "Autobiography can be a mourning for the perpetual loss of a name—one's proper word-thing." Should autobiography then be nothing but allegory? I met you and have lost my name. What a ruinous relation? You (w)rite me (over) with these words: "Dear person for whom I have no name." This is communication. You exist in relation to me (and others) in another time, a time of relations, an historical materiality of time imagined. Benjamin is critical of the illusory linearity of traditional autobiography. We do not remember the past, we re(w)rite it each time we give each other a present. This is a ruinous notion of the present. Thus, for Benjamin (1986, pp. 25–26), "memory is not an instrument for exploring the past but its theater. It is a medium of past experience, as the ground is the medium in which dead cities lie interred." Benjamin's autobiographical reminiscences are based not in linear narrational "sequence and what makes up the continuous flow of life" but in a self-ruining structure of "space, of moments and discontinuities" (Benjamin, 1986, p. 28). Benjamin collapses time in a sentence that re(w)rites the past continuously as discontinuity. This for Benjamin is the work of memory—reading oneself backwards. "There is no chronological ordering of his reminiscences," because time is reconceptualized as space (Sontag, 1981, p. 115). Did you say this as well? I don't remember exactly. I remember your black Converse sneakers, deep dark circles beneath your eyes beautiful, your sharp wit and laughing on our way to the ruins.

"I never laugh at death, no matter how often and regularly I am the cause of it" (Rice, 1976, p. 15). You wrote this quoting an *Interview with a Vampire*. This is what differentiated Benjamin's epistemological practice from the vampires'. To his melancholy Marxism was added the gift of surrealism, a revolutionary laughter at death in dying. "The melancholic always feels threatened by the domination of the thing-like, but surrealist taste mocks these terrors. Surrealism's great gift to sensibility was to make melancholy cheerful" (Sontag, 1981, p. 124). According to Benjamin, "The only pleasure the melancholic permits himself, and it is a powerful one, is allegory" (Sontag, 1981, p. 124). Benjamin was always working, re(w)riting, ruining his relation to things. This much he shared with the vampires: a desire for ruins.

"She shook her head. 'The ruins,' she said. 'It was always the ruins. . . . In my grandfather's time it was the ruins, and it is the ruins again.' "

Whenever Benjamin (w)rote of ruins, a given image was never far from his pen—the image of *Paris, Capital of the Nineteenth Century.* This also Benjamin shared with the vampires: "The very name of Paris brought a rush of pleasure" (Rice, 1976, p. 204).

"We must bypass Vienna [said the vampire]. We need our language, our people. I want to go directly to Paris . . . the first capital of western Europe" (Rice, 1976, p. 202). A century later *Capital* would lose its center. So would the vampires.

Paris, the Capital of the 19th Century

The terrorists wore masks and many senior year trips to Paris were canceled by high schools in the suburbs. The United States was drawing blood from civilian populations in Libya in the middle of the night, and the next day, on television, they were wondering if the kids and their parents would get a full refund. They were canceling their trips to Paris because there were terrorists and they wore masks. The terrorists wore masks like actors and Ronald Reagan, an actor, was President. He hoped the children would get a full refund on their ruined trips and said so, on television. No one seemed able to recognize the terrorists. They wore masks. It was a matter of consumer affairs.

In a Cafe, Not in Paris

This is an intervention. At gatherings where people come together to criticize literature, when someone is acknowledged as having a question, this is an intervention. This is a question. Here are its words. I am sitting at a cafe in Boston at the Isabella Stewart Gardner Museum with pen, paper, and a coffee, how romantic. I used to come here often when interpellated-in a romance with an other who guarded its visual treasures, aesthetic icons seized by a wife of 19th-century capital, a patroness of representation, definer of good taste. This was her duty: to bless us with an abundance of dead paintings and call them beauty. The ruins of art. They please the eyes that pay.

A waitress poses over my coffee and I (w)rite myself in relation. Why am I here? She is not the waitress I came to flirt with but I find myself called out by her beauty nonetheless. The ruins of art? I am inscribed once again by desire and slain within a historical narrative that is not entirely of my own choosing. Am I making this up? Where does this story come from? Where do I? I am picked up by my pen and make history. I write: REMINDER: Insert here quote from Karl Marx, The Eighteenth Brumaire of Louis Bonaparte.

> Men [and women] make their own history, but they do not make it just as they please; they do not make it under circumstances chosen by themselves, but under circumstances directly found, given, and transmitted from the past. The tradition of all the dead generations weigh like a nightmare on the brain of the living. (Marx, 1978, p. 595).

Benjamin was reading this text, The Eighteenth Brumaire, when visiting Brecht in Denmark. That is, it was reading him, re(w)riting itself in history through him. He was also thinking about theater. This much I remember about Benjamin. He wrote that "memory is not any instrument for exploring the past but its theater." Why am I here? I can't remember exactly. Is this theater? The waitress pours me more coffee and poses, how romantic. Are we flirting? Why this way? Would she pose like this, would I, had we not turned ourselves on before the television? Would we play these roles? Is this theater? She is too young to have seen "General Electric Theater," but I'm certain that she's seen Reagan and some fashion magazines. I can tell by the pose. Is this a kind of language? I'm beginning to forget. This is ruining our relationship. Once again, I (w)rite: REMINDER: Insert here second quote from The Eighteenth Brumaire.

> The beginner who has learnt a new language always translates it back into his [or her] mother tongue, [she or] he has assimilated the spirit of the new language and can produce freely in it only when [she or] he moves in it without remembering the old and forgets it in his [or her] ancestral tongue. (Marx, 1978, p. 595).

REMINDER: Instruct the reader that this is an allegory. This is not something new. This is a repetition. Is this the meaning of primitive romance, a CAPITAL idea? Benjamin was thinking about theater and the ruins of memory, about the forgetting that is our history and Marx's Eighteenth Brumaire. He was visiting Brecht in Denmark. Unlike Benjamin, Brecht believed that things could be made perfectly clear. Brecht was a Marxist but not melancholy. He criticized Benjamin's desire for allegory. He demanded that theater remember the truths of history without forgetting. According to Sontag (1981, p. 122), Brecht's was a "very . . . Un-Jewish sense" of history. Moreover, Brecht was a modernist, whereas Benjamin appears to anticipate more ruinously the postmodern, the mass-mediated image culture of late capital. Near Brecht's desk there sat a little wooden donkey around whose neck hung a sign that read: "I, too, must understand it." This was a sign of primitive romance. For Benjamin, things were more complex. Benjamin was nonetheless fascinated by Brecht's desire for precise meaning. REMINDER: Instruct the reader that Sontag (1981, p. 122) (w)rites that "Benjamin's 'masochistic' . . . relation to Brecht, which most of his friends deplored, shows the extent to which he was fascinated by this possibility." Why? Was this "masochism" related to a narrative of frustrated desire on the part of a Jewish son for recognition from a father that remained absent and bourgeois? Hannah Arendt suggests this. Of Benjamin, she (w)rites that "his father never recognized his claims, and their relations were extraordinarily bad" (Arendt, 1969, p. 27). Is this gossip or is Arendt re(w)riting the story of Oedipus in historically material terms we forget. This is our history. She (w)rites, "If Freud had lived and carried on his inquiries in a country and language other than the German-Jewish milieu which supplied his patients, we might never have heard of the Oedipus complex" (Arendt, 1969, p. 27).

Benjamin left his father's home in Germany for Paris, just as Nordic fascism projected its ruinous real upon the imperial screen. They were shooting images of purification and blood sacrifice into the blond veins of those for whom primitive romance had become a CAPITAL idea. But what if he had stopped in Vienna first? Lacan did, but that's another story. Then again Lacan was a "ladies man" (Gallop, 1982). A waitress poses over my coffee and I (w)rite myself in relation. Why am I here?

In Paris, Not a Cafe

" 'Let me explain,' I began. 'I know that you're a master vampire. I respect you. But I'm incapable of your detachment' " (Rice, 1976, p. 236).

The vampire had come to Paris to discover their origin. It was the capital of the 19th century.

" 'I understand,' said the master vampire . . . 'I saw you in the theater, your suffering, your sympathy with that girl . . . [Y]ou die when you kill, as if you feel you deserve to die, and you stint on nothing. But why, with this passion and this sense of justice, do you wish to call yourself a child of Satan!' " (Rice, 1976, p. 236).

He was referring to one of the more significant traps of primitive romance: the cult of evil. This trap consumed much of the potential resistance of alienated bourgeois artisans during the 19th century. It lingers still, now magnified electronically, close-circuited through every television set and Walkman. A desire to stray from the path of proper narrative, yet without ruining the base structure of the story itself, its historical destination: a CAPITAL idea. The pleasure of flirting promiscuously within fixed boundaries inscribed in time. Perhaps this represents an uncertain step to the left, a temporary slide carnally into knowledge of the fourth person, *la petite mort*, a trembling gesture of transitory self-loss, our consolation for the night. But at dawn, many more things remain to be undone. The ruinous potential of this evil is far from realized materially in history. Benjamin (1986, pp. 186–187) made note of this and wrote: "The seduction was too great to regard the Satanism . . . as a pendant to art for art's sake. . . . If, however, one resolves to open up this romantic dummy, one finds something usable inside. One finds the cult of evil as a political device, however, romantic, to disinfect and isolate against all moralizing dilettantism."

" 'I'm evil, evil as any vampire who ever lived! I've killed over and over and will do it again.' This, the apprentice vampire said to the master. The master replied, 'Why does that make of evil? Is evil a great perilous gulf into which one falls with the first sin, plummeting to the depth?' " (Rice, 1976, p. 236) This is a warning against primitive romanticism, of reducing evil to a single thing that can be counted upon clearly, to falling once and for all time into love and out of history.

She was dying to know the truth about this, to get these things under control, to name everything and so she asked, "What was it like making love?" (Rice, 1976, p. 210).

"I was walking away from her before I meant to, I was searching like a dim-witted mortal man for cap and gloves. 'Don't you remember?' she asked" (Rice: 1976, p. 210).

He remembered a time entwined with another. It was late at night and evil. They had taken shelter from the moon on his rug. Her nipples were erect but her eyes hesitant and he was trying not to think of his performance, like in the movies. She realized that they didn't even know each other's proper names and speculated that maybe he'd kill her and hide the body.

"I stopped, feeling her eyes on my back, ashamed, and then I turned around and made as if to think, where am I going, what shall I do, why do I stand here?" (Rice, 1976, p. 210).

This frightened her. Her nipples were erect but her eyes hesitant; why was she here? She lifted her blouse above her head, exposing her neck with a filmic gesture of sex and asked, "What was it like making love? Don't you remember?"

"It was something, hurried, I said, trying now to meet her eyes. How perfectly, cold blue they were. How earnest. And it was seldom savored . . . something acute that was quickly lost. I think it was the pale shadow of killing.

'Ahh . . .' she said. 'Like hurting you as I do now . . . that is also the pale shadow of killing" (Rice, 1976, p. 210).

This is a question. Did they lose themselves in intercourse on the rug that night, or were they lost in the solitary desires of another story: a romantic simulation of death? This is a warning against primitive romanticism, of reducing evil to a single thing that can be counted upon clearly, to falling once and for all time into love and out of history. But why am I writing this to you? This is a question. This is gossip. This is an allegory. You quoted the following words, re(w)riting them onto a sheet of paper, placing this paper in an envelope, and licking the stamp. You quoted neither my name nor yours. These are the words you wrote: "Evil with infinite gradations and without guilt . . . And I would be the protector of your pain." I read these words with a ruinous pleasure and with melancholy.

With care,

Without a certain name

A Postscript, The First

This is not a love letter, yet it had been a long time and he had wanted to quote to her from Benjamin.

A Postscript, The Second

In a letter to Gerhard Scholem dated April 17, 1931, Benjamin imagined himself "like one who keeps afloat on a shipwreck by climbing to the top of the mast that is already crumbling. But from there he has a chance to give a signal leading to his rescue."

A Postscript, The Third

Benjamin's last chance to signal came on September 26, 1940. The Fascists had taken Paris and Gestapo agents had seized each page of writing, each quotation from his apartment. He had arrived at the Spanish border to learn that only that day his exit was blocked. It was the middle of the night and he took his own life. "Sometimes one has to cut one's way through with a knife. Sometimes one ends by turning the knife against oneself" (Sontag, 1981, p. 117).

A Postscript, The Fourth

The death of the author: on history, allegory and autobiography; a quote. "In allegory the observer is confronted with . . . history as a petrified, primordial landscape. Everything about history that, from the very beginning, has been intimate, sorrowful, is expressed in a face—or rather in a death's head . . . [T]his is the form in which human subjection to nature is most obvious and it significantly gives rise not only to the enigmatic question of the nature of human existence as such, but also of the biographical historicity of the individual. This is the heart of the allegorical way of seeing" (Benjamin, 1977, p. 166; Owens, 1984).

A Postscript, The Fifth

Writing in the fifth person plural. I wish you well. Thoughts of you pass ruinously and often. "The boy seemed on the verge of saying something more, but the hand that rested on the table, slid forward on the boards, and his head lay down beside it as he lost consciousness" (Rice, 1976, p. 345).

ACKNOWLEDGMENTS

A note of thanks to Avery Gordon, Jackie Orr, Sandra Joshel, Andrew Herman, Marc Driscoll, and other members of the Parasite Cafe for their support, encouragement, and constructive criticism in the development of this manuscript.

References

Acker, K. (1978). Blood and guts in high school. New York: Grove Press.
Acker, K. (1986). Don Quixote. New York: Grove Press.
Arendt, H. (1969). Introduction. In W. Benjamin, Illuminations. New York: Schocken Books.
Baker, H. A. (1984). Blues, ideology and Afro-American literature. Chicago: University of Chicago Press.
Barthes, R. (1977). Image, music, text. New York: Hill and Wang.
Baudrillard, J. (1983). Simulations. New York: Semiotexte.
Baudrillard, J. (1987). Forgetting Foucault. New York: Semiotexte.
Benjamin, W. (1969). Illuminations. New York: Schocken Books.

Benjamin, W. (1977). *The origin of German tragic drama.* London: Verso.

Benjamin, W. (1986). *Reflections.* New York: Schocken Books.

Clifford, J. (1988). *The predicament of culture: Twentieth century ethnography, literature and art.* Cambridge, MA: Harvard University Press.

Daly, M., & Caputi, J. (1987). *Webster's first intergalactic wickedary at the English language.* Boston: Beacon Press.

Feuerbach, L. (1983). The essence of Christianity. In G. Debard, *Society of the spectacle.* Detroit: Black and Red Press.

Foucault, M. (1973). *Madness and civilization.* New York: Vintage Books.

Gallop, J. (1982). *The daughter's seduction: Feminism and psychoanalysis.* Ithaca, NY: Cornell University Press.

Gil, A., & King, J. (1981). Why theory? In Gang of 4, *Solid gold* (album). Burbank, CA: Warner Bros. Records.

Hollier, D. (Ed.). (1988). *The college of sociology 1937–39.* Minneapolis: University of Minnesota Press.

Hurston, L. N. (1981). *Tell my horse.* Berkeley, CA: Turtle Island.

Irigaray, L. (1985). *Speculum of the other woman.* Ithaca, NY: Cornell University Press.

Jackson, G. (1970). *Soledad brother: The prison letters of George Jackson.* New York: Coward-McCann.

Kroker, A., & Cook, D. (1986). *The postmodern scene: Excremental culture and hyperaesthetics.* New York: St. Martin's Press.

LeFebvre, H. (1984). *Everyday life in the modern world.* New Brunswick, NJ: Transition Books.

Levi-Strauss, C. (1986). Structures elementaires de la parente. In H. Cixous & C. Clement, *The newly born woman.* Minneapolis: University of Minnesota Press.

Lunn, E. (1982). *Marxism and modernism: A historical study of Lukács, Brecht, Benjamin and Adorno.* Berkeley: University of California Press.

Marx, K. (1978). The eighteenth brumaire of Louis Bonaparte. In R. C. Rucker (Ed.), *The Marx-Engels reader.* New York: W. W. Norton.

Mills, C. W. (1956). *White collar.* New York: Oxford University Press.

Morrison, T. (1970). *The bluest eye.* New York: Washington Square Press.

North, O. L. (1987). *Taking the stand: The testimony of Lieutenant Colonel Oliver L. North.* New York: Pocket Books.

Owens, C. (1984). The allegorical impulse: Toward a theory of postmodernism. In B. Wallis (Ed.), *Art after modernism: Rethinking representation.* New York: New Museum of Contemporary Art.

Pfohl, S., & Gordon, A. (1986). Criminological displacements: A sociological deconstruction. *Social Problems, 33*(6), S94–S113.

Reed, I. (1988). *Mumbo jumbo.* New York: Vintage Books.

Rice, A. (1976). *Interview with a vampire.* New York: Ballantine Books.

Richmond, M. (1984). *Reading Georges Bataille: Beyond the gift.* Baltimore: Johns Hopkins University Press.

Scott-Heron, G. (1981). B movie. In *Reflections* (album). New York: Arista Records.

Sontag, S. (1981). *Under the sign of Saturn.* New York: Vintage Books.

Spivak, G. C. (1974). Translator's preface. In J. Derrida, *Of grammatology.* Baltimore, MD: Johns Hopkins University Press.

Spivak, G. C. (1977). Glas-Piece: A compte rendu. *Diacritics, September.*

Spivak, G. C. (1987). *In other worlds: Essays in cultural policies.* New York: Methuen.

Wittig, M. (1971). *Les guerilleres.* New York: Aron Books.

CHAPTER 11

Some Thoughts on How and When to Predict in Criminal Justice Settings

Peter Schmidt and Ann Dryden Witte

Introduction

It is inconceivable that we would live our lives without predictions of "what will happen." We get up and listen to the weather *forecast* to decide how we will get to work and what we will wear. We continue our day by making decisions based on the "likely" economic outlook and the prospects for the organization for which we work (e.g., the sales of our firm, or the student enrollment and likely funding of our university). We return home to discuss the "career outlook" with our children. It is clear that forecasts and predictions play major roles in our daily lives.

Predictions play no lesser role in the lives of organizations, with larger and more sophisticated organizations dealing with larger "clienteles" generally using more formal predictions in more wide-ranging ways than smaller organizations. Our criminal justice system is no exception in this regard. Decisions have to be made, and they are inevitably made on the basis of predictions of future events. The predictions may be intuitive, clinical, anamnestic, or based on statistical models.

In this chapter we will consider the "proper" role of prediction in criminal justice decision making. We will also consider the accuracy of forecasts that is currently possible and that can be expected

PETER SCHMIDT • Department of Economics, Michigan State University, East Lansing, Michigan 48823.   ANN DRYDEN WITTE • Department of Economics, Wellesley College, Wellesley, Massachusetts 02181.

from the best methods currently available. Specifically, in the next section, we consider the use of prediction in criminal justice and some of the important issues currently being discussed in connection with making such predictions. We begin with a discussion of the ethical and legal issues that arise when making and using forecasts in criminal justice settings. We next turn to more technical issues that must be addressed if forecasts are to be made. These include the type of data that should be used in research that seeks to predict future behavior, the selection of a criterion variable and explanatory variables for prediction models, and the selection of a statistical methodology. In the penultimate section of the chapter, we discuss reasonable goals for prediction research in criminal justice. The final section contains our conclusions.

Prediction in Criminal Justice

There is a long history of prediction in criminal justice, as in many other areas. Individuals working in the criminal justice system must make decisions, and these can be improved if the policymakers are better informed about what the future is likely to hold. For example, police officers must determine whether or not to arrest a suspicious character, and prosecutors whether or not to bring a case to trial. Judges must decide whether or not to grant pretrial release, and for convicted offenders what type of sentence to impose. Correctional officials must determine the security level and activities of their charges, and parole boards must decide whether to release an inmate before the expiration of his or her sentence. Most criminal justice policymakers base their decision at least in part on their prediction of the likely future actions of the individual whose fate they are considering.

Historically, and in many cases today, predictions of the likely future actions of an individual are made informally on the basis of "experience" or "clinical judgment." However, it is realized increasingly that predictions emanating from statistical models tend to be more accurate than predictions made using either clinical or informal methods, and that statistical predictions can provide a valuable decision aid to criminal justice decision makers.[1]

There have been several recent reviews of the prediction litera-

[1]For example, see Gottfredson (1987), Gottfredson and Gottfredson (1986), and Monahan (1981). Gottfredson and Gottfredson (1986, p. 247) conclude after an extensive survey: "In virtually every decision-making situation for which the issue has been studied, it has been found that statistically developed predictive devices outperform human judgements."

ture and we will summarize the conclusions of these reviews, adding some insights of our own.[2] Having just completed a large-scale prediction project for the National Institute of Justice and the North Carolina Department of Correction, we are in a good position to step back and carefully consider the "when" and "how" of prediction in criminal justice.

Ethical and Legal Issues

The overriding issue in criminal justice prediction research is the ethical one, which has been debated extensively.[3] The major question that each criminal justice researcher and administrator must answer is: When and how is it appropriate to use prediction for criminal justice decision making? We feel that it is important to answer this question carefully.

Our professional experience convinces us that statistical prediction can be a very valuable decision-making tool. However, producing useful predictions often requires great care and considerable statistical sophistication. Further, predictions can be used in many ways. In the material that follows we will summarize the suggestions for use of predictions in criminal justice and indicate the way in which we would feel most comfortable using predictions derived from our work. It should be pointed out that we disagree (in spite of the fact that we have similar training and have worked together for the last 15 years) on how predictions should be used and what the proper role of the "scientist" is.

In our work prior to our most recent project, we have been careful not to make individual predictions, even though the group predictions that we did present were derived from such individual predictions.[4] As far as we are aware, the North Carolina Department of Correction (for which we carried out our research) has also refrained from using our models for the purpose of predicting whether or not a given individual would return to crime. However, the recent call for selective incapacitation has led both the department and us to rethink our positions. The department is under pressure to more effectively use scarce

[2] The reviews we will draw most heavily on are by Farrington (1987), Farrington and Tarling (1985a), Gottfredson (1987), and Gottfredson and Gottfredson (1986).

[3] For good summaries of the ethical issues, see Blumstein, Cohen, Roth, and Visher (1986), Farrington (1987), Morris and Miller (1985), and Tonry (1987).

[4] See Schmidt and Witte (1976, 1978, 1984). To obtain group predictions, we made individual predictions for each member of the group and cumulated the resulting predictions.

prison space. We are concerned that our models will be used to make individual predictions, even if we refrain from explicitly doing so.

In the work that we have completed most recently (Schmidt & Witte, 1988), we make and report results for individual predictions. We did this primarily out of scientific curiosity concerning the ability of our models to predict individual behavior. However, our comparison of the individual predictions and the actual behavior of the prison releasees we studied leads us to quite different conclusions. Schmidt concludes that our results are scientifically interesting, but that the predictions we are able to make should not influence criminal justice decision making. His reasons for believing this relate primarily to the fact that we are not able to predict with what he regards as sufficient accuracy. He would be quite willing to use predictions if we could predict with sufficient accuracy. Witte sees a potentially broader range of uses for our research. Readers should judge for themselves. We will simply report our results and conclusions and summarize the conclusions of the other respected researchers.

In our most recent research, we are able to identify a group of prison releasees that has over a 50% chance of reimprisonment and a group that has less than a 30% probability of returning to prison after release. In the jargon common to this type of research, we have a "false positive" rate of slightly less than 50% and a "false negative" rate of slightly less than 30%. What do we conclude? Different things! Schmidt concludes that "we do not dismiss the importance of a discussion of the ethics of a policy of selective incapacitation, or of other similar policies, but we believe the point is basically moot until models are developed that predict more accurately than is currently possible" (Schmidt & Witte, 1988, pp. 5–6). Witte agrees that predictions should be improved, but suggests that our ability to predict who *will not* return to crime is sufficient to allow the (predicted) probability of return to serious crime to be one piece of information used in selecting *convicted offenders* for *less harsh* treatment than they might otherwise receive.

In a very interesting and thoughtful paper, Morris and Miller (1985) suggest that prediction studies seek to provide criminal justice decision makers with actuarial tables structured like those widely used by life insurance companies. These tables would indicate, for groups with various characteristics, the probability that a member of the group would return to criminal activity. It is this type of information that Witte would feel comfortable providing to criminal justice decision makers. She, like Schmidt, feels that our recent work should not be used to provide decision makers with predictions of truly *individual* behavior. That is, she would provide decision makers with the probability that an individual with certain characteristics (e.g., three prior convictions for a property offense) would return to crime, but not indicate whether or not a particular individual would do so.

Neither of us ascribes to the traditional position of economists and many other scientists: "Our job is to produce science, and it is the policymaker's job to decide how to use it." Witte ascribes to a more "utilitarian" or "limited retributivist"[5] approach to the use of actuarial predictions. She sees a steady increase in researchers' ability to predict[6] and a need for the criminal justice system to make rapid decisions regarding the treatment of convicted offenders. Such decisions are almost always made at least partially on the basis of the likely predicted future behavior of the offender. She feels that such predictions are likely to be more accurate and less prejudicial if they are based on carefully developed statistical models. Schmidt's disagreement with this position is more practical than theoretical. Although we can predict better than before, we can still not predict very well, and to introduce statistical models to make such predictions risks granting the prediction process a spurious appearance of precision. Such an appearance might allow predictions to be used in ways that would be inappropriate.

Our positions regarding the use of prediction are divergent, but perhaps less so than the positions of others who have thought carefully about the use of prediction in criminal justice decision making. The spectrum of opinion ranges from that of the strict retributivists (see Monahan, 1981, for a discussion), who see no role for predictions in criminal justice decision making, to that of the strict utilitarians such as Posner (1977), who believe that predictions of future dangerousness are central to criminal justice decision making. Most recent statements by criminal justice researchers have tended toward the utilitarian perspective, while some legal scholars seem more open to the "just desserts" model of sentencing (e.g., Tonry, 1987). Perhaps the most controversial of the utilitarian proposals is "selective incapacitation" (Greenwood, 1982; Wilson, 1983). Under a policy of selective incapacitation scarce prison space would be allocated to those who are predicted to be high-rate, serious offenders. Proposals for selective incapacitation have brought forth strong reactions. We feel that our ability to predict who will return to prison, although it is

---

[5] See Tonry (1987) for a discussion. This is a position that Tonry ascribes to Norval Morris, former dean of the University of Chicago School of Law.
[6] Even as late as 1985, Morris and Miller reported that an ability to identify a group that had a 1-in-3 chance of returning to serious crime was the "state of the art" in prediction research. It should be noted that Morris and Miller were interested in violent crime, while we are interested in all offenses leading to reimprisonment.

good by comparison with previous criminal justice prediction studies, is not sufficient to warrant the use of our predictions to help implement a policy of selective incapacitation.[7]

Witte feels comfortable with Gottfredson and Gottfredson's (1986, p. 279) call for using prediction for "selective deinstitutionalization"[8] and Morris and Miller's (1985) suggestion that an increase in penalties because of prediction of likely future return to serious crime is acceptable so long as punishment is not increased beyond that which would be justified as deserved punishment independent of predictive information. Schmidt does not feel comfortable with either of these positions.

Having agreed to disagree about the arena in which we feel comfortable using prediction, we are left with the issue of deciding how to use the information that is available to actually produce predictions. This is an issue that has considerable scientific content, and, not surprisingly, we agree in our conclusions.

In justice settings, the information used for predictions generally consists of extensive data on the attributes, experiences, and activities of certain individuals. The use of such information for prediction generally involves two steps. First, a set of individual data is used to estimate a model. Second, the model is used together with information on individuals and sometimes structural variables to predict the individuals' future behavior. We believe that the way in which one should use information is quite different in step one and step two of this process. Furthermore, in our opinion, ethical issues arise only in step two of this process.

In step one of the prediction process, when one is estimating the prediction model, we believe that all information relevant to the behavioral outcome of interest should be used. Our reasons for believing this are statistical: Failure to use relevant variables will lead to biased estimates of the parameters of the prediction model. We should be very clear. We advocate the use of such controversial variables as race, ethnic group, sex, age, and religion when estimating a prediction model if these variables help to explain the behavior that one is seeking to predict. For example, in our recent work we seek to predict the return to prison of releasees from North Carolina's state prisons. Race and sex are strongly related to return to prison. Because this is so, we use such variables when estimating our models.

The inclusion of such variables when the parameters of the prediction model are estimated will help to purge other parameter esti-

---

[7] Recall that our false positive rate is only slightly less than 50%; that is, only slightly more than half of those we predict to return to prison actually do so.

[8] Recall that our false negative rate is less than 30%.

mates of the effects of these controversial variables. Recall that the parameter estimates in multivariate models are interpreted as indicating the effect of the variable (e.g., drug addiction, employment opportunities) on the criterion when all other explanatory variables in the model are held constant. Thus, for example, when we include race and sex in the models we estimate, we can interpret the findings for other variables as indicating the effects of these variables (e.g., previous record, drug addiction, age) on the probability of return to prison, controlling for the effect of race and sex. By including race and sex in our model, we have in a sense purged other parameter estimates of their effects. These results are clearly to be preferred to results obtained from models that omit race and sex when estimating the models. The estimated coefficients of explanatory variables in this latter type of model will often indirectly reflect racial and sexual differences as well as the independent effect of the explanatory variable under consideration.[9] For example, since previous record and employment opportunities are correlated with both race and sex, the "true" effect of these variables on future criminality will be misstated in models that omit these variables. The coefficient on previous record and employment opportunities in such models will inadvertently reflect not only the independent effect of these variables but also the effect of sex and race on return to crime. We will have inadvertently contaminated our model with a hidden potential for discrimination if we omit such variables as race and sex when estimating the model.

The second step in prediction is to use the model estimated in step one to predict future behavior. At this stage, selection of the variables to be used clearly involves ethical and legal issues. Consider the admonition of the Panel on Research on Criminal Careers: "Characteristics such as race, ethnicity, and religion are especially unacceptable as candidate predictors because they have no relationship to blameworthiness, . . . and their use affronts basic social values" (Blumstein et. al., 1986, p. 8). Further, as pointed out by Tonry (1987), the use of race, ethnicity, political beliefs, religion, and possibly sex for prediction is unlikely to meet the constitutional standards laid down by the Supreme Court. However, the use of other factors (e.g., prior record, age, status variables such as employment, addiction, and marital status) is nearly always permitted by the Court if there is no discriminatory intent and if the factors are used to form a "rational basis" for classification.

We would strongly oppose using the predictions of our fully specified model (including race and sex) for criminal justice decision mak-

[9]To be more precise, the effect of these variables will be reflected to the degree that they are correlated with the particular variable under consideration.

ing even if it were legal. We believe that an individual's race or sex should have no effect on the way in which the criminal justice treats the individual. In other words, our position is that race and sex should be included when the model is estimated, but information on race and sex should not be used when the model is used to make predictions.

The important statistical and practical issue is how much the failure to use such "unacceptable" information in step two compromises our ability to make accurate predictions. We explored this issue in our recent work (Schmidt & Witte, 1988). To do so, we first predicted recidivism using a fully specified model and information on all variables in the model, including race and sex. We then made predictions using the parameter estimates from our fully specified model but ignoring the information that we had on race and sex. Encouragingly, we found little loss of predictive power as a result of failing to use the available information on these two variables.[10]

What Sample Should Be Used to Estimate the Prediction Model?

Prediction models should be estimated using large samples of individuals who are as representative as possible of the group for whom predictions are to be made. For example, when the North Carolina Department of Correction asked us to estimate a model that would allow them to predict the likelihood that an individual would return to their system, we asked them to supply us with release cohorts. For our recent work, we received extensive information on two release cohorts: (1) all individuals released between July 1, 1977, and June 30, 1978, and (2) all individuals released between July 1, 1979, and June 30, 1980. Each of these cohorts contains approximately 9,500 individuals; they certainly qualify as large.[11] They are also quite representative of all releasees from the North Carolina prison system during the 1975–1985 time period. Such samples are clearly reasonable to use when estimating models to predict return to prison of North Carolina releasees. However, models estimated with such samples will be of limited use for decision makers in other jurisdictions (e.g., Arizona,

---

[10] See Petersilia and Turner (1987) for an extended discussion of the effect of omitting the racially correlated variable when making predictions of recidivism.

[11] Approximately half of the individual records in each cohort lacked information on one or more of the variables used in our analysis. It should also be noted that our data set unfortunately contained no structural variables. The number of usable records was 4,618 in 1978 and 5,739 for 1980. These are still large data sets, although they do differ in some ways from the full cohort. See Schmidt and Witte (1988) for details.

California, Massachusetts) or for decisions makers at other points in the criminal justice system (e.g., the police, prosecutors, courts).

With such large samples, we were in a rather luxurious position. Most past prediction studies have had sufficiently small samples that they used all sample members to estimate the prediction model. With our large samples, we pursued a different course. We split each of our cohorts randomly into two parts: an estimation sample (of approximately 1,500 individuals) that we used to estimate the prediction model, and a validation sample that we used to evaluate the predictive accuracy of the model.[12] We justify this approach on both practical and statistical grounds. As a practical matter, the models we use are very expensive to estimate, and estimation costs go up substantially as either the sample size or the number of parameters to be estimated increases. Our computer budget would not have allowed us to evaluate the wide variety of models that we did had we chosen larger estimation samples. Statistically, it is always best to check the ability of models to predict for individuals who were not used to estimate the model. This is possible only if information on such individuals is available. Our validation samples contained such information.

The approach we adopt, splitting the available observations into estimation and validation samples, is widely used and generally accepted as "good practice" in statistics. However, statisticians are now beginning to suggest that there are alternative ways of using the data that may be more efficient.[13] Specifically, they suggest the use of jackknifing and bootstrapping techniques. These techniques create multiple samples from the data and then proceed to estimate and predict using all available samples. The multiple models estimated with such techniques allow one to explore how sensitive model selection is to the particular sample used. The multiple predictions produced by jackknifing and bootstrapping techniques allow one to better assess the "shrinkage" that is likely when one predicts for individuals who were not in the set of data used to estimate the model. Such methods would have been prohibitively expensive in our recent research, but they may be more feasible in other contexts and as computing costs continue to decline.

---

[12] Our estimation samples contained 1,540 observations (one-third of the number of usable observations) for 1978 and 1,435 observations (one-fourth of the number of usable observations) for 1980. We limited our estimation samples to approximately 1,500 observations to limit our (considerable) computational costs; this number of observations yielded estimates with adequate precision.

[13] Copas and Tarling (1986) provide a good discussion of these issues. Their discussion explicitly considers criminal justice prediction. They also provide references to statistical literature.

Selection of Variables

In order to estimate a prediction model one must select both the criterion variable (the thing to be predicted) and a set of explanatory variables. We will discuss these choices in turn.

The most commonly used criterion variable in criminal justice modeling is simply an indicator of whether or not the individual participated in the activity of interest (e.g., failed to appear for trial, committed a new offense) during the period over which his or her activities were observed.[14] Such a variable is referred to as a binary variable since it generally assumes a value of either 1 (indicating that the individual participated in the activity) or 0 (indicating that the individual did not participate).

The criterion variable in our recent work was the length of time between release from North Carolina's state prisons and return thereto. This dependent variable is clearly more informative than the binary criterion variable described above, since it also incorporates information on the *timing* of return to prison.[15]

There have been increasing calls for use of a criterion variable that incorporates information on the timing of the event of interest; for example, see Blumstein *et al.* (1986), Farrington and Tarling (1985), and Stollmack and Harris (1974). The National Academy of Sciences Panel on Research on Criminal Careers concludes that future development of prediction models "should be aimed at improving the classification of offenders in terms of their frequency of offending and their residual career length. While these career dimensions are not directly observable, their values can be inferred using statistical techniques that analyze time to recidivism" (Blumstein *et al.*, 1986, p. 9).

There are three compelling reasons for considering the timing of an activity rather than just the traditional binary criterion variable. First, from a statistical point of view, the timing of an activity contains valuable information that it is statistically inefficient to ignore. Second, estimation of the distribution of the length of time until an activity occurs allows one to predict the rate of the activity for any desired period, not just for the particular follow-up period found in the data used to estimate the model. For example, estimation of the distribution of the length of time until recidivism allows one to predict the rate of recidivism for any desired period after release, not just for the follow-up period. Finally, use of the timing of the activity as the cri-

---

[14] For recent examples of the use of this binary criterion variable, see Berk and Rauma (1983), Farrington and Morris (1983), Menard and Covey (1983).

[15] Note, however, that our dependent variable does not reflect the seriousness of the offense.

terion variable brings to the fore and allows researchers to deal with the fact that few if any follow-up studies last long enough to allow observation of all potential activities of interest. This failure to observe an act of interest that will eventually occur is called *censoring* in the statistical literature. Use of the timing of the activity as criterion variable allows one to explicitly deal with this issue.

We next turn to the problem of what explanatory variables (if any) should be used in a prediction model. The answer is—it depends. Our own thinking has changed somewhat as a result of our most recent work (Schmidt & Witte, 1988). We have long been advocates of the inclusion of relevant explanatory variables in prediction models (see, for example, Schmidt & Witte, 1976, 1978, 1984, Witte & Schmidt, 1977). Our position has contrasted rather sharply with that of criminal justice researchers such as Stollmack and Harris (1974) and Maltz and his colleagues (e.g., Maltz, 1984; Maltz & McCleary, 1977) who have generally not used any explanatory variables when estimating prediction models. These researchers have simply fit a statistical distribution to the data on the timing of offense. We will summarize our current position in this debate.

We still believe that it is best to include explanatory variables in prediction models. However, in our recent work we found that models that did not explicitly include any explanatory variables were able to predict as well as those that did for *random samples of prison releasees*. Thus, researchers with no "better" explanatory variables than we had (and ours weren't that bad, but did not include structural variables) who did wish to predict for random samples of the prison population may save time and money by using models that do not explicitly incorporate explanatory variables rather than more complex models that do incorporate such variables. However, models without explanatory variables will predict precisely the same behavior (probability distribution) for everyone.

We consider this an interim position since we believe that as better theoretical models and better explanatory variables become available, models with explanatory variables will predict better than models without such variables even when predictions are made only for *random samples of the population*. By reducing the variance of the prediction for each individual in a group, we ought to reduce the variance of the predictions for group averages (e.g., the recidivism rate). An analysis of the timing of an activity that does not use explanatory variables amounts to an analysis of its *marginal* distribution, whereas an analysis using explanatory variables amounts to an analysis of the distribution of survival time *conditional* on these variables. It is a standard result that the variance of the conditional distribution is less than the variance of the marginal distribution. In a linear regression model, the ratio of these two variances is 1 minus the R^2 of the regression (the portion of the variance of the dependent variable not "explained" by the explanatory variables). Similar considerations apply in more complicated models, such as survival models (i.e., models of the timing of an activity); the variance of predictions will be reduced to the extent that the variance of the event to be predicted is "explained" by observable explanatory variables. In our recent work, and in most other work in criminology, the proportion of the variance in the dependent variable that is explained by explanatory variables is rather small. (The equivalent of R^2 in our models was on the order of .10.) However, with better models and better data, we presume that this proportion can be (and will be) increased. If so, we should find that models with explanatory variables will predict more accurately than models without them, even for random samples of releasees.

Having discussed the case of prediction for random samples of releasees, we now make the important point that it is essential to include explanatory variables in the model if one wishes to predict for nonrandom samples or for individuals. This is most obvious in the case of prediction for individuals, since a model that does not contain individual characteristics could only predict the same probability of recidivism for everyone, and this would not be very useful. In the case of prediction for nonrandom samples of individuals, the usefulness of explanatory variables is that they allow one to correct for differences between the group used to estimate the model and the group for which the prediction is to be made. As a simple example, suppose one has estimated a model for the timing of recidivism using data on a random sample of releasees (of all ages), but wishes to make predictions of the rate of recidivism for a group of youthful offenders. There is little hope of accurate predictions unless the statistical model contained age as an explanatory variable. As a more detailed example, in our most recent work we estimated models for the timing of recidivism using random samples of individuals released from prison in North Carolina in FY1978 and in FY1980. The rate of recidivism is higher for 1980 releasees than it is for 1978 releasees. When we fit models without explanatory variables to the 1978 data, they consistently underpredict the rate of recidivism in the 1980 data. However, when we fit models that contain explanatory variables to the 1978 data, they predict the 1980 releasees' recidivism quite accurately. In other words, differences in observed characteristics of the releasees appear to explain adequately the differences in recidivism rates of the 1978 and 1980 cohorts. In general, models with explanatory variables will generate more accurate predictions because they can adjust for changes in the characteristics of the group for which predictions will be made.

The most frequent use of prediction research in criminal justice in the past has been to predict future case loads (e.g., number of crimes, number of court cases, number of prison inmates), to evaluate various innovative management techniques (e.g., better case management in prosecutor's offices) and programs, and to provide estimates of the probability of a future activity of interest for individuals. Models without explanatory variables can be used to project case loads and to evaluate programs applied to random samples of the population. However, evaluation of programs applied to nonrandom samples and individual prediction will require models that explicitly incorporate explanatory variables. It strikes us that many or most prediction exercises will involve predictions for individuals or for nonrandom groups of individuals. If so, models with explanatory variables should be the mainstay of criminal justice prediction research.

There is an additional reason why it may be worthwhile to include individual characteristics in models of time until recidivism, which does not relate directly to prediction. Inclusion of explanatory variables enables one to make statements about the effects of demographic or environmental variables on return to criminal activity, and these may be interesting in and of themselves. For example, in our recent work we found that the time until recidivism is significantly related to age, race, sex, marital status, alcohol or drug abuse, and prior record. Such findings are clearly of interest to criminal justice researchers and practitioners.

Selection of a Statistical Methodology

Selection of a statistical methodology should be based on the distribution of the criterion variables, conditional on the explanatory variables, if there are any. Recall that models without explanatory variables simply fit a single distribution to the timing of the event of interest.

We have suggested that prediction studies analyze the length of time until an event of interest (e.g., return to crime) occurs. The distribution of the timing of events contains a number of unusual features that call for some care in statistical analysis. First, the distribution is generally skewed to the right. For example, most individuals who return to crime do so quite quickly, although a few do return only after a substantial period of refraining from crime. Second, the observed distribution of the timing of an event of interest is generally censored on the right. This occurs because follow-up periods in criminal justice research are not generally long enough to observe al individuals who will ultimately participate in an activity doing so. For example, in our recent work using information on releasees from the North Carolina prison system, our follow-up period ranged from 46 to 81 months. These follow-up periods are among the longest we are aware of in studies of recidivism. Approximately one-third of the individuals in these release cohorts returned to prison during this follow-up period; two-thirds did not. Some of these latter individuals will eventually return to prison, but we do not observe the timing of their return. It is for this reason that the timing of return is said to be *censored*. It is inappropriate either to ignore the individuals who do not return to prison or to set their date of return at the end of the follow-up period.[16] Third, in many criminal justice applications the probability that an individual who has not previously participated in an event of interest will do so during a given time period (known in the literature as the *hazard rate*) is not monotonic. For example, when modeling the length of time until prison releasees return to prison, we found that the probability of return (for those who had survived until the time under consideration) increases for the first few months, peaks, and then declines rapidly. (See Figures 1 and 2 for the pattern of return to prison for our 1978 and 1980 validation samples.) The final notable feature of survival times is that they are nonnegative by definition and may take on a wide range of values.

Analyses of the timing of events of interest have a long history in biostatistics and operations research but have been used relatively infrequently either in criminal justice or in the social sciences more generally. Such analyses are generally referred to as *survival analyses* or *failure time analyses*. We will use these two terms interchangeably since both refer to whether or not an event will occur. It is this type of analysis that we suggest for extensive use in prediction research in criminal justice applications.

Such models specifically take into account the censoring of observations on timing by reflecting the fact of censoring in the likelihood function that is used to estimate the model. Both parametric models (which assume a particular distribution for the timing of the event of interest) and nonparametric models have been used. Nonparametric models merely faithfully reflect the patterns actually observed in the data. As is clear from Figures 1 and 2, the probability of failure in a given month jumps around a good bit. Undoubtedly the more radical departures from the overall trend are due to chance or random events. For example, in Figure 1 note the large and unexpected dip in the

---

[16] See Brannas and Eklof (1985) for a recent example of work that is statistically sophisticated but still ignores the censoring issue. The issue was, however, not central to their work since only 5% of their sample were not observed to participate in the activity they were analyzing.

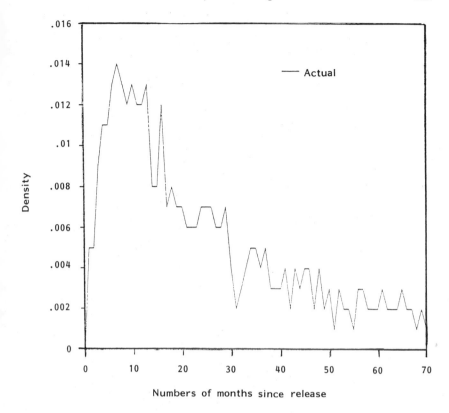

Figure 1. Actual recidivism—1978 validation sample.

density at 30 months. Such chance occurrences cannot be expected to occur in other samples. For example, there is no large dip in month 30 observed in Figure 2. We and a number of other researchers (e.g., Chaiken & Rolph, 1981) see nonparametric methods such as life table analyses and Cox's proportional hazards model as best used in preliminary analyses. They can provide a very useful standard against which to judge various parametric models. However, a good parametric model will "smooth" the temporal variation in probability of return, and this should result in improved predictions. The potential problem in using a parametric model is that the model can be (and in practice always is) wrong, in the sense that it represents only an approximation to the true distribution being modeled. The strength of parametric models will be realized only if a "correct" distribution (one that adequately reflects the major aspects of the timing of the event being studied) is chosen. Indeed, an adequate parametric model may yield predictions that are much worse than those from a nonparametric model.

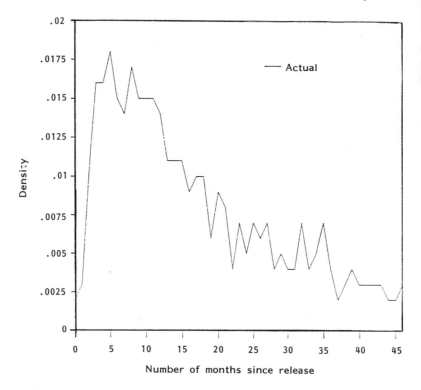

Figure 2. Actual recidivism—1980 validation sample.

To make the above discussion more concrete, consider our work with parametric and nonparametric survival models to analyze the length of time between release from prison and return thereto for releasees from the North Carolina prison system (Schmidt & Witte, 1988). We began by estimating nonparametric models. These models could predict the recidivism rate for similar samples quite well but were not able to predict the probability of recidivism during a particular month (the density) or the probability that an individual who had survived up to that point would return to prison during the month (the hazard rate) very accurately. We next carefully considered the important features of the timing of return to prison (see Figures 1 and 2). The first obvious feature of the distribution of the timing to return to prison is that both the hazard rate and the density are nonmonotonic. For example, in both 1978 and 1980, the hazard rate rises for approximately the first 6 months after the release, and then it falls. such nonmonotonic behavior of the hazard rate is apparently rare in most applications of survival analysis. One can readily find examples of a constant hazard rate (radioactive decay), a rising hazard rate (older light bulbs are more likely to fail), or a decreasing hazard rate (the longer one survives the surgery, the less likely one is to die of complications of the surgery), but not of a nonmonotonic hazard rate.

Unfortunately, most of the work that has used survival models to study the timing of events of interest to criminal justice researchers has simply adopted models from biostatistics or operations research without properly considering the peculiarities of the criminal justice application.[17] Since most applications of survival models in criminal justice involve recidivism in some way, criminal justice applications will generally require specialized survival models that allow the hazard rate to be nonmonotonic.

A second important aspect of survival time in our application is that once hazard rate begins to fall, it falls very quickly, since very few individuals who have not returned to prison within 2 to 3 years do so later. This indicates that we have to select a model that allows for a rapidly falling hazard rate once the hazard rate begins to fall. An extremely simple and effective way to do so is to recognize the fact that not all individuals would ultimately return to prison, even if we observed them for the rest of their lifetime.[18] This was not an issue for biostatisticians (all people do eventually die) or operations researchers (all light bulbs do eventually burn out). Following Maltz and McCleary (1977), we will refer to a model in which the eventual recidivism rate is less than 1 as a *split model*. In such a split model, the probability of eventual recidivism is an additional parameter to be estimated. Split models tend to imply rapidly falling hazard rates, because the surviving population is increasingly made up of individuals who will never fail. They fit our data very well, and we suspect that they will also be useful in many other survival analyses in justice applications.

With extensive effort we found a statistical model that fits our recidivism data quite well.[19] We call this model the logit lognormal

---

[17] For examples of this work, see Carr-Hill and Carr-Hill (1972), Harris, Kaylan, and Maltz (1981), Harris and Moitra (1978), Maltz (1984), Maltz and McCleary (1977), and Stollmack and Harris (1974).

[18] In our recent work (Schmidt & Witte, 1987), we estimate that the rate of recidivism would be approximately 50% if we were to follow all individuals in our cohort until death. That is, we estimate that the probability of eventual recidivism for a new releasee from the North Carolina prison system is 50%.

[19] We first tried models based on the exponential (the most commonly used distribution in criminal justice applications), lognormal, log-logistic, Weibull, and LaGuerre distributions. All of these distributions except the LaGuerre distributions are commonly considered in the failure time literature. None of these distributions fit our data very

model, and it has two important features.[20] First, it is a split model, so that it implies that not everyone would eventually return to prison. However, rather than assume that this probability is the same for all individuals, we let it vary across individuals according to a logit model. Second, we assumed a lognormal distribution for the timing of recidivism (for those who would return eventually). This distribution allows the hazard rate to increase, reach a peak, and then decline, which is the pattern that we observe in our data. This model fits the data very well and yielded very satisfactory predictions for our validation samples. However, in comparing parametric models to nonparametric models, it is important to stress both aspects of our experience. We had to search very hard to find a parametric model that predicted better than the nonparametric model; but, when we did, it predicted much better.

What Are Realistic Goals for Prediction Research?

Although there is general acceptance of the proposition that statistical prediction surpasses informal or clinical prediction,[21] there is also pessimism concerning the ability of more sophisticated models to improve our ability to predict recidivism. For example, both Far-

well. They all tended to overpredict recidivism for the period immediately after release, to underpredict recidivism for the next year or so, and to overpredict recidivism for periods long after release. The overprediction for periods long after release results from the fact that all of these models assume that everyone will eventually fail. For our application, this implies that all prison releasees will eventually return to prison, which, fortunately, does not appear to be the case.

We next considered split models, in the sense of Maltz and McCleary (1977). In a split model, it is assumed that not all individuals will eventually return to prison, and the probability of eventual recidivism is an additional parameter to be estimated. The distribution that is assumed for time until recidivism is understood to be relevant only for the fraction of the sample that will eventually fail. We tried the five distributions listed above for the timing of recidivism conditional on eventual recidivism.

Finally, we estimated models that allowed explanatory variables to affect both the probability of eventual recidivism and the timing of recidivism for those who will eventually fail.

[20] Our logit lognormal model assumes that explanatory variables affect the probability of eventual recidivism according to a logit model. Explanatory variables, however, do not affect the timing of recidivism for those who eventually will return to prison. The timing of recidivism is assumed to follow a lognormal distribution with constant mean and variance. That is, our model of the timing of recidivism is a model without explanatory variables.

[21] See Farrington and Tarling (1985a), Gottfredson and Gottfredson (1986), and Monahan (1981).

rington and Tarling (1985a) and Gottfredson (1987) conclude that the use of more sophisticated statistical methods has not enabled criminal justice researchers to predict more accurately than Burgess (1928) did by giving equal weight to all explanatory variables. This is quite discouraging, and although Farrington, Gottfredson, and Tarling call for further work on statistical methods, they are clearly not overly optimistic regarding the ability of more sophisticated models to achieve major improvements in prediction.

Our own recent work was clearly centered on using more sophisticated methods, and we believe that this work illustrates the benefit of doing so. In 1985 Morris and Miller characterized the state of the art in prediction research as predicting one true positive for every two false positives (pp. 15–16). More recently, Farrington (1987) concluded that few well-designed prediction exercises will manage to keep both false positive and false negative rates below 50%. In our work, we obtained a false positive rate of 47.2% and a false negative rate of 27.7%. That is, of the individuals who we predicted would return to crime, slightly over half actually did so, and of the individuals who we predicted would remain crime-free, over two-thirds actually did so. We believe that this provides convincing evidence of the usefulness of developing more appropriate statistical models for criminal justice prediction. We believe that the pessimism of Farrington, Gottfredson, and Tarling is unfounded. However, we should point out that the model that we used to predict was, indeed, quite sophisticated.

Since we have gone on record as believing that improvements in predictive ability are still possible, it is worthwhile to ask what it is likely to be possible to achieve in the best of all possible prediction settings. Suppose we had an extremely well-developed theory of crime and we were actually able to observe the actions of potential criminals and of those who respond to them (e.g., police, prosecutors, judges). Further, suppose we were able to collect information on all variables relevant to criminal activity. Next, assume that we had carefully chosen an appropriate statistical method, and we used this method and the data we collected to estimate a model of criminality. How well should we expect this model to explain individual criminality?

There is a considerable body of work in the economics literature reporting estimates of models with individual data, in which the dependent variable is the wage rate, hours of work, or some such similar variable. The experience in that literature is that it is rare to be able to explain more than half of the variation in the dependent variable. Why should this be so? There are two basic reasons. First, there is inherent randomness in individual behavior, and this element of uncertainty will remain even if we perfectly estimate the perfect model. Second, there are factors that affect individual behavior that we are unlikely to measure perfectly (or ever know about). For example, when estimating wage equations we are unlikely to have perfect measures of such important variables as motivation, and we have to worry about measurement error even in such well-defined variables as age and education. The random element that we observe will be larger as the importance of such omitted variables in explaining the criterion variable increases.

We would expect that criminal activity has a much larger random element than wages or hours of work and, thus, that we may never be able to explain more than 30% or so of the variation in common measures of criminality. The reasons are relatively straightforward. First, it seems to us quite likely that the criminal decision would be subject to far larger random or chance effects than are wages or hours of work. Second, we are likely to be forced to omit far more relevant explanatory variables when we estimate a crime equation than when we estimate an equation designed to explain wages or hours of work. Wages or hours of work are determined by the economic structure and the joint decisions of employers and workers, while criminal activity requires the congruence of proclivity and opportunity. While it is quite possible to observe many relevant characteristics of the economic structure, employers, and workers, it is much more difficult to measure the factors that lead to a willingness to commit criminal acts and even more difficult to find variables that will accurately reflect the opportunities for crime that the potential criminal faces. As a result, we are likely to omit far more relevant explanatory variables from a crime model than from a wage model, and we are again left with the conclusion that the degree to which explanatory variables will explain variation in the criterion variable is far greater for employment than for criminal activities.

We are not discouraged by our likely inability to explain the majority of the variation in criminal activity. Models that explain a significant portion (even if not the majority) of the variation in crime are clearly useful for both theory and policy. Rather, we believe that it is useful to consider the possible explanatory power of statistical models so that we evaluate prediction research against realistic rather than unattainable goals.

To date, prediction research in criminal justice has been far from the ideal described above, and, as might be expected, the level of explanation obtained has been far below 30%. After careful consideration of the literature, Gottfredson (1987) concludes that the proportion of the outcome variance explained rarely exceeds 15 to 20% and is most frequently lower. The studies that Gottfredson was considering overwhelmingly use the traditional binary criterion variable. As discussed previously, in our recent work we used a more informative criterion variable, the length of time from release until return to prison. With this dependent variable we are seeking to explain not only *who* returns to crime but also *when* they return. Since we are making greater demands on the model, we would, in general, expect to obtain lower explanatory power than if we were seeking to explain who returns to crime. Actually, we obtained explanatory power that is quite similar (an R^2 equal to .10 for 1978 and .12 for 1980) to that of studies that use a binary criterion variable.[22] We feel that this is quite good in the present circumstances and could probably be approximately doubled if we were to more carefully consider the way in which we use our explanatory variables. Better data would allow further improvement.

The ultimate test of prediction research is not variance explained, but rather ability to predict. As we reported earlier, we were able to predict far more accurately than has been traditional in criminal justice research.

Conclusions

We are now ready to answer the question that we posed in the title of this chapter: How and when should one predict in criminal justice settings? We are in much greater agreement on the "how" than on the "when" portion of this question, and hence we will summarize our conclusions regarding "how" first.

One should predict with the best statistical and criminological theory available, using the timing of the event of interest as the criterion variable. The data used to estimate prediction models should be as representative as possible of groups for whom predictions are to be made, and should contain information for as long a follow-up period as possible. The prediction model should incorporate a carefully selected set of explanatory variables. It is in the selection of explanatory variables that criminological theory can be most helpful.

The prediction model should be estimated using parametric survival techniques. Furthermore, the model should be a split model in the sense that the probability of eventual participation in the activity should be estimated, rather than assumed to be equal to 1. Researchers should choose with considerable care a distribution for the timing of the event being studied. In making this choice the investigator should

[22] Gottfredson and Gottfredson (1986) obtain R^2s from .09 (using association analysis) to .14 (using multiple regression analysis) with a binary criterion variable.

carefully consider the pattern of the hazard rate and density for the data being used. Our work leads us to believe that the hazard rate will be nonmonotonic for most criminal justice applications, and the analyst should consider distributions such as the lognormal and log-logistic that explicitly allows for this pattern in the hazard rate.

Prediction models should be estimated using all independent variables that help explain the timing of the event being studied. We feel very strongly about this point and wish our position to be very clear. When estimating prediction models, criminal justice researchers should include such controversial variables as race, sex, and religion if these variables help to explain the timing of the event under consideration, even though these variables will not be considered in actually making predictions from the model. The predictions of models that have been estimated using these controversial variables will be less prejudicial and discriminatory than predictions from models that exclude such relevant variables when the model is estimated. The advice to include these variables when the model is estimated is in no way in conflict with our opposition to the use of such explanatory variables as race, sex, and religion in making predictions. (The models used to predict should have been estimated including these variables, but the actual predictions should not take these variables into consideration.) This raises an important practical issue. How well can we predict when we exclude some relevant explanatory variables when making predictions? Our own work and the work of Petersilia and Turner (1987) leads us to believe that the exclusion of these "unacceptable" variables when predictions are made will not substantially degrade our ability to predict.

This brings us to the "when" question for prediction research. The simple fact is that we disagree on this issue. Schmidt believes that we should not at this point use predictions from statistical models for criminal justice decision making. He believes that we need better models before we use such models to make important decisions regarding the extent and type of restrictions to place on suspected or convicted offenders. By way of contrast, Witte believes that our models are now good enough (although far from perfect) to inform some types of criminal justice decision making. She believes that prediction models can provide useful "actuarial tables," which would provide decision makers with the probability that groups with various characteristics (e.g., older, first offenders who are married and not addicted to either alcohol or drugs) would or would not return to criminal activity. Decision makers would, of course, use such information as they saw fit. However, a number of studies indicate that decisions can be improved when such information is available. Witte would not advocate the use of such tables at all points in the criminal justice system but would rather see such tables used to justify fewer restrictions on the freedom of convicted offenders who are less likely to return to criminal activity. Both Witte and Schmidt strongly oppose the use of currently available statistical predictions to implement a policy of selective incapacitation.

References

Berk, R. A., & Rauma, D. (1983). Capitalizing on random assignment to treatments: A regression-discontinuity evaluation of a crime-control program. *Journal of the American Statistical Association, 78,* 21–27.

Blumstein, A., Cohen, J., Roth, J. A., & Visher, C. A. (Eds.). (1986). *Criminal career and career criminal* (2 vols.). Washington, DC: National Academy Press.

Brannas, K., & Eklof, J. A. (1985). Criminal policy and recidivism—An empirical study on Swedish data (Working paper). Umea, Sweden: University of Umea, Department of Statistics.

Burgess, E. W. (1928). Factors determining success or failure on parole. In A. A. Bruce, E. W. Burgess, & A. J. Harno (Eds.), *The workings of the indeterminate sentence law and the parole system in Illinois.* Springfield: Illinois State Board of Parole.

Carr-Hill, G. A., & Carr-Hill, R. A. (1972). Reconviction as a process. *British Journal of Criminology, 12,* 35–43.

Chaiken, J. M., & Rolph, J. E. (1981). Methods for estimating crime rates of individuals (Report of the Rand Corporation to the National Institute of Justice, R-2730-NIJ).

Copas, J. B., & Tarling, R. (1986). Some methodological issues in making predictions. In A. Blumstein, J. Cohen, J. A. Roth, & C. A. Visher (Eds.), *Criminal career and career criminal* (Vol. 2, pp. 291–313). Washington, DC: National Academy Press.

Farrington, D. P. (1987). Predicting individual crime rates. In D. M. Gottfredson & J. Tonry (Eds.), *Crime and justice: An annual review of research* (Vol. 9). Chicago: University of Chicago Press.

Farrington, D. P., & Morris, A. M. (1983). Sex, sentencing and reconviction. *British Journal of Criminology, 23,* 229–248.

Farrington, D. P., & Tarling, R. (1985a). Criminological prediction: The way forward. In D. P. Farrington & R. Tarling (Eds.), *Prediction in criminology* (pp. 258–268). Albany: State University of New York Press.

Farrington, D. P., & Tarling, R. (Eds.). (1985b). *Prediction in criminology.* Albany: State University of New York Press.

Gottfredson, S. D. (1987). Prediction: An overview of selected methodological issues. In D. M. Gottfredson & J. Tonry (Eds.), *Crime and justice: An annual review of research* (Vol. 9). Chicago: Chicago University Press.

Gottfredson, S. D., & Gottfredson, D. M. (1986). Accuracy of prediction models. In A. Blumstein, J. Cohen, J. A. Roth, & C. A. Visher (Eds.), *Criminal career and career criminal* (Vol. 2, pp. 212–290). Washington, DC: National Academy Press.

Greenwood, P. (1982). *Selective incapacitation.* Santa Monica, CA: Rand.

Harris, C. M., Kaylan, A. R., & Maltz, M. D. (1981). Refinements in the statistics of recidivism measurement. In J. A. Fox (Ed.), *Mathematical frontiers in criminology.* New York: Academic Press.

Harris, C. M., & Moitra, S. (1978). Improved statistical techniques for the measurement of recidivism. *Journal of Research in Crime and Delinquency, 15,* 194–213.

Maltz, M. D. (1984). Recidivism. Orlando, FL: Academic Press.

Maltz, M. D., & McCleary, R. (1977). The mathematics of behavioral change: Recidivism and construct validity. Evaluation Quarterly, 1, 421–438.

Menard, S., & Covey, H. (1983). Community alternatives and rearrest in Colorado. Criminal Justice and Behavior, 10, 93–108.

Monahan, J. (1981). Predicting violent behavior: An assessment of clinical techniques. Beverly Hills: Sage.

Morris, N., & Miller, M. (1985). On "dangerousness" in the judicial process. In M. Tonry & N. Morris (Eds.), Crime and justice: An annual review of research (Vol. 7, pp. 1–50). Chicago: University of Chicago Press.

Petersilia, J., & Turner, S. (1987). Guideline-based justice: Implications for racial minorities. In D. M. Gottfredson & J. Tonry (Eds.), Crime and justice: An annual review of research (Vol. 9). Chicago: University of Chicago Press.

Posner, R. A. (1977). Economic analysis of law. Boston: Little, Brown.

Schmidt, P., & Witte, A. D. (1976). Determinants of criminal recidivism (Report to the North Carolina Department of Correction).

Schmidt, P., & Witte, A. D. (1978). Determinants of criminal recidivism: Further investigations (Report to the North Carolina Department of Correction).

Schmidt, P. & Witte, A. D. (1984). An economic analysis of crime and justice: Theory, methods, and applications. Orlando, FL: Academic Press.

Schmidt, P. S., & Witte, A. D. (1987). How long will they survive?: Predicting recidivism using survival models (Report to the National Institute of Justice).

Schmidt, P. S., & Witte, A. D. (1988). Predicting recidivism using survival models. New York: Springer-Verlag.

Stollmack, S., & Harris, C. M. (1974). Failure rate analysis applied to recidivism data. Operations Research, 23, 1192–1205.

Tonry, M. (1987). Prediction and classification: Legal and ethical issues. In D. M. Gottfredson & J. Tonry (Eds.), Crime and justice: An annual review of research (Vol. 9). Chicago: University of Chicago Press.

Wilson, J. Q. (1983). Crime and public policy. San Francisco: Institute for Contemporary Studies Press.

Witte, A. D., & Schmidt, P. (1977). An analysis of recidivism, using truncated lognormal distribution. Applied Statistics, 26, 302–311.

Index

ABA, *see* American Bar Association
ABA Model Rules of Professional Conduct, 32
Abortion, 23, 27n, 73, 107, 218
Accidents, 73
Acker, Kathy, 218, 237
ACLU, *see* American Civil Liberties Union
Acquired Immune Deficiency Syndrome (AIDS), 23, 163, 209
Addiction, 71, 72, 85, *see also* specific types
Adjudication, 56, 57
Adultery, 59
Affirmative action programs, 27
Africa, 57, 58, 128, 129
    precolonial, 17
Age, 78, 92, 93, 94, 192
    justice and, 190
    recidivism prediction and, 252, 253, 258, 259
AIDS, *see* Acquired Immune Deficiency Syndrome
Albania, 44
Albanians, 140
Alcohol abuse, 59, 73, 85, 94, 259
Algeria, 45
Allocation, 119
    defined, 117
Alternative Dispute Resolution, 190, 202
AMA, *see* American Medical Association
American Bar Association (ABA), 25, 34
American Civil Liberties Union (ACLU), 26n-27n
American Medical Association (AMA), 25
American Nazi Party, 27n
American Trial Lawyers' Association, 25
Anastasia, 161
Anomie, 73

Anticipatory societal reaction, 82
Antifeminist movement, 86
Antisocial behavior, 92
Arbitration, 43, 56, 57
Arendt, Hannah, 241
Aristophanes, 129, 139
Asia, 128, 133
Assamese, 133
Assassination, 43
Australia, 22
Authority, 4
Automobile industry, 204, 205
Automobile theft, 180
Avoidance, 2, 43, 49-53, 54, 56, 58, 60, 61
    defined, 49

Baker, Houston, 219
Banishment, 43
Bank burglary, 87
Bar associations, 19, 25, 28, 31-32
Bar examination, 23, 30n
Bataille, George, 217-218
Baudelaire, Charles, 229, 237
Baudrillard, Jean, 215, 217, 220, 221, 222
Beating, 3, 43
Bedouin nomads, 44, 59
Belgium, 18
Bengal, 128
Benjamin, Walter, 216-218, 228-231, 232, 236-239, 240, 241, 242, 243-244
Ben-Yehuda, 74
Berger, P.L., 82
Bigamy, 145
Binary variables, 256, 267
Bingham, Jonathan, 144
Biography, fraudulent, *see* Fraudulent identification and biography
Blackletter rules, 20